# AND SO I SING

# AND SO I SING

## AFRICAN-AMERICAN DIVAS OF OPERA AND CONCERT

## ROSALYN M. STORY

### Amistad

New York, New York

Amistad Press, Inc.
1271 Avenue of the Americas
New York, New York 10020

Distributed by:
Penguin USA
375 Hudson Street
New York, New York 10014

First published in February 1990 by Warner Books as An Amistad Book.
First issued as an Amistad Press, Inc. trade paperback with an additional Preface in February 1993.

Printed in the United States of America
10 9 8 7 6 5 4 3 2 1
Library of Congress Cataloging-in-Publication Data

Story, Rosalyn M.
    And So I Sing : African-American divas of opera and concert
Rosalyn M. Story.
        p. cm.
    Originally published : New York : Warner Books, c1990. With new
pref.
    Includes bibliographical references and index.
    ISBN 1-56743-011-2 (pbk) $12.95
    1. Afro-American singers—Biography. 2. Women singers—United
States—Biography. I. Title.
[ML400.S88 1993]
782.1'092'2—dc20
[B]                                                                    92-43559
                                                                       CIP
                                                                       MN

*Book design by H. Roberts*

*To my mother and father,*
*Mable and Algrim Story*

There are many people whose generous contributions to this book, in the forms of support, encouragement, and friendship, helped make it a reality. My thanks go to:

William Winspear, for his interest and generosity in supporting this project.

John Ardoin and David Hedges for their patient and painstaking reading of this manuscript.

Plato Karayanis, Roger Pines, and the staff of Dallas Opera, in Dallas, Texas, for their support.

Dr. John Hope Franklin, for his enthusiasm for the subject and for encouraging me early in the writing.

Alex Burton, who provided his new IBM personal computer for a longer period than either of us expected, and never complained once.

Arthur LaBrew, for making available his excellent research on the life of Elizabeth Taylor-Greenfield.

Thanks also go to Wayne Shirley, music specialist at the Library of Congress in Washington, D.C., Janet Sims-Woods and the staff of the Moorland-Spingarn Research Center at Howard University, the Howard University Channing Pollock Collection, the Marian Anderson Collection at the University of Pennsylvania Van Pelt Library, the Schomburg Center for Research in Black Culture, the Chicago Lyric Opera, Tulsa Opera, the Metropolitan Opera, Opera News, Pamela Johnson at Essence Magazine, George Price, Thurlow Tibbs, of the Evans-Tibbs Collection in Washington, D.C., Bob Oskam, and Harvey-Jane Kowal. Many thanks to my literary agent, Carol Mann, and especially my editor, Charles Harris, whose enthusiasm and belief in this project encouraged and inspired me.

And to the following people who allowed themselves to be interviewed, I express sincere gratitude:

Leontyne Price, Martina Arroyo, Grace Bumbry, Shirley Verrett, Leona Mitchell, Mattiwilda Dobbs, Reri Grist, Camilla Williams, Gloria Davy, Joan Sutherland, Richard Bonynge, Cynthia Clarey, Betty Allen, Marvis Martin, Charlotte Holloman, Hilda Harris, Gwendolyn Bradley, Barbara Hendricks, Florence Quivar, Wilhemina Fernandez, Jennifer Jones, Barbara Moore, Vinson Cole, George Shirley, Sylvia Lee, Benjamin Matthews, Wayne Sanders, Virgil Thomson, Calvin LeCompte, Jonathan Morris, Simon Estes, Todd Duncan, Gregg Baker, Warren Wilson, James DePreist, Ethel DePreist, and Marion Cumbo.

Sometimes the sun unkindly hot,
My garden makes a desert spot;
Sometimes a blight upon the tree
Takes all my fruit away from me;
And then with throes of bitter pain
Rebellious passions rise and swell;
But—life is more than fruit or grain,
And so I sing, and all is well.

—*Paul Lawrence Dunbar*

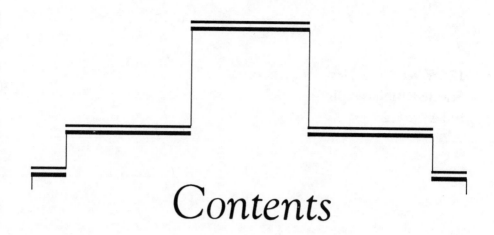

# Contents

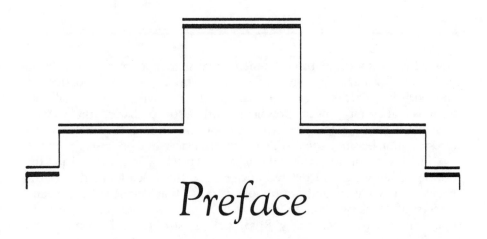

# *Preface*

AFRICAN-American family trees are unlike those of other races and cultures. The separation of slavery has withered and broken the sturdiest of branches and severed all but the toughest leaves. Threads of kinship, however thin, are vital. So when my grandmother died in the 1960s and I learned that she and Rosa Parks had been first cousins, it was as if a long-hidden configuration of limbs and leaves had survived to find new life and purpose.

Grandmother, who was older than Rosa, left Montgomery, Alabama, and the South in the 1920s and never looked back. She selected her suitors from among those black men who had an eye to the North, believing as many blacks did, that the South was best viewed through a rear-view mirror. I can only imagine that both grandmother and grandfather had had their fill of riding in the backs of Montgomery's buses, and of bending to the will of whites. By the time Rosa Parks' arrest for non-compliance with Montgomery's segregated bus laws advanced her to the front of the Civil Rights Movement, Grandmother's children were grown with children of their own. The cousins likely had not been close, but as southern black women, they shared more than the bond of blood. Both women were quiet, hard-working, dutiful and devout, and both harbored enough spiritual wealth and self-worth to challenge whatever aberrant powers prevailed. Both also combatted the stay-in-your-place code of the pre-civil rights South. Indeed, Rosa Parks was arrested, not because she didn't know her place, but because she did.

As I set out to write a book about black women in opera, the notion of knowing and defending one's rightful place loomed over the pages of newspapers and scrapbooks I found that detailed the lives and careers of black women in this overwhelmingly white profession. In opera there have been many Rosa Parkses, strong black women who stood their ground quietly and firmly, knowing that their place was wherever they chose to be.

They knew that it was only a matter of time before the rest of the world knew as well. From the first diva, Elizabeth Taylor-Greenfield, to the modern artist, the black opera singer has achieved as much by changing the face of classical music in the last century as black women who pioneered for civil rights. Just as Rosa Parks anchored the movement for equality in Montgomery, Ida B. Wells Barnett fought against the evil of lynching in the South, and Mary McLeod Bethune crusaded for the education of blacks, Marian Anderson and the great artists who preceded her foraged a new order in a world where black voices were often ignored, and at best, severely underrated. Bethune herself heard Anderson's Lincoln Memorial concert in Washington, D.C., on Easter Sunday, 1939. Spirits were high, as it was the culmination of weeks of intense debate between Anderson fans and the Daughters of the American Revolution, who forced Anderson to find concert space in the open air of the city after refusing her use of Constitution Hall. "I came away almost walking on air," Bethune said. "My hopes for the future were brightened. All fear has vanished. We are on the right track—we must go forward."

Since I began this book in the fall of 1986, people have often asked me why I chose to write a book on black divas. The project seemed a natural course for a black violinist whose only role models in classical music were the women who sang so-called 'serious' literature. Marian Anderson and Leontyne Price were icons who presented me with a universe of possibilities. They showed me that art, once created, belonged to the world at large, and to sing the music of Mozart one did not need a European pedigree. In my realm of impressions, their music belonged to the same spectrum of artistic influences that included Miles Davis' "cool" period, Mahalia Jackson's searing gospel, and Aretha Franklin's reign in the 1960s as the "queen of soul." Anderson and Price intrigued me because even though racism positioned them against the wind, they prevailed like titans, with genius, courage and grace.

This book was born of a much smaller project. In 1986, while living in Tulsa, Oklahoma, and working as a violinist with the Tulsa Philharmonic and as a reporter for the Oklahoma Eagle (Tulsa's black weekly), I was assigned a story on Metropolitan Opera soprano Leona Mitchell. An Oklahoma native, Leona was to appear with Tulsa Opera Theater as Aida. The angle was obvious—small-town black girl returns to her grass-roots home as an international star. Leona's story was as moving and inspiring as her singing. I wrote the piece, then proposed a similar article to *Essence* magazine, who had done little in the past to cover blacks in the classical arts. *Essence* accepted the proposal and expanded the assignment to explore opera's "new guard" of young, black divas. Leontyne Price had retired with much fanfare from the Metropolitan Opera, and younger stars like Mitchell, Jessye Norman, and Kathleen Battle stood poised for similar greatness.

Researching the *Essence* article (June '86) taught me many things, most important of which is that some of the greatest stories of black heroes are still waiting to be told. For more reasons than can be sufficiently discussed here, great gaps exist in the chronicling of African Americans in history in all but the most popular areas; the best-known blacks in sports, the most popular entertainers, the most controversial political activists and statesmen. (Not surprisingly, given the nature of the publishing industry, few of these books are written by black authors.) Consequently, opera's great black artists find little room in documented histories—a footnote here, an encyclopedia entry there. In 1986 nothing existed in Books in Print covering the subject in a more than general manner. Rectifying this neglect seemed imperative.

Writing a book about a subject so undervalued and ignored had its advantages and its drawbacks. It was not difficult to convince publishers that there was a need for such a book, but that need carried with it the problem of limited resources. My research took me to library reading rooms, university collections and newspaper files to unearth material that would provide a keyhole view into the lives of black divas in the 19th and early 20th centuries, and interviews enlivened my research on some of the recent stars. I spent time with Leontyne Price on the road in Little Rock, Arkansas, before a symphony performance, and visited Grace Bumbry in New York during a Met run of Aida. I spoke to Barbara Hendricks via a transatlantic call to her home in Zurich, and likewise with Reri Grist in Berlin.

I also interviewed artists who, while not black singers themselves, had a more than passing interest in the presence of blacks in opera. I talked with the American composer Virgil Thomson shortly after his

90th birthday on the use of an exclusively black cast for his landmark 1930s opera, "Four Saints in Three Acts," and spoke to Dame Joan Sutherland and her conductor-husband Richard Bonynge, both admirers of black artists, on the vocal differences of black singers. I tried to be as comprehensive as possible in my research, including those singers whose careers were documented, even in the smallest way, in the card catalogues and computerized files of American libraries. Even with my best efforts, some omissions occurred. If "And So I Sing" survives to see a future edition, information on the lives and careers of such worthy artists as Annabelle Bernard, Vera Little, and Leonore Lafayette will amend the present text, as will the inclusion of those singers whose careers have taken flight since the end of the 1980s, when this book first went to press.

In the time since I wrote this book, social concerns among blacks have evolved. New expressions such as "Eurocentrism," "Afrocentrism," and "politically correct" have extended the lexicon, replacing the looser jargon of the sixties, but sharing a similar resonance. If support for racial separation is not on the rise (among both blacks and whites), it is at least true that the "melting pot" theory faces serious reevaluation. As black Americans continue to search for identity, many are hard-pressed to reconcile two distant concepts—loyalty to African heritage and the embrace of European-centered values that dominate American middle-class consciousness. Modern Afrocentric thinking leads to the question: 'Why should black artists perform the music of European composers and neglect the music that stems from their own African culture?

Blacks in opera do not share a monolithic view on this question. Some came to opera because of a passion sparked by exposure to a particular performance. Others were encouraged by their early display of a type of talent that seemed to lean in the direction of classical music—the possession of a strong vibrato, a vast range. Some were inspired by great role models of the past such as Marian Anderson and Roland Hayes. Still others—and this well could be the most popular reason—came to opera because of chance and opportunity. When the brilliant tenor Thomas Young played the dual role of "Street" and Elijah Muhammad in the Anthony Davis opera based on the life of Malcolm X, he clearly proved his abilities in both jazz and opera. But when I interviewed him for an *Opera News* article and asked him why he focuses on opera, he replied, "I simply have had more opportunities to make a living in classical music than in jazz and pop."

Black singers, like everyone else, are looking for regular work, and some depend upon their range of talent and adaptability to styles to increase their employability. As for black opera singers and their racial consciousness, the dilemma is solved by the inclusion of the Negro spiritual in their repertory, the study of the music of classically-trained black composers, and the support of projects that provide opportunities for young, gifted blacks in the arts. Clearly, African consciousness is not lost on many of today's black singers (Texas-based baritone Donnie Ray Albert once wore a Kente cloth while performing on a recital that featured the works of black composers). Black artists, consciously or unconsciously, present their careers as a reflection of their cultural makeup—a synthesis of the African and the European, embodying the best of both creative worlds. Blacks will continue to sing the music of the European masters, just as whites will continue to perform and enjoy the music of the great masters of African-rooted jazz and rhythm and blues. As poet-author Maya Angelou said: "All art belongs to all the people, all the time." It is this synthesis of the African and the European, the coupling of cultures, that forms the basis for this book.

Black women bring a host of influences and ideologies with them to opera as well as their spirituality, their strengths and passions. When black women sing the works of Puccini and Mozart, there is a potential for added richness, a new point of view. The exclusion of blacks from opera for so many generations impoverished both the artists and the artistic world from which they were barred. Imagine if Leontyne Price had been born 50 years earlier, during a time when she would not have been allowed on an American opera stage. Imagine if she, like the 19th century diva Greenfield, had been denied training because of her race. Such a loss, given the knowledge of Price's contribution to the entire world, would be incalculable. In *And So I Sing* I have tried not only to supply portraits of the greatest artists for future generations of students of black art and culture, but also to rescue from history's shadows the lost legacies of geniuses born too soon.

# Introduction

IN his autobiography *5000 Nights at the Opera,* former Metropolitan opera manager Rudolf Bing tells an interesting story. One night in the 1950s, during a performance of *Lucia* starring Lily Pons, Bing was sitting in the lobby of the old Met when he heard a great commotion at one of the doors. It seemed a little black boy had sneaked into the orchestra section to catch a glimpse of the stage, and was being brusquely removed by one of the ushers. Bing took the little boy's hand and told him he could listen if he stood in the aisle by the door. After listening for a few minutes, the boy came out and said in a respectful, well-mannered tone, "Thank you, I've had enough." Impressed, Bing said to himself, "This race will go far..."

As far as opera was concerned, Bing's statement was not only prophetic but self-fulfilling, as Bing did his share to help advance the position of blacks in an exclusive white world. Before he took over as general manager of the Met in 1950, blacks were barred from its stage, and Bing's unilateral decision to hire Marian Anderson in the mid-fifties met with a frosty reception from his board of directors. In racially troubled times, it was an unpopular move, but one that was long overdue.

Anderson's historic debut was only one of many events in her life that helped transform her from singer to icon, and it is perhaps because of the notoriety surrounding this quiet woman that it is widely assumed she was the first black "diva." Taken from the Latin, the word means "goddess, divine one." In that sense, Anderson was surely the first black artist of the century to provoke the kind of worshipful adulation associated with the great divas of the Golden Age—Adelina Patti, Nellie Melba, and others. To say that these women were admired is an understatement; they were pampered, adored, extravagantly adorned, and deified. Called nightingales, they lived in an insular world, wrapped in a web of their own mystique and charisma, and were removed from a public who indulged them beyond all practicality. They were divas—prima donnas—and if they were eccentric, spoiled, capricious, and misbehaving, they were allowed to be so.

Anderson, on the other hand, who was neither overtly vain nor spoiled and did not fit any of the other stereotypical "diva-isms," conquered an admiring public with her understated yet powerful presence. Her singing had a hypnotic effect on listeners, as forceful as that of any of the white divas who preceded her, and her queenly comportment—unfettered by the racial hysteria of her time—only enhanced her subtle mystique.

But the story of the black diva begins well before Anderson was born. The black world of the nineteenth century, with its racial volatility and master-slave societal structure, somehow managed to produce great women of song who fought the odds—poverty, prejudice, sexism—and won. They sprang from the most humble circumstances; they were the daughters of slaves, of servants, of washerwomen and itinerant preachers. Privilege, power, and social position were as remote from their experience as is humanly conceivable. Yet from their mouths and souls poured some of the most remarkable sounds of the century.

It is a sad fact that these women—Elizabeth Taylor-Greenfield, Sissieretta Jones, Marie Selika, Flora Batson, and others—are today consigned to oblivion. And yet the fact that they are omitted from the annals of the great artists of history is not surprising. Even today the volumes written on the great singers of opera, past and present, either omit black artists entirely or discuss them minimally as "the black singers," a subgroup apart from the mainstream. Excuses for omission are all too convenient. Before Anderson's career, black artists did not sing with major opera companies—they were not allowed. Hence, any written compendium of the great opera divas could safely ignore blacks, who were forced to restrict their careers to black companies, European houses, and the American concert stage. But had Sissieretta Jones and her contemporaries been permitted their rightful places in American opera, the history of this genre would have been greatly transfigured.

Today, the black diva flourishes in a world that excluded her for generations. From Greenfield and Jones to Anderson, Dorothy Maynor, and Leontyne Price, and on to Jessye Norman and Kathleen Battle, the distance traveled in one hundred years is remarkable. The most successful black artists of today are in demand at every opera house and concert hall in the world, and unlike their worthy predecessors, their place in history is assured. The purpose of this book is to rediscover the black divas of the past and to follow the evolutionary journey from the nineteenth-century artist to her extraordinarily successful modern-day counterpart.

The career of any singing artist is beset with painstaking preparation, strenuous physical demands, rigorous travel, and an almost neurotic obsession with protecting the voice, the most fragile of instruments. Singing is the most organic of all musical pursuits, inextricably tied to physiology, human emotion, and the psyche. Add to that the qualities of blackness and womanhood, with all that each implies, and the result, the black diva, is a wonderment. While other singers of history had only to honor and represent themselves, the black prima donna has had to surmount additional obstacles while shouldering the hopes and expectations of an entire race.

Balancing those burdens is not without cost; in many singers, it has produced an ostensible passivity toward social activism. While black singers have had plenty to be angry about—until recent years all have had to contend with being barred from everything from restaurants to hotels to opera companies—angst and anger have never been conducive to beautiful singing. Thus the life of the black artist is one of restraint and compromise; the singer of the past had to subordinate her inner rage at injustice to the production and promotion of good music. But despite this, few could ignore the profound social statement Marian Anderson made in 1939 as she sang before 75,000 people on Easter Sunday in Washington after being denied the use of Constitution Hall by the Daughters of the American Revolution, or the statement made by Leontyne Price, America's premier artist of the 1960s and 1970s, when she opened the new Metropolitan Opera House at Lincoln Center in 1966. The black diva, in contributing to the awakening of a new social awareness in America, has been quietly, musically aggressive.

This book is not intended as a comprehensive, encyclopedic record, and therefore no attempt has been made to include mention of every notable singer of the past century. Regrettably, there are omissions due to limitations of space. This book is merely an informal biographical collective (with two digressive chapters on spiritual and vocal and visual ethnicity). Its scope is deliberately narrowed to include only those black women who have come up through the American social system—from slavery to freedom and through the civil rights movement—to achieve greatness. Proportion in a book such as this is also a subjective consideration. I have given noticeably more space to several singers I feel have been lost to history, as well as to those who have been pivotal in shaping the direction of music during the explosive era of the struggle for civil rights. Less space has been given to the brilliant younger stars, whose greatest work perhaps lies ahead, and for whom I feel a complete historical portrait would be premature.

Perhaps in future years some researcher will undertake the exhaustive task of documenting the history of black male singers, as well as the black artists of Europe and elsewhere to provide this virtually unexplored subject with a more complete, more global perspective. Meanwhile, I hope that some illuminating insight into the world of the black diva—her life, her legacy, and above all, her glorious artistry—may be found herein.

# ARIA

One morning
natural as air she unfolded
the limbs that threaded
through velvet lowlands
under a hush crying moon.
Arms that once wrung
soured water into careless
dirt lifted themselves
brown in the white heat of noon.
She swelled her shoulders
narrowed by half shade
tenement cells

and from a cavern that drank
a million suns, a voice
that roamed all the Gehennas
of earth and spirit rode out on a sweet wind
and she was singing.

*—Maxine Clair*

# AND SO I SING

# 1

# Sissieretta Jones

*I*T was not the best time to be black. Like a beaten boxer, the South of the late nineteenth century staggered from the devastating blows of war, while carpetbaggers and scalawags swarmed the ravaged states like vultures. For blacks, emancipation glinted with the promise of a double-edged sword. Freed slaves, who just before the war comprised nearly forty percent of the southern population, were eyed with hatred and spite as they grappled with the ramifications of their new-won freedom and, for the first time in their lives, pondered life without bondage. Postwar America hardly provided a fecund environment for the flowering of the black classical musician. Resentment ran high toward blacks not only in the South, but also in the more liberal North, and musical training for even the most gifted blacks was unlikely. In slavery, many blacks had shown themselves to be musical, translating sorrow into song while struggling to survive. But that was folk music. Classical music was as remote from black culture as America was from Europe, and the concept of a skilled black classical artist strained the most vivid imagination.

Perhaps the most interesting artistic revelation witnessed in the antebellum South was the career of a young blind boy named Thomas Bethune. Born a Georgia slave in 1849, "Blind Tom," as he was called, showed prodigious musical talent from an early age. And though he was never taught to play piano, he could perform with extraordinary skill technically advanced pieces from memory after one hearing. Under the aegis of his self-serving owner Colonel Bethune, Blind Tom barnstormed the South, amazing listeners with dazzling demonstrations of the European classics, including works by Bach, Beethoven, and Chopin.

Blind Tom was, of course, an idiot savant, a chromosomal curiosity who parlayed his abnormal gifts into a recital career. But although the nature of his genius transcended intellect, Blind Tom showed white southern Americans in particular something they had never seen—an intimate alliance between a low-born American black and the "highbrow" music of the European composers. The specter of a black classical artist was, at the time, a hazy image, but one that would gather sharper focus in the years to come. Unfortunately, Blind Tom's genius was too rare to inspire a tradition of great black pianists, but black American classical music would not have to wait for another piano-playing savant. Instead, the legacy would belong to classical singers, the black divas, culminating at the end of the century with the artistry of Sissieretta Jones.

Whether Sissieretta Jones was the greatest black performer of the nineteenth century is a matter for speculation, but there can be no doubt about her enormous celebrity. There is no other artist whose fame has more successfully survived the usual oblivion and neglect suffered by the black artists of her generation. Critics were generous with their accolades, lavishing praise upon her and, as often as not, comparing her favorably with the reigning white diva, Adelina Patti. Patti's voice set the standard by which all others were judged, and if Jones' artistry could not always shine under such scrutinizing comparisons, neither could that of any white singer at the time.

Jones was early dubbed the Black Patti, a move combining journalistic circumstance with managerial shrewdness. Almost immediately after the dubiously flattering nickname first appeared in print, she had to resign herself to a label that worked both for and against her. Often, listeners were disappointed in Jones' inability to duplicate exactly Patti's great talent, and reviewers criticized her management heavily for setting the singer up for a standard of comparison she could not live up to. But in spite of the "perilous sobriquet," as one reporter put it, Jones was soon able to establish herself as an individual artist with her own special talent.

Adelina Patti, the Italian-American prima donna who captured the hearts of opera lovers in the late 1800s, was a diva "to the manner born" and destined for deification. Courted by nobility, worshipped by audiences and critics alike, she floated through the world of opera and concert music with ease, grace, and immutable perfection, possessing a compelling childlike beauty and a voice that never ceased to enrapture her public. Even George Bernard Shaw, a tough critic and latecomer to Patti's crowded gallery of admirers, acknowledged her special gifts, praising "that wonderful instrument with its great range, its birdlike agility and charm of execution and its unique combination of the magic of a child's voice and the completeness of a woman's." Patti's career spanned five decades; toward the end she made a mini-career of farewell concerts for twenty years. Finally, she did retire, with all the pomp and panache of an exiting diva, to her private castle in Wales.

Doubtless, Sissieretta Jones' managers felt invoking Patti's name would lend a certain cachet to their star's billing and draw curiosity seekers eager to witness a black version of their ideal. "How would a *black* Patti sound?" they surely wondered. And since the public was interested in anything even vaguely resembling their demigoddess, they came in droves to find out.

They liked what they heard, and the more they heard, the more they liked. By all accounts, Sissieretta Jones had a phenomenal voice and solid training to back up her lofty billing. Whether she sounded exactly like Patti seemed not to be the issue, for the two women had obviously dissimilar styles and types of vocal endowment. But the critics and public seemed to agree that Sissieretta Jones was to blacks what Adelina Patti was to whites—a Queen of Song.

On a less grand scale, Jones enjoyed a career as one of the most sought-after concert artists of either race. She performed before four U.S. presidents. On her tours in South America and the West Indies, heads of governments and wealthy private citizens showered her with diamonds, gold, rubies, and pearls as tokens of admiration. At one concert in New Jersey, 1,000 people were said to have been turned away. White, well-heeled vacationers at New York's idyllic summer retreats flocked to see her, and of an outdoor summer park concert in Saratoga, one journalist wrote, "Every chair, bench or seat of any kind, or anything that could be used as a seat was taken and still sixty percent of the people stood during the entire program. The romantic little lake...was surrounded on all sides by the crowd of between five and six thousand people who were attracted by the phenomenal singer they were anxious to hear." At a performance in Chicago, fans demanded six encores, and, as the custom of the times allowed, often interrupted her singing with sporadic bursts of applause in recognition of a particularly impressive trill, turn of phrase, or breathtaking high note.

Though she never performed in a complete opera, Sissieretta Jones was a diva in every other sense of the word, and sang both from the operatic and popular repertories. From Meyerbeer, she sang arias from *Robert le Diable* (Robert the Devil) and *L'Africaine*. Other favorites were Gilda's aria "Caro nome," from Verdi's *Rigoletto*; "Ernani, involami," from *Ernani*; and "Sempre libera," from *La Traviata*. Like Patti, she indulged public taste and sang popular ballads, such as "Comin' Thro' the Rye," "The Last Rose of Summer," "Home Sweet Home," and "Swanee River." No matter what she sang, the crowds were large and enthusiastic. After a concert at the National Theater in Washington, D.C., the *Washington Post* wrote, "Probably no voice of our time has made such an impression by its vibration, its purity, and its natural flexibility. Nature in her case seems to have taken a special delight in showing how she can shower her gifts, irrespective of training or of birth. She has here produced a cantatrice, who...sings with 'full throated ease,' and sweeps away with the majesty, compass, and brilliancy of her tones, all criticism and prejudice."

The music press found her intriguing. An attractive woman of medium height and build, she captivated them with her pleasing appearance, gentle manner, and impeccable taste. She dressed stylishly, and often was described as elegant and majestic. Photographs show her in beaded, laced gowns of silk or satin with voluminous skirts, and wearing long, white gloves.

As if noting some new species of performer, journalists described her in excessive detail. A Canadian reporter wrote:

> Upon the platform, Madame Jones is very attractive. She has a perfect figure, a pretty natural carriage, and a pleasant, girlish face lit with dark, soft eyes. Her dress is the perfection of richness and good taste; a combination of form and color that gives the dusky skin effective setting. Her hair, of heavy, dusky black, without ever a kink or curl, is coiled in a Grecian knot at the nape of the neck, showing a prettily shaped head.

And sometimes the comments were comically absurd. "Her teeth," effused another writer, "would be the envy of her fairer sisters and the despair of dentistry. Her rather thin lips are fond of exposing heir [sic] even rows of snowy teeth."

If audiences were not accustomed to seeing an appealing black presence on the concert stage, they were even less prepared for the unusual quality of her singing. She had a big voice that spanned nearly two and a half octaves, from a low C to a high E. Her upper notes were described as clear and bell-like, and her lower register was said to have the depth of a contralto. She was not above showiness; once a journalist reported her "taking the A above the staff and holding it for.

**Sissieretta Jones**

fifteen seconds" in an immodest and unmusical display of vocal athletics that delighted her audience. Though she was weak in florid coloratura passages, she mastered the broad, expressively lyric ones, reminding more enlightened critics of dramatic soprano Lillian Nordica more than the sweet-voiced Adelina Patti. And her enunciation, everyone said, was perfect.

Though Jones was born with talent, it was her training and background that led her from an indigent upbringing as the daughter of an ex-slave to the most prestigious concert stages in the world. She was born Matilda Sissieretta Joyner in Portsmouth, Virginia, on January 5, 1869, the only child of Jeremiah Malachi Joyner and his wife, Henrietta. Her father was a native of the Carolinas and was his master's body servant during the Civil War. A devoutly religious man, Joyner became an Afro-Methodist minister and preached in Portsmouth. When the war ended, Joyner undoubtedly found the Reconstruction South, with its economic malaise and volatile racial climate, a less than desirable place for his family. In 1876 he accepted the call to a ministry in Providence, Rhode Island, and took his wife and daughter north.

Providence, at the time, was one of many bright northern beacons luring blacks from the uncertainty of the postwar South and promising opportunities for jobs and comparative racial harmony. Even its name suggested the kinder vicissitudes of fate. It was not perfect—its history had been scarred with race riots in 1824 and 1831—but by the 1870s the city had a thriving, progressive black community, due to years of intense migration from the South. For a time Rhode Island had the second largest black population of the northern states, after New Jersey. Race relations in the state were healthier than in most; black men had been voting since 1842, and by 1866 Providence's public schools were integrated.

Joyner took on odd jobs in Providence to supplement his income from the church, and he and his wife, both musically gifted, sang in the church choirs. And from the start, Sissieretta loved to sing. "When I was a little girl...I would go about singing," she later told an interviewer. "I guess I must have been a bit of a nuisance then, for my mouth was always open." A born performer, the youngster would stand on top of chairs, tables, and bureaus and "perform" for anyone willing to listen. Even in her preschool years, she showed remarkable vocal prowess. She attended the Meeting Street and Thayer Street schools, both with integrated faculties and student populations. She sang at school functions and at festivals at the Pond Street Baptist Church. At fifteen, she entered the Providence Academy of Music and studied with M. Mauros and Ada Lacombe, a retired professional singer.

Though information from this period of Sissieretta Joyner's life remains obscure, she was reported to have married David Richard

Jones on September 4, 1883, when she was fourteen. The couple had one child, who died in infancy. Richard Jones, described in newspaper articles as a "handsome mulatto from Baltimore," was said to have worked as a newsdealer and hotel bellman. Relatives tagged him, probably more accurately, as a gambler—he showed a fondness for race tracks—and a spendthrift. Later, when he took over handling his wife's business affairs after a run-in with her professional manager, he showed himself to be a serious liability to her career, spending her money flagrantly and failing to earn any of his own.

But even her husband's ne'er-do-well character and feckless behavior could not thwart Sissieretta's career. At eighteen, she began studying privately at the New England Conservatory in nearby Boston, and was coached by Luisiana Cappiani of New York. Even while studying, she began to establish a reputation, giving successful performances before 5,000 at Boston's Music Hall for the Parnell Defense Fund and at Providence's Sans Souci Gardens. She made her New York debut in 1888 in a Bergen Star Concert at Steinway Hall, and a month later sang at Philadelphia's Academy of Music.

That same year, her performance at Wallack's Theater in New York (she was the first black artist to perform there) alerted the metropolitan press to a new and, as some saw it, novel presence in the world of serious concert music. The details of this occasion are disputed by many sources. Some newspaper accounts claim the event was a private performance for the New York press in which the Tennessee Star Concert Company, organized by Florence Williams, performed before departing on an eight-month West Indian tour. Others claim a Metropolitan Opera scout heard Jones at the performance and was so impressed that he arranged a West Indian tour specially for her. In either case, the singer was engaged with the Tennessee Star Concert Company, a troupe of black musicians, to perform in major cities in the West Indies. The tour reportedly covered, among other islands, Jamaica, Barbados, and Haiti, and lasted eight months. On the islands Jones was hailed the "greatest singer of her race" and was presented with medals laden with precious stones, and with other valuable jewels from generous admirers. A miniature gold crown set with jewels was a gift from residents of Kingston; an inscribed gold ivy leaf was given to her by American residents of Colon; and a group of Haitians presented her with a gold medal set with diamonds. After returning to the United States, a short tour of several eastern seaboard cities was arranged; she sang with baritone Louis Brown in Virginia, Maryland, Washington, D.C., Delaware, and Connecticut. Another successful tour to the West Indies with the Tennessee Jubilee Singers (one of many groups capitalizing on the success of the famed Fisk Jubilee Singers) followed in 1890.

It was during the period following her New York debut that Jones was labeled the "Black Patti" by the *New York Clipper*, a theatrical journal. From then on, managers and concert advertisers, attempting to draw crowds with Patti's magical name, clung to the sobriquet, sometimes excluding Jones' real name on programs, reviews, and concert advertisements. Jones adamantly disapproved of the title, no doubt realizing that comparison was inevitable and pointless. "I do not think I can begin to sing as Patti can," she told a *Detroit Tribune* reporter, "and I have been anxious to drop the name. That is impossible almost, now it has become so identified with me." She feared audiences would think she considered herself Patti's equal. To a *Detroit Evening News* writer she insisted, "I assure you I do not think so. But I have a voice and I am striving to win the favor of the public by honest merit and hard work. Perhaps some day I may be as great in my way, but that is a long way ahead."

The name stuck, and remained with her for the rest of her life. In some cases, Jones' fears were realized; many critics saw the label as exploitative, pretentious, and a cheap enticement. "'Black Patti' should not seek to attain popularity or inveigle the coy goddess of liberty as she appears upon the American dollar by fake advertising," reprimanded one music journalist. "The 'nom de plume' under which she is announced is an unnecessary reflection upon her race. Besides, she is only brown, not black. The comparison with artists which her assumed title excites [*sic*] detracts from the favorable impression which much of her work makes."

A more sympathetic reviewer, John S. Van Cleve of the *Cincinnati Gazette*, took a softer line on the issue but pointed out the futile temerity in any artist daring to compete with Patti, the Queen of Song, during her uncontested reign. "The label...," he said, "both helps and hurts. It certainly does pique curiosity and draw people into the concert room, but it sets up a standard of comparison which neither she nor any other vocalist of our generation can successfully meet." To some, Patti's name was sacrosanct, and to invoke it as a commercial inducement was sacrilege.

Presumably, Patti heard word of her younger namesake, but whether the two divas met is not known. A reporter from the *Pittsburgh Dispatch* claimed Patti attended one of Jones' performances, was impressed, and "paid her ebony-hued competitor a personal tribute," but other glaring errors in the reporter's account cast doubt on this claim. The event was the well-publicized Grand African Jubilee held at New York's Madison Square Garden in April 1892, shortly before Patti was to perform there. A huge success, it was easily the turning point of Jones' career. Before the event, the *New York Times* announced the three-day extravaganza, featuring Jones, the Alabama Quartet, and a "chorus of

400 colored people," with instrumental music furnished by Jules Levy and his military band. Jones sang the cavatina from *Robert le Diable*, "Swanee River," Ettore Celli's vocal waltz "Farfella," and the aria "Sempre libera" from *La Traviata*.

The *New York Morning Advertiser* described the program: "The performance of which the Black Patti was the dark star was termed a Colored Jubilee, and consisted of quartet, chorus singing, fancy dancing, some show of sparring, and closed at a late hour with a cakewalk." It was a fashionable affair, the ideal setting for the unveiling of a new, unusual star destined for rapid ascent. The jubilee was a potpourri of varied entertainment with New York's most talented black performers, and Sissieretta Jones, the *Advertiser* added, was the "pièce de résistance of the bill."

Attended by 75,000 people and reviewed by New York's formidable press corps, the Garden concerts had the city's music community buzzing about the talented black soprano. Sissieretta Jones, suddenly catapulted to the forefront of the American concert scene, was stunned by the magnitude of her popularity. "I woke up famous after singing at the Garden, and didn't know it," she later remarked. And if Jones wasn't convinced of her fame, forthcoming responses from the public and press would reinforce the notion. The year 1892 was pivotal for the twenty-three-year-old singer; having gained approval from New York's demanding music community, her career hit its stride. Earlier that year, in February, she performed in the White House Blue Room at the invitation of President and Mrs. Benjamin Harrison. After her performance of "Home, Sweet Home," the Meyerbeer cavatina, and "Swanee River," the First Lady was so pleased that she presented Jones with a bouquet of White House orchids. In later years, Jones became a regular guest at entertainments for Washington dignitaries, singing for U.S. Supreme Court Chief Justice Fuller and presidents Grover Cleveland, William McKinley, and Theodore Roosevelt.

Though details are scant, sometime during this period Jones signed a three-year contract with Major J. B. Pond, manager of the American Lecture and Musical Agency in New York. Pond was a shrewd, savvy businessman who managed the careers of sopranos Euphrosyn Parepa-Rosa and Clara Louise Kellogg, humorist Mark Twain, and clergyman and abolitionist leader Henry Ward Beecher. He had a knack for knowing what the public wanted, and was able to combine the talents of Jones, white cornetist Jules Levy, and Russian violinist Lilli Dolgorouky and parlay them into an exciting program of popular and serious music. Levy played cornet solos and conducted his Sousa-style military band in lively marches, then later in the program conducted accompaniments for both Dolgorouky and Jones. Sissieretta was the hit of these evenings, a centerpiece surrounded by other talented performers. Later, Pond hired Alberta Wilson, a black pianist from Brooklyn, to accompany her. Critics praised Wilson, an apparently gifted player, and marveled at the rare sight of an accomplished black pianist on the concert stage. Eventually, other well-known black performers such as poet Paul Lawrence Dunbar, baritone Harry T. Burleigh, and Joseph Douglass, violinist and grandson of Frederick Douglass, were engaged to round out the programs, which had become a showcase for diversified entertainment and something of a forum for the best black talent of the day.

Critical raves abounded as Jones, Levy, and company traversed the Midwest and Northeast and performed at a variety of venues. New York's Carnegie Hall, Central Music Hall in Chicago, the Academy of Music in Philadelphia, and the National Theater in Washington, D.C., were a few of the auditoriums where Jones sang before throngs of thousands. She performed at the Pittsburgh Exposition, where Pond demanded and got $2,000 for her week-long engagement—reportedly the highest salary ever paid a black artist. By the time she appeared at the Chicago World's Fair in 1893, she had established herself as a major box office attraction. Though the "Black Patti" label still followed her relentlessly, critics had become tolerant of it, and sometimes even sympathetic, focusing more attention on the artist's performance and less on her sensational billing. "Madame Jones is not a Patti," said a reporter for the *Louisville Post*, "but she is an artist." And a writer for a New York weekly agreed: "If Madame Jones is not the equal of Adelina Patti, she at least can come nearer it than anything the American public has heard."

Unfortunately, the American public was to see less of Jones in the months following the World's Fair performance. Mishaps, managerial problems, and slow attendance at concerts began to break her stride. Her relationship with Pond soured, and a string of legal entanglements, salary disputes, and lawsuits ensued. According to the press, Jones' husband, Richard, arranged some concerts in Baltimore and Brooklyn without Pond's consent. Pond, the couple claimed, had effectively dismissed Jones from his management while she was engaged in Troy, New York, leaving them free to make their own arrangements. Pond met the accusation with indignation and steadfast denials. Further, he said, since the concerts were arranged without his permission, their contract had been breached. He refused to pay the Black Patti $150 owed her according to the terms of their contract. Also, he filed for an injunction against Jones to bar her from singing under any other manager. Meanwhile, a local paper reported the Joneses' version: that Pond previously told Levy he wanted to "get rid of the Black Patti and her husband" and Levy could "have them if he wanted them."

Apparently, Pond denied the conversation with Levy and filed for the injunction to certify his exclusive authority over Jones' career. At first the request for an injunction was denied, but later one was granted while Jones was appearing, under Richard's management, in Newark, New Jersey. A *Newark Evening News* article dated June 27, 1893, reported the story: "Yesterday Judge McAdam of the Superior Court of New York, granted an injunction restraining the Black Patti from singing under any management other than Major J. B. Pond. Despite this, she says she will sing all week. Her husband, who is now managing her, says it will be all right if 15 percent of the receipts are sent to Major Pond."

According to a later article, Jones was eventually able to overturn the injunction, and her husband took over the management of her concerts.

Another incident during a scheduled Ohio tour was equally embarrassing. Pond was still managing Jones, and arranged for an E. S. Jones, of Jones and Velder in New York, to control advertising and pay expenses for a tour of Cincinnati, Columbus, Dayton, and Indianapolis. Things went according to plan in Cincinnati, although expenses were barely covered. But in Dayton, E. S. Jones skipped town with all the money from ticket sales and left a stack of unpaid bills. Sissieretta made apologies to the concert organizers and, not wanting to disappoint her audience, performed without pay. In Columbus, creditors were also left unpaid. Jones sang the first of the two planned Columbus concerts without pay, and the second one was cancelled. The morning of the cancelled performance, Jones apologized publicly in the local newspaper:

> Will you kindly allow me to state through your paper that E. S. Jones, who has made a fiasco of the concerts at the Auditorium last night and tonight, is not my manager as many have told me they supposed. My manager is Major J. B. Pond of New York. E. S. Jones and his partner J. C. Velder simply contracted with Major Pond for my services at the two concerts to be given in Columbus. I am very sorry that anyone has been misled in the matter, and that on account of Messrs. Jones and Velder not meeting their obligations, those friends who had purchased tickets for the concert advertised for tonight have been disappointed. Thanking you very kindly for your courtesy, I am very sincerely yours,
>
> Sissieretta Jones, The Black Patti

As if the singer's credibility had not suffered enough, a misunderstood no-show in Chicago made matters worse. A black-owned Chicago newspaper, the *Conservator*, exposed a ruse involving Jones and black composer-violionist Will Marion Cook and his partner, a man named Morris. Jones agreed to sing in Chicago with the understanding that she would receive $300 in advance of the concert. Morris and Cook, the concert contractors, could raise only $100 by the specified date but continued to sell tickets to the concert, knowing Jones was not committed. Cook supposedly borrowed $200 from orator Frederick Douglass, who also was to appear on the program, along with baritone Harry T. Burleigh and tenor Sidney Woodward, and sent the money to Jones well after her deadline. The money arrived too late for Jones to consider coming. To add to the confusion, the performance had been billed as the debut of Cook's new opera, *Uncle Tom's Cabin*, in which Jones was supposed to star. Jones, of course, did not show, and no opera was mentioned. A performance took place with Woodward and Burleigh supplying the only musical entertainment.

Though hard luck and the bad faith of those around her temporarily edged Jones' career off its track, she managed to carry on. There were a few notable appearances in 1894, one of which linked her with one of the world's greatest composers. Antonín Dvořák, then director of the National Conservatory in New York, conducted a concert of black students of the Conservatory to benefit the *New York Herald's* Free Clothing Fund. The Bohemian composer, long an admirer of blacks and their music, had just written his *New World* Symphony (No. 9, E minor) inspired in part by black folk melodies. Jones was not a student at the Conservatory but, because of her reputation and strong following, was invited to sing. Her "Inflammatus" from Rossini's *Stabat Mater* was well received, and the program ended with Dvořák conducting Jones and Harry T. Burleigh in the composer's own arrangement of "Swanee River."

Details of the next few years of Jones' life are vague. Reportedly, a European tour was arranged by Morris Reno, president of the Carnegie Hall Association, and Jones sang in England, Germany, and France. In England she gave a command performance for the Prince of Wales and sang at the Royal Opera House at Covent Garden. Jones called her Covent Garden performance "one of the most exalted triumphs of my career." Europe loved her, too, but even there the Black Patti tag followed. In Berlin, she sang shortly after an appearance by Adelina Patti, and the *Berliner Zeitung* wrote: "No sooner had the real Adelina Patti departed than a most worthy substitute appeared in the person of Madame Sissieretta Jones, the 'Black Patti.'"

Unfortunately, the life of Sissieretta Jones is like a puzzle with pieces missing. And despite extant clippings and memorabilia (her personal scrapbook at Howard University contains hundreds of reviews), no complete picture is possible. Thus, as with many details about her career, much of Jones' personal life remains clouded in mystery. One such "missing piece" would contain details about her relationship with her husband, Richard. It was no secret that Richard was not an asset to

Jones' life or career, and sometime between 1893 and 1898 the couple divorced. Whether they parted amicably or quarrelled is not known. But given Richard's penchant for gambling, his apparent love for liquor, his habit of spending money recklessly, and his inability to keep a job, the latter assumption probably comes closer to the truth. Whatever the situation, Sissieretta filed for and was granted a divorce, charging drunkenness and nonsupport, and her marriage of more than ten years was over.

It is not inconceivable that Sissieretta Jones used the period following her European tour and her divorce as a time for reflection and reassessment. She had survived unscrupulous management and a disappointing marriage, and escaped both relatively unscathed. She had been the toast of two continents; Europe and America both had praised her singing over the past eight years. On the stage she was a unique presence—intelligent, disarmingly attractive, and as an artist, entirely professional. However, she was not white. And as a black woman in the nineteenth century, albeit a great artist, she was subjected to the same attitudes that beleaguered most blacks in nineteenth-century America.

While traveling, Jones made a point of avoiding southern cities. Born in the South, she had left early with her parents, but surely was aware of the prejudice against blacks there. "It would not be pleasant, I fear," she once told a reporter for the *Detroit Evening News.* "Louisville is as far as I go." But a Louisville incident years later may have changed her mind about that city. At a performance at the Masonic Temple Theater, blacks were not allowed on the orchestra floor but were permitted to sit in the balcony. The balcony filled up quickly while the orchestra floor was only half-filled with whites. Instead of allowing the overflow of blacks to occupy the remaining ground floor seats, the management turned them away. As the *Louisville Courier-Journal* reported, "The first floor at Masonic Temple was occupied by quite a large audience of Louisville's 'regular theater goers and music lovers' last night, and the gallery was packed with colored people...."

Jones noticed the odd division and was furious. "It's so strange," she told a Louisville reporter after the concert. "I never saw anything like it before—putting the colored people off in the gallery and leaving all those vacant seats downstairs. I felt very much disappointed. I never before had such an experience, and I could not help feeling it."

But even the northern cities were not always free from such problems. Audiences often were divided by race, and decent hotel accommodations, when not prearranged by her white manager, were difficult to get. At Cincinnati, Jones complained about the situation: "We had so much trouble at the hotels..." she said. "We had to search and search before we—Mrs. Wilson and I—could find a nice place."

For the most part, Jones seemed to take such difficulties and disappointments in stride, but being excluded from opera because of her race was perhaps the biggest disappointment she had to face. She referred to it constantly. Once she mentioned she was considering an offer from Mascagni, the composer of such verismo operas as *Cavalleria Rusticana*, to appear in his new work *Scipio Africanus*. He may have offered, but it is doubtful he could have gotten whites to produce it with Jones playing the lead and whites playing subordinate roles. Years later, a more realistic Jones said she would love to sing in one of her favorite operas, *L'Africaine* by Meyerbeer, but sadly added, "They tell me my color is against me." She apparently agreed to sing the role of Topsy in Will Marion Cook's opera based on *Uncle Tom's Cabin* at the Chicago World's Fair in 1893, but that never materialized. And it was rumored that Abbey, Schoeffel, and Grau, managers of the Metropolitan Opera, approached her for roles such as Selika in *L'Africaine* and Aida but, for reasons never disclosed, would not hire her. (An 1892 fire that gutted the Metropolitan building stopped all production plans, but apparently no attempts were made to engage Jones after the opera house's reconstruction.)

Yet critics agreed Jones had dramatic flair as an artist. Her voice, with its rare ability to combine power and pathos, might have added much to an opera role. As a *Philadelphia Times* writer put it after a performance at the Academy, "The thought was irresistible that she would make a superb Aida, whom her appearance, as well as her voice, suggested."

Finally, Jones found a way to satisfy her desire for the opera stage, and as a result, she turned a corner onto the path that would take her to the end of her career. The Black Patti's Troubadours, a multifaceted act organized by New York theatrical proprietors Voelckel and Nolan, occupied the next years of Jones' life and provided a forum for her operatic talent. Performing a mixture of comedy sketches, acrobatic acts, and grand opera, the troupe was organized with Sissieretta Jones as the main attraction. The show, which toured the country and was an unqualified success, consisted of three parts: the opening comedy sketch; an olio, or vaudeville-styled section, during which actors, singers, acrobats, and jugglers performed in specialty acts; and the "Operatic Kaleidoscope." During the Kaleidoscope, Jones, assisted by an ensemble of singers, orchestra, and chorus, performed scenes from *Carmen, Faust, Il Trovatore, La Bohème, Rigoletto,* and other operas from the popular repertory, replete with costumes and scenery. Engaging, lighthearted, and full of variety, the Troubadours' show contained everything from low comedy to high musical drama and appealed to all classes and races.

While the operatic scenes were the drawing, the success of the Black Patti's Troubadours depended largely on its minstrel format. An outgrowth of white minstrelsy as presented by the Virginia Minstrels and the Christy Minstrels, black minstrelsy reached its peak in the early 1900s, but its popularity continued well into the twentieth century. Jones was no stranger to the minstrel show; she had performed with the short-lived Georgia Minstrels at the Dockstader's Theater in New York in 1889.

The Black Patti's Troubadours and other traveling minstrel shows were historically significant; they were springboards from which a number of black artists launched successful careers in the theater. Though minstrelsy presented blacks as naive, slap-happy buffoons, the art form gave blacks an opportunity to benefit financially by capitalizing on their own stereotypes (as whites had been doing for years), and provided valuable theatrical experience. Popular comic characters such as "Jim Crow" and "Zip Coon" were based on the stereotyping of blacks as guileless, unintelligent, and childlike, but they were fundamental prototypes in an idiom that provided employment for talented black actors, comedians, and singers. As James Weldon Johnson explained in his 1933 book *Black Manhattan*:

> Minstrelsy was, on the whole, a caricature of Negro life, and it fixed a stage tradition which has not yet been entirely broken. It fixed the tradition of the Negro as only an irresponsible, happy-go-lucky, wide grinning, loud laughing, shuffling, banjo playing, singing, dancing sort of being. Nevertheless, these companies did provide stage training and theatrical experience which, at the time, could not have been acquired from any other source.

Troupes like the Troubadours spawned such successful artists as minstrel and vaudeville star Ernest Hogan, the comedy team of Williams and Walker, and composers Bob Cole and Billy Johnson. In the early going, Cole and his collaborator, Johnson, formed the musical backbone of the Troubadours, composing songs, writing skits, and directing the show. But the talented tandem only lasted a year with the company. After a row with managers Voelckel and Nolan in which Cole was denied a request for more money, the songwriting team left the group, took their musical scores and several sympathetic colleagues with them, and started their own company. Voelckel and Nolan tried unsuccessfully to have Cole arrested for theft and prevented from performing, but the Cole troupe was able to produce the hit show *A Trip to Coontown*, which was lauded as a major breakthrough in black musical comedy and the first successful all-black theatrical production in New York. Whether Sissieretta Jones was sympathetic to Cole and Johnson's plight during their short tenure with the company is not known, but both groups were successful on the road, despite Voelckel and Nolan's plan to destroy the dissident group by blacklisting them and booking the Troubadours' performances in the same cities just prior to Cole's scheduled openings.

For Jones, the concert artist, minstrelsy was a different way of life, with its colorful characters and motley group of black performers. It also posed different problems. A group of forty or fifty blacks traveling across the country at the turn of the century was an easy target for hate groups sponsoring anti-black activities, and the problem of lodging for blacks naturally increased with the size of the group. The Black Patti's Troubadours, like many other traveling minstrel groups, toured the country in specially built railroad cars, mainly for protection against the hazards of life on the road. As Robert C. Toll explains in his minstrel history *Blacking Up*, customized transportation vehicles for black minstrel groups was "more a matter of convenience and necessity than a display of opulence. In addition to providing a place to stay, the cars also carried stocks of food and had secret compartments to hide performers who had offended local whites."

Whites, though, comprised at least half the Troubadours' audience. From New York to Texas, they came to see the Black Patti in her new element. And although the shows concentrated heavily on satire and farce, Jones' fans sought her out for the same reasons they had thronged to see her before—her magnificent voice. Accordingly, critics embraced the Troubadours' brand of entertainment, seeing it as charmingly multifaceted and more sophisticated than other competing groups. "These 'Troubadours' undoubtedly boast more black talent than any other like enterprise that ever was brought to public notice," proclaimed the *Detroit Free Press*, and the *Evening News* agreed: "Without exception the Black Patti Troubadours company is the best colored theatrical organization that has visited this city. Every member of it seems to be a star."

But despite the public's enthusiasm, the concert singer was not completely happy as the star of her own minstrel troupe, and said as much to a writer for the *New York Dramatic Mirror* after appearing at Proctor's Pleasure Palace, a New York vaudeville auditorium, early in 1896. Jones said she much preferred to sing in concert, as "there are so many things in a vaudeville performance to distract the attention of the audience that they are not in a proper frame of mind to enjoy straight singing." Jones stated her intention to return to the concert stage after her run at the Pleasure Palace, but it was not to happen. Her intended brief foray into vaudeville and minstrelsy lasted nineteen years, until her retirement.

Inevitably, the popularity of the minstrel show waned in the years before and during World War I, as audiences and performers became more sophisticated and less inclined toward demeaning "darky humor."

And with the decline of minstrelsy came the demise of Black Patti's Troubadours. The last few performances saw poor attendance, with the management struggling to make the payroll. Jones was distraught by the dissolution of her company. After its final performance at New York's Gibson Theater in 1916, she paced backstage, waiting hours with her chorus members for paychecks that subsequently bounced at a nearby bank on Broadway. A young boy in the chorus later recalled: "The night we waited in the theater, she was so distressed. . . . she came and kissed each one of us saying, 'My dears, I am terribly distressed about this, but this is show business.'" After two decades on the road, the Black Patti's Troubadours was bankrupt, and minstrelsy was dead. Ironically, a genre that had laid important groundwork for black professionals in the theater was a casualty of its own making, a victim of its own success. Serving a noble purpose, it brought a multitude of black singers and actors into the theater, only to be outgrown by them and abandoned for more serious and dignified theatrical pursuits.

Jones returned to her home in Providence on Wheaton Street. Her mother was ailing and needed looking after. The years passed, and apart from a concert at the Grand Theater in Chicago, she never sang professionally again. She spent her years quietly, taking care of her mother until she died and singing occasionally at the Congdon Street Baptist Church. Out of charity, loneliness, or both, she took in two homeless boys who were wards of the state. Poverty eventually forced her to sell most of the property she had accumulated—four houses in Providence, her jewelry, and most of her medals from the West Indian tours. And when funds from the sale of her property ran out, Jones went on relief.

In 1933 she became ill. A charitable friend, William Freeman, paid the taxes on her house, and her water, wood, and coal bills. During this time she corresponded with her cousin, Melvina Newsome, in letters tinged with sadness and resignation. Despite her despair and illness, Jones, sixty-four and dying, seemed to find solace in her spiritual convictions. "I have been very sick," she wrote. "I went out for the first time to Communion service Sunday. I asked the Lord to give me strength and he answered my petitions. So you see how good my Savior is. I shall continue to pray and to trust in the Lord and serve Him until he is ready for me."

On June 24, 1933, at the Rhode Island Hospital in Providence, Sissieretta Jones died penniless, of cancer. And the woman who had sung for four U.S. presidents, filled nearly every major concert hall in the country, and had been heralded as one of the great singers of her time was given a grave by friends to escape burial in Providence's "Potter's Field." Her remaining possessions were assigned to the state.

The *Afro-American*, a New England paper, reported the contents of her house weeks after her death:

> Her parlors still contain four valuable large paintings . . . gold gilt chairs, gold clock, gold candlesticks, settees of wonderful rich red brocade with gold fleur de lis, her walnut piano and autographed pictures of other stage celebrities, among them the autographed pictures of Cole and Johnson with their famous song, "Mudder Knows," Madame [Nellie] Melba and Bohn Poles, dated 1904. . . . She still retained her two beautiful fur coats and her wonderful wardrobes of her evening gowns, loaded with sequins, her gorgeous airgret [*sic*], gloves and other finery.

Though destitute, Jones had held on to a few precious vestiges of her days of fame, reminders of her pioneering career as the first black prima donna. In life, her career was not what it could have been; in death, it would be relegated to near obscurity. Indeed, some thought she had died years earlier. When Flora Batson, another well-known black soprano and Providence native, died in 1906, a photograph of Sissieretta Jones appeared in *Musical America* with a caption saying "the Black Patti" had died. Rumors began to fly that Jones was not the original Black Patti. Jones herself was disheartened by the mistake. Thus, for the black artist to whom little respect was accorded and who was forced to abandon her own name and link herself superficially with a white star, even the memory of what she had been was not safe from confusion and abuse.

Sissieretta Jones struggled as an artist, fighting daily for dignity and artistic survival in a world that viewed her as, at best, a freakish imitation of a white ideal. Refusing to see her only as the gifted singer she was, the public lauded her with left-handed praise: the "dusky diva," the "chocolate-hued" songstress, the "Black Patti." Critics acknowledged her beauty, but never without qualifications: "The Black Patti is of pure Negro blood," said one reporter, "*nevertheless* [emphasis added], she is of very pleasing appearance." The comparisons with Patti were ludicrous; there was no comparing the two. Patti was the idol of millions, demanded at least $4,000 nightly, and retired to her opulent Welsh castle, complete with private theater. Jones rarely earned more than $300 for one appearance and retired, largely forgotten, to a life of poverty.

Jones had to deal with mismanagement, critics whose highest praise was often condescending, and a public bewildered by the presence of a sophisticated black artist. But despite the inequities, indignities, and abuses Jones faced, her contribution to the music of black women in America is immeasurable. Though she never reached the heights of an Adelina Patti, she forced whites to see blacks as potentially talented, capable, dignified beings. Jones was an artist whose determination to give out music was resolute and unhindered by the shortcomings of a society unprepared for her likeness. "I love to sing," the diva once said. "Singing is to me what sunshine is to the flowers; it is our life. The flowers absorb the sunshine because it is their nature. I give out melody because God filled my soul with it."

# 2

# Pioneers and Pathfinders

*H*OW did a black singer with the polish and poise of Sissieretta Jones come to be in the late nineteenth century, given the racial predisposition of much of the post–Civil War American population? Could such a woman have envisioned herself a diva without role models to emulate? One can only speculate on whether Jones heard the great singers of the day in concert; she apparently heard the great Patti in the latter's declining years (Patti retired in 1903 and died in 1919), the Australian Nellie Melba, and possibly the Americans Lillian Nordica and Clara Louise Kellogg. But serious black singers before Jones were scarce, and none attained her measure of fame. Thus, her sources of inspiration from black singers were limited at best. Years before Jones was born, however, an even less socially sympathetic era produced another great soprano who lays claim to the title of first, if not the greatest, black concert artist of the century.

For Elizabeth Taylor-Greenfield, born a slave in the South of the 1820s, the road to recognition and respect as a vocal artist was perhaps more difficult than that of any other singer who ever attempted a career. She had nothing in her favor, except raw talent and courage. She was not beautiful; in fact, she was regarded (mostly by white reviewers) as awkwardly unattractive. She was largely self-taught; no reputable teacher dared take her or any other black singer as a student for fear of jeopardizing his career. Riots often were threatened where she sang, and a phalanx of policemen protecting the halls where she sang was not unusual. Although she sang mostly in the Northeast, blacks frequently were barred from her performances. When they were allowed in, they were hustled to the balcony, the place "appropriated for them." (The ticket prices alone must have kept many blacks away; they were $1, twice the average admission price for concerts.) The black press attacked Greenfield's ethics, outraged that she permitted herself to be an instrument of segregation. At a concert in the Midwest, some well-dressed blacks tried to enter with tickets in hand and were refused. "We told them we had been permitted to hear Jenny Lind on her first and last visit to Ohio," wrote J. I. Gaines in the *Voice of the Fugitive*, "but it was to no avail." He commented further, "We cannot believe that Miss Greenfield would suffer herself to be exhibited by a set of pro-slavery scamps after she is apprised of the fact that her own people are insulted and abused through her." Greenfield answered the attacks with separate concerts for black audiences.

If Sissieretta Jones was considered a novelty, Greenfield was a curiosity, with all its attendant implications. For white music patrons in the early nineteenth century, the very idea of a refined voice emerging from an African-looking woman evoked a myriad of reactions, from amazement to amusement. Greenfield not only had to endure prejudice from whites, but derision. More than once the sight of the ungainly black woman, led onstage by a visibly repulsed white usher, was enough to provoke laughter and gave her concerts the atmosphere of a carnival freak show.

But Greenfield had a voice the likes of which the American public had seldom heard from any singer, white or black. Jenny Lind, the Swedish singer and the current sensation, provided the vocal standard at the time, but with a voice spanning three and one-half octaves, the untrained Greenfield surpassed the "Swedish Nightingale" in range and was said to rival her in natural ability and production of sound. Certainly with more training she would have been a force to reckon with. In May 1852, a *Toronto Globe* writer marveled at Greenfield's ability, noting "the amazing power of the voice, the flexibility and the ease of execution." He continued, "The higher passages were given with clearness and fullness, indicating a soprano of great power. She can, in fact, go as low as Lablache and as high as Jenny Lind, a power of voice perfectly astonishing."

As low as Lablache? Greenfield could, in fact, sing higher than

Lind, but perhaps the writer was given to a fit of hyperbole in comparing her to the famous Italian basso Luigi Lablache, whose range extended to the low E-flat. Certainly, it was Greenfield's phenomenal range, from a low G in the bass clef to an E above high C, that attracted most of her listeners. Her extraordinary low register was said to have the full, rich sonority of a baritone, and her high notes, though some critics complained of thinness, were evenly and effortlessly produced. And her sense of pitch, critics said, was flawless. "A more correct intonation, there could not be," glowed one reporter. "She strikes every note on the exact center, with unhesitating decision, and unerring truth." Though her ability to sing in the baritone register was admired by most, it offended one *New York Daily Tribune* critic, who said, "The idea of a woman's voice is a feminine tone; anything below that is disgusting. It is as bad as a bride with a beard on her chin and an oath in her mouth. We hear a great deal about woman's sphere. That sphere exists in music, and it is the soprano region of the voice." The reporter's words, mirroring the moral strictures and prejudices of the times, illustrate the unusual difficulties with public attitude that Greenfield had to surmount in her trying career. Not only did she defy tradition by establishing a career in a field monopolized by whites, but she dared to challenge existing musical proprieties by singing in musical territory dominated by men.

Greenfield was born in Natchez, Mississippi, in the middle 1820s, of the union between a full-blooded African man and a Seminole Indian woman. Both were slaves, the property of Elizabeth Holiday Greenfield, a wealthy landowner with estates in Louisiana and Mississippi and stocks in banks in Mississippi and Pennsylvania. Shortly after Elizabeth was born, her mistress moved to Philadelphia and joined the Society of Friends, a Quaker anti-slavery group. She freed Elizabeth's parents and gave them enough money to establish a home in Liberia. Elizabeth remained with her mistress in Philadelphia. Before her death, Greenfield set up a trust for Elizabeth's mother and arranged for Elizabeth to receive $100 a year for the rest of her life, along with a $500 bequest. Elizabeth's healthy endowment allowed her freedom from the menial work she might otherwise have been consigned to and gave her time to pursue her passion—music.

Though she was twenty before performing in public, as a child she showed talent by teaching herself to play guitar and piano, accompanying herself as she sang. With the help of a local amateur musician, she refined her voice and skills and was soon singing at local private parties, amazing her hearers with her raw-edged but affecting musicality.

When her benefactress died in 1845, Elizabeth moved to western New York to stay with friends. No matter where she went, she attracted people with her unusual voice. While en route to Buffalo, she entertained a small gathering and, as a result, acquired another patroness. She sang for the Buffalo Music Association in 1851, and through their auspices gave concerts in the area. She had no manager until late in 1851, when she signed a three-year contract with Colonel J. H. Wood, a former museum manager from Cincinnati. With Wood, Greenfield toured upstate New York, Massachusetts, Rhode Island, and major midwestern cities. A typical program included arias from *The Daughter of the Regiment* and *Lucrezia Borgia* by Donizetti, ballads by Bellini, and Verdi's "Ernani, involami." After intermission, Greenfield sat at the piano and accompanied herself to slow, moving songs such as Bishop's "Like the Gloom of Night Retiring," in the bass clef. When a reporter for the *Buffalo Commercial Advertiser* heard her, he immediately tagged her "the Black Swan," an unlikely title since, as a writer later pointed out, swans are not known for their singing. Nonetheless, the label stuck and, as with Sissieretta Jones, it followed her permanently, to the exclusion of her own name.

But the *Advertiser* reporter was impressed, and said so: "Miss Greenfield possesses a voice of great purity and flexibility, and of extraordinary compass; singing the notes in alto, with brilliancy and sweetness, and descending to the bass notes with a power and volume perfectly astonishing." Other reviewers were not so generous, dwelling on her lack of professional training, her lack of stage presence, and her size and color. "She has a fine voice," allowed a reviewer, "but does not know what to do with it."

Racial epithets dominated many of her notices. A *Cincinnati Enquirer* journalist called her the "African Crow." Another writer estimated her weight at between 275 and 300 pounds, noting "her voice is more refined than her person." The *Detroit Daily Advertiser* told its readers: "The Swan is a plain looking, medium sized, woolly headed, flat nose negro woman, and no one would suppose there was any more enchantment...in her than a side of leather." And another reporter went to inordinate lengths to describe her physiognomy: "The Swan is of good figure and form, with a full bust, containing organs more completely adapted to the development of the vocal powers and qualities, than those of any other human being whose voice we ever listened to, or tested.... her complexion not exactly ebony, but approaching it as nearly as the brownest black can possibly do; her features, but slightly modified from the pure African lineaments—retaining the low forehead, the depressed nose, and the expansive mouth, without the bulbous labia."

For all their awkward commentary, the music press seemed aware of the obstacles Greenfield had to overcome as the first black exponent of serious music. And most agreed that, given the proper training from someone like Manuel Garcia, the teacher of Jenny Lind and foremost

**Elizabeth
Taylor-Greenfield**

musical pedagogue of the day, she might have rivaled the great artists. Apart from the amateurish help of a few friends, Greenfield had little training in musical execution. Said a *Toronto Globe* reporter, "It must be confessed that Miss Greenfield has a very heedless way of throwing her notes about, has far from perfect command over them, and wants the knowledge of ornamental points, which can only be given by instruction from the best masters." But even after offering more money for instruction than the going rate, she could not persuade white teachers to take her as a student. As a white writer for the *Anti-Slavery Standard* said, "Being of an outcast and despised race, she has never enjoyed the privilege even of listening to our great singers." Thus, the world of American concert music in the middle nineteenth century denied Greenfield exposure and refused to train her, while reproaching her for remaining untrained.

After one of her concerts, an Ohio journalist admitted his prejudice and pondered his dilemma in fairly assessing the voice of such an unseemly artist. "We know the natural prejudice that we all have against her color," he admitted, "and it is very difficult to divest one's self entirely of them and criticize fairly and justly in such a case." Another journalist solved the problem. "Upon the suggestion of another," he wrote, "we listened to her without looking toward her during the entire performance of 'The Last Rose of Summer' and were at once and satisfactorily convinced that her voice is capable of producing sounds right sweet."

Those who did look in her direction found Greenfield sartorially inelegant and lacking in style, dress and poise being essential elements of success for concert artists of pre–Civil War America. The fact that Greenfield was not properly schooled in the genteel arts bothered even those who otherwise championed her cause. After a concert in Utica, New York, one woman took the liberty of advising the singer on the proper dress for a stage artist. In a letter to Greenfield, she wrote:

> I have a few suggestions to make, respecting your dress. You were dressed with great modesty and with much simplicity; still there are some things it would be well for you to lay aside. Wear nothing in your hair, unless it be a cluster of white flowers. Let your dress be a plain black silk. . . . Wear muslin under sleeves and white kid gloves— always. Dress very loosely. I would advise no whalebones (but perhaps you are not prepared for that reform). . . . If you tire of the black silk, a steel colour would be a good change—but these two are preferable to all others.
>
> Your pocket handkerchief should be unfolded and somewhat tumbled, not held by a point in the center; perhaps it would be better to have it in your pocket, quite out of sight—the piece of music is enough for the hands.
>
> I rejoice in the dignity of your deportment and in the good hours you keep [*sic*]. I have said this much in relation to your dress, because I know how important it is that, in the midst of all the prejudice against those of your colour, that your appearance should be strikingly genteel.

Despite whatever ostensible shortcomings Greenfield might have had as a professional concert artist, her performances were popular, and in 1853 she arrived at a landmark engagement in her American career. On March 31, she made her New York City debut at Metropolitan Hall, drawing a crowd of 4,000. Though musically favorable, the limitations surrounding attendance at the concert aroused the ire of the black community. A *New York Times* ad announced, "No colored persons can be admitted as there is no part of the house appropriated for them." Letters threatening disruption of the concert and damage to the building worried managers so much that police were called to guard the hall. An apologetic Greenfield placated the irate blacks by agreeing to repeat her concert at the Broadway Tabernacle for five black church congregations. "I regret that you have been debarred from attending the concert to be given at Metropolitan Hall this evening," said Greenfield, replying to the request for the extra concert from a group of black ministers, "but it was expressly stated in the agreement for the use of the hall that such should be the case."

A packed house at the Metropolitan Hall greeted Greenfield with boorish laughter as the singer was escorted to the piano by a white usher, who, as the *New York Herald* reported, "seemed afraid to touch her with even the tips of his white kids, and kept the Swan at a respectable distance." But the derision subsided when Greenfield sang. While most of the press acknowledged her natural ability, the *New York Times* dismissed her singing as unworthy of comment: "It would be perfectly ridiculous to attempt a criticism of the Swan's singing. She has some notes in her voice that are musical, and which might possibly be improved by cultivation, but at present there is not the faintest approach to the latter qualification. The attraction, we imagine, was the novelty of the exhibition rather than the talent which might be exhibited in the singing."

Other journals were sympathetic to the point of recommending that Greenfield seek a more liberal environment outside of the country for her work. "We advise Elizabeth Greenfield to go to Europe and there remain," said the *New York Daily Tribune*. The suggestion was appropriate; Greenfield had been planning a trip for months and departed for England days after her New York debut.

In Britain, Greenfield doubtless had hopes of finding a good teacher, honing her vocal technique, and escaping the savagery of the American public and press toward her color. While much of mid-nineteenth-century America saw blacks in general as slaves, former slaves, or potential slaves, and saw black stage performers as minstrel buffoons, England's image of blacks was not so narrow and demeaning. Greenfield soon made friends among London's music community and literati, friends who would be useful in her career. Among them was the American writer Harriet Beecher Stowe, author of *Uncle Tom's Cabin*. Stowe helped sponsor concerts in the city and introduced her to the Duchess of Sutherland, who arranged performances for her at Stafford House. Of one performance Stowe wrote in her memoir, *Sunny Memories*:

Miss Greenfield stood among the singers on the staircase, and excited a pathetic murmur among the audience. She is not handsome, but looked very well....A certain gentleness of manner and self-possession, the result of the universal kindness shown her, sat well upon her. Chavalier Bunsen, the Prussian ambassador, sat by me. He looked at her with much interest. "Are the race often as good-looking?" he said. I said, "She is not handsome compared with many, though I confess she looks uncommonly well today."

Miss Greenfield's turn for singing now came, and there was profound attention. Her voice, with its keen, searching fire, its penetrating vibrant quality, its timbre as the French have it, cut its way like a Damascus blade to the heart. She sang the ballad "Old Folks at Home," giving one verse in the soprano, and another in the tenor voice. As she stood partially concealed by the piano, Chavalier Bunsen thought that the tenor part was performed by one of the gentlemen. He was perfectly astonished when he discovered that it was by her.

Lord Shaftesbury was there. He came and spoke to us after the concert. Speaking of Miss Greenfield, he said, "I consider the use of this hall for the encouragement of an outcast race a consecration. This is the true use of wealth and splendor, when they are employed to raise up and encourage the despised and forgotten."

With tutelage from her newly acquired accompanist Sir George Smart, organist and composer to Queen Victoria's Chapel Royal, Greenfield's singing became more refined. She sang for England's royalty, and on May 10, 1854, she gave a command performance for Queen Victoria at Buckingham Palace. The London critics raved, praising the power and purity of her voice. "Miss Greenfield sings 'I Know That My Redeemer Liveth,' with as much pathos, power and effect as does the 'Swedish Nightingale' Jenny Lind," said the *London Times*. And the *Morning Post* lauded her expansive range. "This lady is said to possess a voice embracing the extraordinary compass of nearly three octaves," it said, "and her performance on this occasion elicited the unmistakable evidence of gratification." When Greenfield returned to the United States in July 1854, New York critics acknowledged her newfound musical maturity, saying the Swan "now sings in true artistic style and the wonderful powers of her voice have been developed by good training."

Greenfield eventually returned to Philadelphia, where she continued to give concerts and set up a studio for private teaching. And when her career ended, she left a musical legacy that would have far-reaching effects. One of her students, tenor Thomas Bowers, had a professional career, traveling and singing with Greenfield under Wood's management. Bowers, in turn, taught others. Greenfield died in 1876, but the Swan's song echoed long into the future. As the first of black women concert artists, she left an impression of accomplished artistry and unfailing courage etched onto the cultural consciousness of her era. Greenfield was a trailblazer, ruggedly cleaving a pathway into unfamiliar and unfriendly territory and paving a smoother road for singers who followed.

The year 1876 proved a landmark in the history of the black American prima donna. Elizabeth Greenfield's death signaled the end of an important chapter in history and the beginning of another. It was a year that saw milestones in two other careers: Sissieretta Jones was fortuitously taken by her parents from the troubled South to culturally fertile New England, where her important career could grow and thrive, and in San Francisco Marie Selika (c. 1849–1937), another important artist, made her professional debut.

Though Selika's career as coloratura was eclipsed by Sissieretta Jones in later years, for a time she held forth as the preeminent artist and biggest drawing card of the day. Born Marie Smith, she borrowed the pseudonym from the lead character Selika in *L'Africaine*. Petite and demure-looking with refined features, Marie Selika was heralded as the "Queen of Staccato," a title she earned from her exemplary singing of show pieces such as Mulder's "Staccato Polka." The piece, showing off her solid two-octave range (from C to C) and her flair for ornamentation, became her signature work. She was reportedly the first black concert artist to sing at the White House (during the Hayes administration), preceding Jones by more than ten years. And like Greenfield, she sang for the Queen of England (in 1883).

By coincidence, the small town of Natchez, Mississippi, produced two great black prima donnas. Some twenty years after Greenfield, Selika also was born there. Details about her birth, early life, and parentage are scant and conflicting. But Selika's childhood was apparently peripatetic, as she traveled from Mississippi to Ohio, to San Francisco, to Chicago, and finally to the East. How and why she moved from place to place is not known, but wherever she went, she sought good music instruction and found it. In San Francisco she studied with Giovanna Bianchi, and in Ohio her vocal precocity attracted a wealthy family who arranged for her instruction there. In Chicago she studied with a coach named Farini. She settled in the Northeast, and in Boston was said to have replaced the indisposed Hungarian soprano Etelka Gerster at a concert one evening, to critical acclaim. In 1878 the black press announced the engagement of the young singer to perform the title role in *L'Africaine* at the Philadelphia Academy of Music. However, this may well have been an apocryphal report, as there is no other surviving account of what would have been a remarkable first.

Information on Selika's performance at the White House is also incomplete. But it is known that on November 13, 1878, a few months after the Colored Industrial School Children had sung in the East Room, Selika gave a program with her husband, baritone Sampson Williams, in the Green Room. After an introduction to President and Mrs. Rutherford Hayes from Marshall Fred Douglass, Selika sang "Ernani, involami," the Thomas Moore ballad "The Last Rose of Summer," Harrison Millard's "Ave Maria," and the "Staccato Polka." Her husband, a well-known artist who performed under the stage name "Signor Viloski," sang the Bliss ballad "Far Away." Though Selika was only about twenty-nine years old at her White House performance, her following was evidently sizeable and ardent. It is possible President Hayes knew of the singer before he became President, as Selika lived in Ohio during his two terms there as governor.

Selika and her husband toured the European capitals together and garnered good reviews from the Continental press. While Williams was a competent singer, Selika was the main attraction and the major reason for the duo's success. In Paris *Le Figaro* applauded her "very strong voice of depth and compass, rising with perfect ease from C to C," and added, "she trills like a feathered songster." In Berlin the *Tagblatt* said her singing "roused the audience to the highest pitch of enthusiasm." While in England in 1883, Williams apparently corresponded with the erudite writer James Trotter, who would later become Selika's manager. From Williams' descriptive letters came the reports of successes in England, Scotland, France, Germany, and Belgium, which Trotter related to the public through a black newspaper, the *New York Age*. Williams noted the respectful treatment of blacks on the Continent, particularly in Belgium. Trotter wrote, "Here as elsewhere in the line of their travels, himself [Williams] and Madame Selika have never once been slighted on account of their color, and at the most elegantly appointed hotel in Brussels they could not have received more polite attention had they been Madame Patti and husband. What a lesson for our as yet uncivilized America!" Later that year came Selika's command performance for Queen Victoria in St. James Hall in 1883, England's final stamp of approval for any singer of international repute.

Poised, attractive, and endowed with unusual talent, Selika must have been an engaging presence to concertgoers. But in the late 1800s her career lost momentum. Many sources say that teaming with her less-talented husband and booking concerts with him inhibited her career and limited its potential. Despite the unwillingness of some contractors to book the duo, Selika continued to perform with Williams, and the couple toured Europe again from 1887 through 1892, lived in Germany for a year, and performed in the West Indies. In 1893 she returned to Ohio, established a music studio, and continued to concertize. Chicago's black press reported on her performance in that city during the summer of the World's Fair. Interestingly, Sissieretta Jones was also performing in Chicago that summer, and the presence of the two black divas naturally prompted comparisons. The *Chicago Gazette* wrote: "Among our singers Madame Selika by common consent of connoisseurs still holds first place," but then said of Jones, "Public opinion ... proclaims her the greatest coming singer."

Selika and Williams moved to Philadelphia, where, in 1911, Williams died. Selika retired from the concert stage but in 1916 began teaching at the Martin-Smith School of Music, founded by violinist David Martin and located in Harlem on West 136th Street. In 1919 the respected *grande dame* of concert music was given a testimonial at St. Mark's Hall by her admirers. Selika died in New York in 1937 at age eighty-seven.

Extant reviews of Selika's performances suggest that she somehow was spared the usual pejorative racial references, perhaps because, unlike Jones and Greenfield, she did not look African. Her skin was fair, her hair long and straight, and she was not, as a reporter had said of Greenfield, "black in earnest." But as the first successful black coloratura, she captivated the public with her awesome display of vocal pyrotechnics. She thoroughly impressed British impresario James Henry Mapleson, who heard her sing once in a Philadelphia concert. A passage from his memoir reveals the Englishman's eagerness to hear the diva, as he ventured alone into the black section of the city.

> Whilst at Philadelphia, the head-waiter of the hotel informed me that a very grand concert was to take place, for which it was very difficult to obtain tickets, but that a prima donna would sing there whom he considered worthy of my attention. In due course he got me a ticket and I attended the concert, which was held in the extreme quarters of the city. On entering, I was quite surprised to find an audience of some 1,500 or 2,000, who were all black, I being the only white man present. I must say I was amply repaid for the trouble I had taken, as the music was all of the first order.
>
> In the course of the concert, the prima donna appeared, gorgeously attired in a white satin dress, with feathers in her hair, and a magnificent diamond necklace and earrings. She moreover wore white kid gloves, which nearly went to the full extent of her arm, leaving but a small space of some four inches between her sleeve and the top of her glove. Her skin being black, formed, of course, an extraordinary contrast with the white kid. She sang the "Shadow Song" from *Dinorah* delightfully, and in reply to a general encore, gave the valse from the *Romeo and Juliet* of Gounod. In fact, no better singing have I heard.

**Marie Selika**

Mapleson stayed for the remainder of the concert of black artists. Though Selika impressed him with her vocal prowess, he didn't offer her an opera contract, as he did for the young black baritone who followed her on the program.

> I immediately resolved upon offering him an engagement to appear at the opera house in London as Renato in *Un Ballo in Maschera*, whom Verdi, in one version of the opera, intended to be a coloured man; afterwards to perform Nelusko in *L'Africaine*, and Amonasro in *Aida*. Feeling certain of his success, I intended painting him white for the other operas. After some negotiations I was unable to complete the arrangement. He preferred to remain a star where he was.

In his memoir Mapleson gives no hint as to why the nameless young baritone appeared more deserving of a contract than Selika. Nevertheless, his enthusiasm for them both points out the difference between Europe and America regarding acceptance of the black artist of the nineteenth century.

With inroads laid carefully by singers like Greenfield and Selika, the public began to see the black diva no longer as an anomaly, but as a refreshing and welcomed presence on the concert stage. Other singers appeared, each with her own special persona and distinctive style of singing.

Flora Batson, a contemporary of Sissieretta Jones and fellow resident of Providence, Rhode Island, may have been slightly shadowed by Jones' towering stature but still enjoyed a worthy career. Also endowed with an enormous range, Batson was called the "Double Voiced Queen of Song." Her bearing was called "unaffected and almost childlike."

Like Jones', the singer's career began humbly in Providence's black churches. But by the age of nine, she was attracting hundreds to the Bethel Church, where the child star was the featured soloist. By thirteen, she was singing professionally, and in 1883 she attracted the attention of J. G. Bergen, a white concert manager who hired her to sing in his Tennessee Star Concert Company. The company was a successful touring organization and springboard for many well-known black artists, including baritone Harry T. Burleigh, tenor Sidney Woodward, and, at one time, Sissieretta Jones. When Batson joined the group, Nellie Brown, a black soprano from New Hampshire, was the star of the company. Due to a calendar conflict, the prima donna had to cancel one evening, leaving a vacancy Batson was ready to fill. She stepped in at the last minute, caused a sensation, and became the company's new star. Bergen took a liking to her personally as well, and on December 13, 1887, the two were married. Afterward, with Bergen as her husband and manager, Batson's career took flight, and soon she was booked all over the country and the world.

Naturally, the white diva name tags poured forth; a New York paper called her the "colored Jenny Lind," while the *Chicago Inter-Ocean* called her the "Patti of her race," no doubt aiding the inevitable confusion with Sissieretta Jones. The *Charleston News and Courier* called her a "highly cultivated mezzo-soprano [though her voice extended throughout both the soprano and mezzo ranges] of great sweetness, power, and compass," and a Lynchburg paper said she had "the sweetest voice that ever charmed a Virginia audience." In Victoria, British Columbia, the *Colonist* said, "the indescribable pathos of her voice in dramatic and pathetic selections wrought a wondrous effect." Batson toured the world three times, singing for Queen Victoria, Pope Leo XIII, Queen Lil of Hawaii, and New Zealand's native royal family. But her relationship with Bergen was short-lived; in 1896 they separated. Batson subsequently partnered with black basso Gerard Millar to sing "operatic specialties" with the South Before the War Company, and at the turn of the century performed with the Orpheus MacAdoo Minstrel and Vaudeville Company in Australia. Batson died on December 1, 1906.

Though not as well known, Anna Madah and Emma Louise Hyers formed a singing duo and toured the country performing to great acclaim in the late nineteenth century. Born in Sacramento in the early 1850s, the sisters showed prodigious talent early and, through the prudent supervision of their ambitious father, enjoyed long and successful careers. Anna Madah, a soprano of considerable gifts, was said by the *New York Evening Post* to possess a "flexible voice of great compass, clear and steady in the higher notes." The writer also praised Emma's beautiful contralto, calling it "a voice of great power and depth." As children the singers had studied with opera singer Josephine D'Ormy.

As a duo, they made their professional debut at the Metropolitan Theater in Sacramento in 1867, and began their first tour in 1871. Anna and Emma delighted audiences and critics in Missouri, Illinois, and Ohio, and after a performance in Salt Lake City in which they sang arias from Donizetti's *Linda di Chamounix*, the press noted Anna's effortless high E-flat, her birdlike trills, and Emma's dark, rich timbre. Their father engaged other popular singers, among them tenor Wallace King and baritone John Luca (oldest son in the famed family of concert singers), to fill out programs and expand the duo to a trio or quartet. The group worked its way eastward, and performed at Steinway Hall in New York. A successful appearance in 1872 at Patrick Gilmore's World Peace Jubilee concerts in Boston solidified their fame, and by 1875 they formed their own concert company.

Emma Louise Hyers and Anna Madah Hyers

In 1876 the Hyers' father expanded the company to include drama, and a four-act play titled *Out of Bondage* was written specially for them by Joseph B. Bradford. *Urlina the African Princess* and *The Underground Railroad*, written by black playwright Pauline E. Hopkins, were also added to the repertory. In 1883 the group appeared at the Grand Opera House in New York for the Callendar Consolidated Spectacular Minstrel Festival, then toured west. Two white concert managers, Charles and Gustave Frohman, had plans to organize a Colored Opera Troupe around the talented sisters and Marie Selika, but the company never materialized.

Emma and Anna continued to tour the country together performing *Out of Bondage* until the mid-1890s. Afterwards, they began to appear in separate ventures: Emma joined a company performing *Uncle Tom's Cabin* in 1894, and Anna joined John Ishman's minstrel production "Octoroons" to sing opera excerpts.

Shortly before the turn of the century, Emma died, and Anna traveled to Australia with the All-Star Afro-American Minstrels. She returned to the United States in the early 1900s and retired to her home in Sacramento.

Other talented singers emerged and centered their careers mostly around New England. But as the century ended and public tastes altered, the black woman as concert artist fell out of fashion. Adelaide and Georgina Smith of Providence, Estelle Pickney Clough, Edna E. Brown (sister of Nellie Brown), Rosa and Sadie DeWolf, and Rachel Walker all had respectable careers. Desseria Plato's Azucena in Verdi's *Il Trovatore* with Farini's Grand Creole and Colored Opera Company in New York brought her a modicum of recognition. Recitalists Annie Pindell and Amelia Tilghman also attracted audiences for a time, but none of these singers reached the heights of their stellar antecedents. Whether the decline in popularity was due to the inevitable attenuation of a trend or a dearth of world-class talent is difficult to say. Perhaps, as in the case of Jones and Greenfield, the black diva in nineteenth-century America could survive only as a novelty, and increased familiarity only lessened her appeal. As Eileen Southern in *The Music of Black Americans* explained:

> The fickle public soon tired of black prima donnas. Although the singers were gifted, well trained, and fortunate in obtaining good management, their careers on the concert stage were relatively short, ranging from three or four years to a dozen or so in most instances. Their white impresarios staged concerts in the prestigious halls of the United States and Europe and arranged for command performances before important persons, but to no avail. By the mid-1890s the black

prima donna had almost disappeared from the nation's concert halls because of lack of public interest.

The determination and conviction of Emma Azalia Hackley represented a glimmer of light at the end of the century. Born in Tennessee in 1867, Hackley was committed to the selfless task of teaching young black artists and helping to advance their careers. As a young soprano she began by giving recitals in Detroit and in Colorado, where she was a student at the University of Denver. After her debut there in 1901, she toured for a while, and in 1904 she organized a one-hundred-voice People's Chorus in Philadelphia. She studied in Paris with the renowned Polish tenor Jean de Reszke for a year, then returned to Philadelphia.

If the black vocal artist was a fading presence at the turn of the century, Hackley did her best to revive it. She held tenaciously to her idea of educating talented black singers, to the detriment of her own singing career, and in 1908 established a scholarship fund for assisting black artists. She founded a school for training and instruction and called it the Vocal Normal Institute. She wrote a series for the *New York Age* titled "Hints to Young Colored Artists." She traveled around the country, lecturing and organizing large choruses in major cities, using their best black singers.

Hackley continued to travel and concertize in her later years, but only to raise money for her institute and its students. She became widely known as an authority on black folk music, promoting the idiom to the delight and edification of American audiences, and was largely responsible for its growing acceptance. Her death in 1922 was untimely; she collapsed while on tour in California, but she is remembered as a crusader committed to the proliferation of the schooled black singer.

It took years, but in due course the black diva regained her place of prominence in the concert world. The die had been cast, and the hard-won gains of Greenfield, Jones, Selika, and others in the American concert hall were irrevocable. The new century promised bolder voices, defiantly stentorian and even less willing to be muted than the proud pioneers of the past. While the major opera companies obstinately continued to refuse the black artist for decades, the concert halls of Europe and America soon resounded with the voices of black women. Having survived the skepticism, derision, and neglect of the nineteenth century, the black woman artist began to benefit from the confluence of new ideas presaging the American civil rights movement. And from the wellspring of talent that is black America emerged some of the greatest and most beloved classical vocalists in musical history.

# 3

# *Marian Anderson: The Voice of a Century*

O N the evening of December 30, 1935, in New York's Town Hall, a waiting audience was restive and expectant. News of a young American singer's triumphs in Europe and return home had brought hundreds to the hall in the middle of the holiday season, but nothing had prepared them for the drama of the event. As if metaphorically unveiling a new work of art, drawn curtains finally parted to reveal a tall black woman, broad boned with a queenly manner, standing poised in the piano's curve. Her face was angular and noble, and like the arched shoulders of a Stradivarius, her pronounced cheekbones defined the perfect chamber for a sound that, as Toscanini had said, "one hears once in a hundred years." With her eyes closed and her face in spiritual repose, she sang—and an epoch began.

On the night of her historic Town Hall concert, Marian Anderson caused a wave of excitement that New York had seldom seen. Even the discomfort of a broken ankle (the curtains had been drawn to conceal the awkwardness of her being wheeled to the stage) could not suppress that surge of sound, with its limitless musical capacity and bottomless soul. New York critics, although forewarned of her talent by their European counterparts, were surprised and exultant, calling her one of the "great singers of our time." Her rise to fame had been more circuitous than meteoric—Anderson herself could give testimony to the early years of doubt and frustration. But in the years to follow, America's preeminent contralto was transformed from singer to symbol to national treasure. She was decorated by presidents, admired by kings, honored by universities, and, at a crucial period in history, embodied the hopes and spirit of an oppressed people with unparalleled dignity.

Few present that evening remembered her first performance at Town Hall more than ten years before. Then, her confidence buoyed by encouraging responses to hometown performances, the young singer had plunged herself into the mainstream of the New York recital world, only to be promptly tossed back by indifferent criticism. At twenty-two, she was far from the artist she later would become. By the time she made her second appearance, she was a different person. Ten years abroad had matured her musicality and solidified her training. Europe, with its polyglot cultures and overlapping of languages from country to country, had settled her linguistic apprehensions and given her first-hand familiarity with the music of the European masters. Triumphs in Scandinavia, Russia, Germany, France, and Austria had restored her confidence, this time irrevocably. News of her successes traveled across the Continent and to the United States. And by the time her stay on the Continent ended, Europe was mourning her departure as America excitedly awaited her return.

Marian Anderson, the shy woman with the "voice of the century," captured the collective heart of the country after Town Hall, and rarely was a performance not sold out for the rest of her long career. Critics were enamoured of the voice as well as the persona. Of a performance in Vienna, *New York Times* writer Herbert F. Peyser wrote: "There can be no question that Miss Anderson, alike by virtue of her great, gorgeous voice, her art of song, the emotional, indeed the spiritual and mystical elements of her nature that repeatedly lend her work the character of a consecration, her dignity, sympathy, and ineffable sincerity of approach, ranks today among the few imposing vocal confrontations of the age."

And critics labored long to describe that unusual voice, with its earthy darkness at the bottom, its clarinet-like purity in the middle, and its piercing vibrancy at the top. Her range was expansive—from a full-bodied D in the bass clef to a brilliant high C. When words failed them, some reviewers simply called it a Negroid sound. One critic called her the black Lilli Lehmann, but the description was hopelessly inadequate—and by now white diva sobriquets were seen as fatuous and insulting. Marian Anderson, they finally admitted, was one of a kind. More than once, her singing of spirituals had left listeners in rapt silence. And with her visceral low D in Schubert's "Der Tod und das Mädchen," she could excite listeners more with one note than other singers could with an entire song. Another *Times* critic, Howard Taubman, praised the "sheer magnificence of the voice" with its "stunning range and volume managed with suppleness and grace."

Henry Pleasants, in his *The Great Singers*, wrote that her lower range had a "Stygian darkness" not to everyone's liking (a curious mythological allusion to hell, especially when considering the spiritual nature of Anderson's art) and said her upper notes "tended toward

Marian
Anderson

stridency." But Kosti Vehanen, the Finnish pianist who accompanied Anderson for years, was moved by the mysterious qualities of her voice at their first rehearsal together and wrote of Anderson in his 1941 biography:

> From where does this sound come? I thought. It was as though the room had begun to vibrate, as though the sound came from under the earth. I could not find the direction of the tone, but it seemed to me that the very atmosphere was charged with beauty—certainly the tone must come from under the earth. It made me think of an exquisite flower that stands alone in a deep forest, where no human being has ever trod, the roots drinking the aged nectar from the soil, rich with every substance that sun, rain and fire can create. Such a flower blooms with a superb loveliness, with a most delicate perfume, trembling with a tenderness never before felt. So the sound I heard swelled to majestic power, the flower opened its petals to full brilliance; and I was enthralled by one of nature's rare wonders.

If any voice in history could inspire such unabashed, lofty prose, Anderson's could. But her voice was only a fraction of the total effect she created as America's foremost contralto and one of its most beloved performers. As a black artist whose height of popularity coincided with racist Nazi furor in Europe, Anderson's presence reminded high-minded Americans of their own social inconsistencies. The ironies were undeniable and blatant; she was her country's premier concert artist but had been turned away from one of its music schools as well as from its hotels and restaurants, and she was often obliged to sing in segregated halls. Europe, even with its encroaching Third Reich and talk of Aryan supremacy, had treated her better. And when she was refused permission from the color-conscious Daughters of the American Revolution to sing in Constitution Hall, the irony ignited a national cause célèbre, expanding her life and career to nearly messianic proportion.

Thus Anderson's artistry became the core of a heroic presence. For blacks she was, and is, a point of pride and a source of inspiration, having raised herself through diligent hard work from Philadelphia's humbler quarters to the forefront of the American concert world. For America, she was a dignified ambassador, traveling from continent to continent and personifying her country's nobler principles through her exalted art and the universal message of her music. As a personality, she was the soul of humility and a refreshing change in the world of self-obsessed concert artists. Her humbleness even affected her grammar. "We felt we sang well," she might tell a reporter, demonstrating her well-known aversion to the implied vanity of self-descriptive pronouns like "I" and "me." Early on, the press saw this pluralization of the self as a grand affectation, but later they were convinced of her genuine belief that her work was invariably the result of a group effort. "The longer one lives," she once said, "one realizes that there is no particular thing that you can do alone. Even the voice, the breath, the motion that you have, to go to a platform to perform, it's not of your doing. So the 'I' in it is very small after all."

Anderson's legendary humility belied both the enormity of the talent and the regal countenance she assumed. Lola Hayes, a New York vocal coach (and in recent years a friend of Anderson) recalled an incident in the 1940s, during the height of Anderson's fame, which bespoke the artist's ability to be both queenly and common. "I went to a concert at Town Hall one night...I don't even remember who was singing," said Hayes. "I went down on the Eighth Avenue subway, and at about Eighty-Fifth Street two ladies got on—a white lady and a colored lady. I thought, 'That lady certainly resembles Marian Anderson,' but I never dreamed that she would be riding the subway. We got off at Town Hall, and finally I said, 'Miss Anderson?' She turned and said 'Yes, my dear?' Just very simple, almost plain. I think she had been visiting with this lady and they simply decided the quickest way to get to Town Hall was on the Eighth Avenue subway."

It would be difficult to envision either Callas or Sutherland at the height of their fame dropping tokens into turnstiles, waiting on platforms, and riding as straphangers. But interestingly, the woman who was not above using New York's public transportation system had an effect on those around her that can be described as mystical. She was inundated with mail from all over the world—from fans, well-wishers, and celebrities. The University of Pennsylvania's Van Pelt Library now houses her massive collection of artifacts, among them letters from such figures as Josephine Baker, Ed Sullivan, Rudolf Bing, and Franklin and Eleanor Roosevelt. One of the most poignantly descriptive impressions of Anderson's simplicity and largesse is found in a letter to her from Vincent Sheean, an American correspondent and admirer of Mahatma Gandhi. Sheean had spent an afternoon with Anderson, discussing the possibility of co-authoring her autobiography. (He ultimately declined the offer, and Anderson later produced *My Lord, What a Morning* in 1956, assisted by Howard Taubman.) Like others who found themselves in Anderson's presence, Sheean was struck by the artist's ability, like other great men and women in history, to imbue simple motions with poetic meaning. Later he wrote:

Dear Miss Anderson,
    I have wanted to tell you that nothing I ever experienced could equal the afternoon I spent with you in respect to acts and words full of meaning. I remember how you built the fire. You were not really

thinking about the fire. You were thinking of the things we were talking about. You told me that the first opera duet you had studied...was "Ebben, qual nuovo fremito t'assal gentile Aida." You told me the first duet you ever sang in your life was in church in Philadelphia and it was with Roland Hayes, something about the going-away or the coming-back of the swallows, by a composer whose name (I'm wrong but this is a guess) was Lensbach. Then you told me about the opera-house in Berlin where poor students could go and get a ticket by pulling a number out of a basket in the lobby. Whatever number you got determined your seat, whether it was the best or the worst in the house. And we spoke of opera in general. Meanwhile the fire grew and blazed, and I declare to you that I have never seen a fire more beautifully built or more beautifully inflamed. You seemed to have done it without thinking about doing it, and yet I remember well how slowly, carefully, you put each piece of wood into the fire while you were speaking. I thought then, and think now, and always shall think: this is a woman like Mahatma Gandhi.

Anderson's Gandhi-like grace, especially imperturbable in the face of racial rebuffs, was a tribute to a highly principled and family-centered upbringing in South Philadelphia. Anderson was born in 1902 to John Anderson, an ice and coal salesman, and his wife, Anna, a former Virginia school teacher. Old-fashioned Christian ethics coupled with traditional morality formed the hallmark of her childhood. Her father died when she was twelve, and her mother, unable to continue teaching because her certificate had been lost in a fire, took in washing. Marian's affinity for music showed early. First a four-dollar violin in a local store window caught her fancy, and a compulsion to own it drove her to scrub steps for pay until the instrument could be hers. Later, the fascination turned inward, to the sound of her own voice. Others soon shared the interest in her ripening talent and paid her to sing. Before long Marian was the principal breadwinner for her mother and two sisters, earning fifty cents, and later a dollar or two, performing as the "baby contralto."

Black Philadelphians had enjoyed a long, rich history of musical sophistication, and even the city's poorer black churches were well known for their gala concerts, featuring the best black talent in and around Philadelphia. The family's church, Union Baptist, was the setting for Anderson's public debut. She might have been called a utility singer for the junior and senior choirs, singing any needed part from high soprano to bass and eventually singing solos. Roland Hayes, the successful black tenor and graduate of Fisk and Harvard universities, was a frequent performer at Union Baptist and took an active interest in the young singer's career. With Hayes as her adviser and mentor, Anderson became a local favorite, singing as many as two and three engagements on a Sunday evening and earning as much as five dollars per concert.

A precocious child, Anderson observed that successful singers studied their art. "All this time I was singing from nature, so to speak, without any thought of how," she later wrote in her autobiography. "It slowly dawned on me that I had to have some training." In her middle teenage years she boldly approached a music school in Philadelphia for instruction, but was curtly informed, "We don't take colored." Anderson's first and most bitter confrontation with prejudice was a jolting revelation. "It was as if a cold horrifying hand had been laid on me," she said. Disappointed but undaunted, she sought private study. Early training began with a local soprano, Mary Saunders Patterson, who donated lessons to the gifted youngster. Later, when Anderson was introduced to Giuseppe Boghetti, a well-known tenor and coach of professionals, a student-teacher relationship began that would last off and on for twenty years, until Boghetti's death in 1941.

When Boghetti first heard of the talented young singer, he was skeptical, but after hearing her sing he was convinced of her potential. "I knew she was a find after five minutes," Boghetti told a *Philadelphia Record* reporter years after their first meeting. "When she first came to me eighteen years ago she had been turned down by a half dozen teachers. Understand, the voice was untrained, raw and wild as prairie grass. There was no placement; the colors weren't blended; there were only one or two tones. But what tones! The first thing she sang was 'Deep River' and Joe Boghetti almost dropped. The timbre nearly swamped me."

With money raised from the church, lessons began with Boghetti. The instructor's "find" was in regular demand soon, traveling to nearby cities by train to sing. Nearly every black church, YMCA, and club within a day's drive called for the services of the young singer, and Anderson, accompanied by a talented neighborhood pianist named Billy King, eagerly obliged. By now her voice was beginning to take on the refinement and coloration of an artist. "The more I sang, the more confident I became," she said. "I was now beginning to feel that my voice was more mature, that it was developing size and responding to Mr. Boghetti's training and the experience of concertizing. My voice was beginning to speak in a new way." Full of self-assurance, she was eager to test the currents of the recital world. Her first Town Hall recital was arranged.

Later Anderson admitted that her Town Hall debut was premature and that little thought had been given to the consequences of an unfavorable response. Her performance was tentative, her manner apologetic. Barely twenty-two years old, she had no knowledge of foreign languages, and it showed. "Miss Anderson sang her Brahms as if by rote," a reviewer noted the next day. It was true. Anderson sang Lieder phonetically, artificially shaping the syllables into a meaningless imitation of German. The critics were sharply honest and reprimanding. Their words cast the singer into a mire of despair. "I was embarrassed that I had tried to sing in one of New York's concert halls without being fully ready," Anderson lamented. "I did not want to see any music . . . I did not want to make a career of it." But the depression after the Town Hall "fiasco," as Anderson called it, was short-lived. With youthful buoyancy and the patient prodding of her coach, Anderson continued to sing and to learn.

When Marian Anderson entered her middle twenties, Boghetti felt his charge was ready for competition. She was a winner the first time out, in a small local contest sponsored by the Philadelphia Harmonic Society. But the Philadelphia Orchestra's upcoming annual vocal competition carried with it the prize of an appearance with the orchestra at Lewisohn Stadium in New York. Painstakingly, Boghetti and Anderson prepared "O mio Fernando" from Donizetti's *La Favorita*. The singer won the event hands down over some 300 participants, and along with it the opportunity to sing with one of the country's greatest orchestras.

On the night of August 26, 1925, 7,500 people, including busloads of family and friends, heard Philadelphia's native daughter sing before the third-largest stadium crowd that summer. The applause was tumultuous and the New York press was ecstatic. "A remarkable voice was heard last night at the Lewisohn Stadium," exclaimed Francis D. Perkins in the *New York Herald Tribune* the next day, and he praised Anderson's singing for its "entire naturalness; all that she had to do, apparently, was to sing, without any need of apparent effort to fill the Stadium spaces. In high and low notes, there was a full rich quality that carried far."

After the stadium concert, Arthur Judson, a well-known artists' representative, lured Anderson into his management with promises of increased bookings and higher fees. But then her career inexplicably stagnated. The $750 per concert figure Judson had promised in their initial conversations was cut to $500 in their final agreement. And the number of bookings, instead of increasing, declined. Three years later, though her earning power had burgeoned and her family was well cared for, Anderson found herself unhappily wandering on a musical plateau. Desultorily, she continued singing the same engagements as when she began: a church concert here, a civic club function there. She was locked in a career that lacked progress or momentum. Frustrated, she changed teachers and began studying with Frank LaForge. She thought a new teacher might revitalize her career and attitude, but nothing changed. Eventually, the answer occurred to her—she would go to Europe and realize a closer proximity to the culture her music reflected. She would perfect her knowledge of the languages, absorb the culture, learn from Europe's best pedagogues, and refine her artistry.

Anderson sailed for Europe in 1925 on the *Ile de France*, compelled and full of purpose, as if obeying a spiritual directive. The wisdom of her decision was confirmed at every turn. She studied in London with money she had been given from a Rosenwald Fellowship, and soon concerts were arranged. In Berlin, after a program of spirituals, a Finnish pianist was so impressed he offered to arrange a tour of Scandinavia for her—and Kosti Vehanen became her accompanist for the next fifteen years. In Finland, audiences were spellbound by the voice and the curiously unfamiliar but intriguing presence of the black American. No less impressed was that country's famous composer, Jean Sibelius, who invited Anderson to sing at his house, then celebrated her performance of his music with champagne. Later Sibelius dedicated one of his songs to her.

Over the next several years, Anderson conquered the European capitals, occasionally returning to the United States to fulfill concert commitments. In Europe, her career experienced an unimagined resurgence. Between September of 1933 and April of 1934, she gave 142 concerts in Denmark, Norway, Sweden, and Finland. The next year she toured Poland, Russia, Latvia, Switzerland, Belgium, Austria, Hungary, Italy, and Spain. By the middle 1930s, word of Anderson's singing had spread throughout the entire continent. But the impact of her music on pre-Hitler Europe, standing as it did so precariously on the brink of disruption, extended well beyond the limitations of singer and song. With a disarming pathos and spirituality never before encountered in that part of the world, Anderson vocalized the tragic suffering of a remote, unfamiliar race, and made the experience of a disconsolate people painfully real to her listeners.

The place was Salzburg, Austria; the year 1935. The occasion marked the summit of Marian Anderson's European success. The flood of musicians and music-lovers to Mozart's home and site of the annual summer music festival was not unlike a pilgrimage to the shrine of a saint. From every corner of the earth, concert-goers besieged the city. Musical excellence was the order of the day, and the small town overflowed with the best and brightest of the musically elite. Conductors Arturo Toscanini and Bruno Walter, the great diva Lotte Lehmann, and others performed before the most sophisticated of audiences, and when they weren't performing, took in the musical offerings of their colleagues. Anderson was to sing on August 18 but was barred mysteriously from performing. A foreign news service later determined that a "non-Aryan" rule, particularly aimed against people of color, was responsible. As mysteriously as that concert was banned, another one was scheduled for August 28, under the auspices of a Mrs. Moulton, a musical hostess.

The list of audience members was impressive. Toscanini, Lehmann, Walter, and the Archbishop of Salzburg were present that afternoon at the Hotel de l'Europe. Anderson began with Bach, Schubert, and Schumann and concluded with spirituals. Vincent Sheean heard her program and, in his vivid memoir *Between the Thunder and the Sun*, wrote:

> In the last group she sang a spiritual, "They crucified my Lord, and He never said a mumblin' word." Hardly anybody in the audience understood English well enough to follow what she was saying, and yet the immense sorrow—something more than the sorrow of a single person—that weighted her tones and lay over her dusky, angular face was enough. At the end of this spiritual there was no applause at all—a silence instinctive, natural and intense, so that you were afraid to breathe. What Anderson had done was something outside the limits of classical or romantic music: she frightened us with the conception, in musical terms of course, but outside the normal limits, of a mighty suffering.

Anderson seemed to come by the ability to communicate "a mighty suffering," the woes and pain of the black race in particular and the human race at large, as naturally as she breathed. The effect was spellbinding. Sheean was not alone in his response. Earlier in the program, the Archbishop was moved to ask Anderson to repeat the Schubert "Ave Maria." She did. And Toscanini, unable to wait until the end of the concert, hastened backstage at intermission to issue his now legendary proclamation: "Yours is a voice one hears once in a hundred years." It was more than a pronouncement; it was an anointment. Although she hardly needed it, Toscanini's blessing would do her no harm. Characteristically, Anderson was embarrassed by the remark—the famous compliment was quoted in articles written about her for the rest of her career. In her autobiography, Anderson said she was so nervous at meeting Toscanini that she never heard the statement, and a friend later relayed the message to her. Perhaps she wondered if he'd actually said it. But if Toscanini felt he had been misquoted, or resented his remark being made public, he never said so.

News of the Salzburg success reached the United States within hours. Herbert Peyser had attended the recital, along with a sizable American contingent. "Before the evening was half over," Peyser wrote in his review, "these Americans were behaving with the same turbulent enthusiasm as the most temperamental Europeans." He went on:

"Once more the sumptuous fabric of this incomparable voice, the singer's marvelous ability to create and sustain lyric moods and the spontaneous elemental appeal of her emotional nature...exercized their overpowering effect." Anderson was, he concluded, "one of the greatest living singers."

After this triumph, Anderson's life and career changed immeasurably. Sol Hurok heard her for the first time in Paris that year. "Chills danced up my spine," he said of the experience. "I was shaken to my very shoes." The impresario hurried to meet her backstage after the performance. He was appalled to learn of the arrangement she had with Judson in the United States. Though she had hired a European manager, she was still giving Judson ten percent of all her earnings. Her American concerts were few and not particularly well attended. Hurok told her he could guarantee her fifteen concerts a season. Anderson, who had never actually signed her contract with Judson, now cabled him with the news of Hurok's offer. If Judson could not match the terms, she said, she would end her agreement with him. Judson backed down, releasing her with his best wishes. In later years, Hurok's guarantee of fifteen concerts expanded to ninety in one season.

The first thing Hurok did for his new artist was to arrange for her proper homecoming, and he quickly organized her Town Hall concert to take place the winter of 1935. A shipboard accident on the way home left Anderson with a broken ankle, and Hurok feared the concert would have to be canceled. Anderson was determined to sing but did not want to solicit sympathy by hobbling out to the piano on crutches. After much discussion, a solution was found—she would be wheeled to the appointed spot behind drawn curtains, which would be drawn again after each group of songs. The curtains and the long gown worked well to conceal the artist's infirmity. Not until the end of the first half of the program did Anderson bother to explain the situation to her listeners. By then, the audience was hers, and the overwhelming success of the second Town Hall recital was assured.

While some reviewers were cautiously complimentary, Howard Taubman of the *New York Times* threw caution to the wind and let the accolades fly. "Let it be said at the outset," he began, "Marian Anderson has returned to her native land one of the great artists of our time." Each following paragraph contained a litany of superlatives, as Taubman spoke of the "genuine emotional identification with the core of the music...the music-making that probed too deep for words...the penetrating command of style." The *Times'* senior critic, Olin Downes, had rushed over from an opera he was covering, and in his opera review the next day found space for a few more words of praise for Anderson's art.

Hurok arranged more concerts, and as fast as he could book them, they sold out. The clamor for Anderson concert tickets dominated conversation in New York music circles. Within a few years, Anderson became one of the five highest-paid concert artists in the country, earning a reported $2,500 a performance. On *Variety*'s box office score for 1939, she was topped only by Nelson Eddy and Lily Pons.

But despite her success, no amount of money she earned could secure her a room in New York's whites-only hotels; for years she used the Harlem YWCA, until finally rooms at the Algonquin in midtown Manhattan were made available through a friend. When she was hired by Twentieth Century-Fox to sing at the opening of the film *Young Mr. Lincoln* in Springfield, Illinois, she was refused as a guest at the Lincoln Hotel. And several restaurants, fearful of upsetting their prestigious clientele, categorically refused any party that included Marian Anderson. Racism still ruled in America, and even an artist like Anderson was not exempt from racial abuse.

The event that made Anderson the reluctant leader of a fledgling movement for equal rights was the refusal of the Daughters of the American Revolution to allow the singer to perform in Constitution Hall in Washington, D.C. A routinely scheduled concert caused the nation's capital to become the controversial focal point of the national news for weeks.

The incident began innocuously. Howard University officials approached Hurok for permission to present Marian Anderson in concert in Washington. Hurok replied with an available date: April 9, 1939. The singer had performed in Washington often, usually on the campus of the university. But by now, Anderson's drawing power was so great that the university officials felt a bigger auditorium was needed.

Constitution Hall, owned by the D.A.R., was suggested. However, Fred Hand, manager of the hall, told the university and Hurok that the National Symphony had booked it for a concert on the proposed date. When it was learned that the hall was being used by the National Symphony for an evening concert, while the Anderson concert was to be held in the afternoon, Hand came back with: "It is the policy of the hall never to book two musical attractions in the same day unless they are under the same management." Constitution Hall officials and the D.A.R. were ready with any reason that seemed convenient for the hall's unavailability.

Hurok knew that the D.A.R. and Constitution Hall's manager were carefully skirting the real issue and pressed further to get a clear statement of the hall's policy regarding race. If the National Symphony had no objection, Hurok asked, could the hall be used that afternoon by Marian Anderson? That, replied Hand, would have to be decided by the D.A.R.

It was weeks before the D.A.R. would admit what was already evident—that it was the policy of the organization not to allow blacks to perform in Constitution Hall. The policy had been adopted in 1932, at the behest of a D.A.R. adviser who claimed that the "best" halls in the District of Columbia did not lease to blacks. (The all-black choir of the Hampton Institute had performed there in 1931; the whites-only policy went into effect soon afterwards.) The D.A.R. board met to discuss reconsideration of the policy to accommodate Anderson, and voted 39–1 to keep the whites-only rule. On February 15, 1939, Hand reported to Charles Cohen, chairman of the Howard concert series: "The hall is not available for a concert by Miss Anderson."

Meanwhile, media coverage of the controversy rivaled coverage of Hitler's campaign in Europe. The *Washington Herald* wrote a scathing editorial decrying the ban by the D.A.R. A few days later the *New York Times* picked up the story. The drama intensified when the Board of Education of Washington denied use of the all-white Central High School Auditorium for the Anderson concert, claiming its policies had to remain consistent with Washington's segregationist or "dual school system." The board discussed the situation in heated sessions. "I am satisfied," said board member Charles Drayton during an open meeting, "that the majority of Washington citizens are opposed to interracial use of public schools. If a precedent of this sort is established, the board will lose respect and confidence of the people and bring about its destruction."

Blacks in Washington were furious. A Marian Anderson Protest Committee was formed. NAACP members, sympathizers, and seventy-three civic organizations banded together and presented a petition with 7,000 signatures to the board to protest the action. Members of the committee picketed the Board of Education building. The school board finally rescinded its decision with a caveat—blacks must not consider the concession a precedent and should not invoke the decision later to gain future use of the hall. When the Anderson committee could not accept the conditions, the offer was withdrawn.

It was weeks before Mrs. Henry Robert, Jr., president-general of the D.A.R., addressed the issue of Constitution Hall publicly with a formal statement. She finally broke the silence with the Daughters' carefully constructed explanation: The hall would be denied to Anderson and other blacks as a result of an "unpleasant experience in attempting to go contrary to conditions and customs existing in the District of Columbia."

"This is not a question for the Daughters of the American Revolution alone to solve," she added. "When the community at large has worked out its problem, the D.A.R. will be willing, as at all times, to adopt its policies to practices and customs in accordance with the highest standards of the community."

The D.A.R. steadfastly stood by its statement, despite the rising storm of protest that focused a national spotlight on the nation's capital. Sympathizers from all over the country galvanized in support of the Anderson committee. In other cities, D.A.R. members became personae non grata; some even resigned from the organization. The NAACP received a deluge of mail from celebrities. Artists such as Kirsten Flagstad, Lawrence Tibbett, Geraldine Farrar, Walter Damrosch, Leopold Stokowski, and Frederick Jagel sent telegrams and letters or publicly expressed their support of the Anderson protest. Violinist Jascha Heifetz, who performed in Constitution Hall during the height of the ordeal, told the *Washington Star*, "I protest as the entire musical profession protests against such a sad and deplorable attitude. To think that this very hall in which I played today has been barred to a great singer because of her race; it made me feel ashamed that there could be such a situation in Washington."

But the drama climaxed when the First Lady, Eleanor Roosevelt, resigned from the D.A.R., citing the ban against Anderson as the reason. Mrs. Roosevelt had long been a fan of the great contralto and years before had invited her to sing at the White House. In her newspaper column "My Day," she wrote on hearing Anderson at that private recital in 1936, "My husband and I had a rare treat in listening to Marian Anderson. I have rarely heard a more beautiful and moving voice or a more finished artist."

Eleanor Roosevelt watched the controversy gather momentum, at first, from a distance. Weeks earlier, at the founding meeting of the Southern Conference on Human Welfare held in Birmingham, she had taken a controversial stand, ignoring the city's segregated seating policy by entering the conference with and sitting beside black educator Mary McLeod Bethune. She wrestled with the idea of resigning from the D.A.R., consulting with friends and advisers before she finally made her decision. To her column readers she wrote:

> The question is, if you belong to an organization and disapprove of an action which is typical of a policy, shall you resign or is it better to work for a changed point of view within the organization? In the past when I was able to work actively in any organization to which I belonged, I have usually stayed in until I had at least made a fight and been defeated. Even then I have as a rule accepted my defeat and decided either that I was wrong or that I was perhaps a little too far ahead of the thinking of the majority of that time. I have often found that the thing in which I was interested was done some years later. But, in this case I belong to an organization in which I can do no

active work. They have taken an action which has been widely talked of in the press. To remain as a member implies approval of that action, and therefore I am resigning.

The Franklin Roosevelt administration viewed the First Lady's resignation circumspectly, but a Gallup poll revealed that sixty-seven percent of the American people were in favor of her decision to leave the D.A.R. With Mrs. Roosevelt's action, the groundswell of protest mushroomed. But the one passive presence in the turn of events was the artist herself.

Anderson was busy with concerts in California and had heard something about trouble with the Washington concert from Hurok's office. She learned about the protests and the Roosevelt resignation from a newspaper headline. Reporters dogged her heels, following her from concert to concert, but in the swirling vortex of confusion Anderson remained its quiet center. She endured the affair with an almost saintly silence. Try as they might, reporters could not pry an unkind word from her or exact an edifying remark. "I don't know any more about this than you do," she politely and repeatedly told a frustrated press corps. And in a way, her reticence further fueled the controversy, adding intrigue to the drama and making the D.A.R.'s action seem even more unconscionable and bullying. Decades later, she told a journalist, "Oh, I forgave the D.A.R. many years ago. You can spend a lot of time hating people."

Meanwhile, in the back of Hurok's mind was a plan that would not only solve the problem, but also bring the affair to a spectacular conclusion. On February 24, he announced that Anderson would give an open-air concert in Washington. He dispatched his press agent, Gerry Goode, accompanied by NAACP president Walter White, to the Department of the Interior to get permission for the free concert. Within minutes Secretary of the Interior Harold Ickes granted permission. The concert would take place on April 9, Easter Sunday, on the steps of the Lincoln Memorial.

Anderson had difficulty reconciling herself to the grandstand nature of an appearance outdoors in Washington before a multitude of thousands conveniently within gloating distance of the Daughters' Constitution Hall. She was not predisposed to political one-upmanship, nor to flamboyant, attention-getting spectacles. As late as the evening before the event she had doubts about performing. Arriving in Washington some days before the concert to visit her accompanist, who was ill, she found the press obtrusive and overbearing. The affair was turning into a circus, and she saw it growing out of proportion. Nevertheless Anderson agreed with the principle behind the concert. "I could see that my significance as an individual was small in this affair," she said. "I had become, whether I liked it or not, a symbol representing my people. I had to appear."

On Easter Sunday afternoon, before a crowd of 75,000 people on the Lincoln Memorial grounds, Anderson stepped onto a platform to begin the most celebrated concert of her career. Seated behind her were political dignitaries, sponsors of the concert who wished to go on record as aligning themselves with the cause. Stretched before her was the largest Washington crowd since Lindbergh's arrival in 1927. The mass of people occasionally pressed forward, and at one point policemen had to contain the restless throng. Anderson was overwhelmed. "There seemed to be people as far as the eye could see," she later wrote. "I had a feeling that a great wave of goodwill poured out from these people, almost engulfing me." The expanse of blacks and whites finally quieted and waited for her to sing. Her voice stifled with emotion, she began with "America," then sang "O mio Fernando," Schubert's "Ave Maria," and three spirituals: "Gospel Train," "Trampin'," and "My Soul Is Anchored in the Lord." The applause was deafening. Articulate as usual, Anderson humbly acknowledged her thanks to the crowd. But the words that most aptly expressed the profound significance of the occasion were from Harold Ickes, who in introducing Anderson said, "There are those . . . who are either too timid or too indifferent to lift up the light that Jefferson and Lincoln carried aloft."

It was more than a concert; it was a celebration of mankind's potential for humanity, and the triumph over intransigence and narrow-minded thinking was poetic. Anderson's "tragic muse," as Vincent Sheean described it, had rallied souls for a unifying purpose, and long after the last musical notes were sounded, the image of the great artist singing at the feet of "the Emancipator" weighed heavily on the American conscience.

The Easter concert had an epilogue: The Department of the Interior commissioned a mural commemorating the event in the form of a contest; the painting by the winning entrant, Mitchell Jamieson, now hangs in the Interior building. During the war years, the Daughters invited Anderson to sing in Constitution Hall for a war benefit by the National Society, even though they wouldn't allow the invitation to act as a precedent for future concerts. Anderson reluctantly agreed to sing, not wanting to deprive the war effort. But not until 1953 did she give her first commercial concert there, with no restrictions or caveats, as part of the American University Concert Series.

The media mania surrounding the D.A.R. controversy ensured that any abuse of Anderson's civil rights from that point on would not go unnoticed by the press. The *Chicago Defender* reported it when Anderson and friends were barred from entering the exclusive Granite

Club in Toronto in 1944. And in 1952, when 250 whites demanded refunds for a concert in Jacksonville, Florida, because it was learned that the hall would be integrated according to Anderson's contract, the *New York Times* ran the story. The *Times* also reported the story when the ban against Anderson's appearance at the Lyric Theater in Baltimore was lifted. Little by little, doors were opening.

But the most significant one yet to be opened to Anderson and other black singers was the stage door of the Metropolitan Opera House. Opera had long been a dream of Anderson's, since she was a child growing up in Philadelphia, listening to borrowed recordings of *Pagliacci* and Galli-Curci's "Una voce poco fa." Once while she was on tour in Russia, director Konstantin Stanislawski offered to teach her the role of Carmen, but she declined the invitation, a move she later regretted. Mary Cardwell Dawson offered her roles in her unique National Negro Opera Company, but Anderson's busy concert schedule would not permit her to accept. For one reason or another, the chance to do opera constantly eluded her.

Throughout its long history, the Metropolitan Opera board had maintained an unstated policy not to hire blacks, even though artists such as Jules Bledsoe, Camilla Williams, and Mattiwilda Dobbs had proven themselves in other opera companies. As early as 1940, white and black Anderson devotees were outwardly restless to see the singer bow before a Metropolitan audience. Carl Van Vechten, a wealthy white dilettante and patron-friend to Harlem's artistic elite, said with a note of sarcasm in a letter to a friend, "There is a terrific movement on foot amongst influential ofays to get Marian Anderson into the Metropolitan Opera House, either as Erda in *Siegfried* or Fricka in *Das Rheingold*." But the movement halted outside the doors of the Met's executive offices.

Then, in 1950, Rudolf Bing became general manager of the Met, and a new philosophy emerged. In his first season, Bing hired a black ballerina, Janet Collins, to dance the triumphal scene in *Aida*. "I never had the slightest question about engaging Miss Collins," Bing wrote in his autobiography. And as far as the Met's board was concerned, Bing had his own way of dealing with them. "I told the board about it after the contract was signed."

As soon as Bing became general manager he wanted to hire Marian Anderson, but her schedule, aging voice (by then she was about fifty), and lack of acting experience posed limitations. She would need a part that required little rehearsal time or stage experience, not much acting ability, and that lay well for a contralto voice beyond its prime. Verdi's *Un Ballo in Maschera*, which the Met planned to do in its 1954-55 season, had such a part, and in 1954 Bing hired Anderson for the role of Ulrica the sorceress. With that decision, she would become the first black to sing with the Metropolitan, the citadel of American opera.

The event had a casual inception. At a party given by Sol Hurok for the Sadler's Wells Ballet Company after a performance of *A Midsummer Night's Dream*, Bing found himself seated next to Anderson. The usual small talk turned to serious conversation when Bing asked her, "Would you be interested in singing at the Metropolitan?" Anderson was elated. She relished the prospect but wanted to make sure the part was vocally feasible. An audition with conductor Dimitri Mitropoulos was arranged. Hearing Anderson sing, Mitropoulos was immediately satisfied, and contracts were signed.

The Marian Anderson Metropolitan debut was an event of mammoth proportion. Tickets disappeared weeks in advance. The morning of the performance, January 7, the weather was typical of New York in winter—cold with blistering wind. But the line in front of the opera house for standing room tickets began at 5:30 A.M., and at mid-afternoon there were still about thirty people in line. "Some of these were Negroes," observed Howard Taubman, "a rare sight on the standees' queue." By performance time, there would be more blacks in the audience than ever before, including some proud concertgoers who previously had not known where the Metropolitan Opera House was nor what actually went on there.

Bing had assembled an all-star cast for the *Un Ballo* revival, including Zinka Milanov, Richard Tucker, Leonard Warren, Roberta Peters, Nicola Moscona, and Norman Scott. Anticipation was great as the curtain lifted for Scene Two of Act One, the only scene in which Anderson performed. As Ulrica, Anderson sat stirring a bubbling cauldron; she soon would prophesy Riccardo's death. (Interestingly, Verdi's description of the character, "*dell' immondo sangue de' negri*," —of dark negro blood—was removed from the libretto.) Anderson began her aria, "Re dell' abisso" tentatively, but by the second part, "E lui," the nerves had settled, and the voice warmed to its usual magnificent sonority.

"No doubt, under the special tensions of the occasion, including the newness of the dimensions and vibrancies of the Metropolitan stage, she wavered in pitch," wrote Olin Downes the next day, "but before the air was finished the singer had demonstrated the same musicianship and instinct for dramatic communication that she had long since demonstrated on the concert stage." For the audience, the performance transcended musical criticism; history had been made as the first black voice to sing opera with the Met resounded throughout the hall. Applause thundered as Anderson came out to take her bow with Zinka Milanov, and, wrote Taubman for the *Times'* front page, "Men as well as women in the audience were dabbing at their eyes."

Color finally had been relegated to its proper place of insignificance, and as Associated Press writer W. G. Rogers noted, "The only color that mattered was the color of her voice, which has been one of the richest and most moving in her generation."

Olin Downes, in a *Times* editorial written at the announcement of the Anderson Metropolitan engagement, echoed the sentiments of most Anderson admirers in calling it a "tardy tribute to her rank and achievement as an artist of international fame." Anderson, at her Met debut, was a *diva emerita*, and she was clearly well past her best vocal years. Obviously, Bing could have given the honor of "first black" to someone younger and musically stronger, like soprano Mattiwilda Dobbs, who had succeeded at La Scala and the Glyndebourne Festival in England, or baritone Robert McFerrin, who was engaged at the Met immediately after Anderson. But the point was clear: Anderson, whose career had quietly and continuously broken barriers, dissolved hostilities, and awakened the consciousness of an entire country, was the only singer whose presence could signify the real meaning of the event. The length and contour of her own journey, from poor prodigy to artist-ambassador in the span of half a century, mirrored the progress of an entire movement of people advancing toward artistic and social equality. Anderson's life, in simple terms, defined that movement.

The 1956 season was Anderson's last in opera. Reasons as to why she was absent from the next season's roster remain a mystery, but popular speculations are probably true. Besides the practical fact that she would have had to take a sizeable cut from her concert fee to sing with the Met, the main reason was perhaps the voice itself. There are few roles in opera suited to a true contralto. Anderson's voice had lost much of its sheen, the vibrato had widened, and even some of the spirituals she sang had to be transposed down to accommodate the darkening patina of age. Critics had begun to voice their feelings on the inevitability facing the aging singer—a delicate subject—and "Should Anderson retire?" was a question discussed in critics' circles. Anderson's most devoted fans, however, did not care. For as long as she was willing to sing, they were elated to listen. As for the Metropolitan, the debut had more than served its purpose, and it did not require an encore. As the young soprano Leontyne Price said years later at a seventy-fifth birthday tribute to Anderson in Carnegie Hall, "Whatever role she did that night, it wouldn't have mattered. Even if she had just walked on stage that night, the singular thing that she did was to make the door open. She did that, and I will be eternally indebted to her."

In 1965 an entire nation of admirers acknowledged its indebtedness when Anderson, after thirty years before the public, announced her retirement from the concert stage. A final world tour included a sentimental farewell concert in Carnegie Hall on April 18 before 3,000 people. "It seems as though Marian Anderson has been with us forever," wrote Harold C. Schonberg for the *New York Times*, "but all good things must come to an end." At Robin Hood Dell, Philadelphia's mammoth outdoor pavilion, 35,000 fans packed in on a June evening, testing the venue's generous limits. "People simply swamped the place, whether they had seats or hadn't," wrote an *Evening Bulletin* critic. "They sat on the aisle steps, on ramps, on flat areas of cement, on grass, on railings, outside the Dell, anywhere space could be found."

Anderson's talented nephew and godson, James DePreist (son of her younger sister, Ethel), conducted the concert. DePreist was only three years old at the time of the D.A.R. controversy, but now, at age twenty-eight, his rising career as a conductor complemented Anderson's concluding one. Winner of the Dimitri Mitropoulos Award and newly appointed assistant conductor of the New York Philharmonic under Leonard Bernstein, DePreist had matured into a musical figure worthy of the event. "It would have been inappropriate for me to conduct for my aunt if I had not proven what I could do on my own," DePreist said. "Her sister, my aunt Alice, had just died a week earlier, so that there were a variety of emotions at that time. It was, obviously, a particularly special moment . . . and you wondered what it would have been like to have been doing that earlier—not in terms of the quality of her voice, but just how wonderful that experience was, that level of artistry that close to you."

Hurok appeared heartbroken at the possibility of losing his star to retirement. "Anderson *cannot* retire," he told reporters, rapping his cane against Anderson's dressing room floor on the day of the New York farewell. "She can do some readings of Lincoln and Jefferson and then maybe sing a few spirituals—it'll go like a house on fire." (In fact, lectures and readings of Aaron Copland's *A Lincoln Portrait* extended beyond her seventy-fifth year.) But after the final singing tour, Anderson announced her plans to spend time on her Connecticut farm with her husband since 1942, architect Orpheus Fisher, and become "a homemaker with a vengeance." "And I hope to do something for children," she added. "I want to roll my sleeves up. I want to do something with my hands and heart and soul."

For her exemplary life and work, honors came in abundance. Her list of achievements and awards, musical and otherwise, is staggering. In 1938 Eleanor Roosevelt presented her with the NAACP's Spingarn Medal. In 1942 she received Philadelphia's prestigious Bok Award and established the Marian Anderson Scholarship Award with the $10,000 prize. In 1943 the Republic of Liberia gave her its highest award, the Order of African Redemption. And the list of honorary doctorates from American universities seems endless—at last count they numbered nearly three dozen. The U.S. State Department in 1957 selected her for a ten-week goodwill tour of India and the Far East that took her to, among other places, Korea, the Philippines, Hong Kong, Taiwan, and Thailand. Recording her every move was the crew of Edward R. Murrow's CBS television show "See It Now," who filmed the 40,000-mile odyssey for a TV special titled "The Lady from Philadelphia." Anderson's great dignity and artistry on the tour brought her a plethora of editorial praise, as she received heads of state with characteristic poise and grace. She was invited to sing at the Gandhi Memorial in India, and in Thailand the king defied royal protocol by standing up to greet her with a handshake.

The role of international goodwill ambassador suited Anderson— so much that in 1958 she was chosen to be one of a ten-member delegation from the United States to the General Assembly of the United Nations. Of the honor Anderson said, "We feel very unqualified," but simply stated her intention as member of the delegation: "We would like to be able to express the working desire for a better understanding." In 1963 she was given the Presidential Medal of Freedom by President Lyndon Johnson, and in 1978 Congress struck a gold medal in her honor.

The contradictions of Anderson's life might have unraveled a lesser soul. The woman who was rudely turned down by a music school was honored by presidents. The artist who could be turned away from a restaurant could draw thousands to a concert hall a few blocks away. But Anderson somehow understood such human irony. As Kipling wrote of those equal impostors triumph and disaster, she treated trials and tributes "the same." Overwhelmed by neither, she saw them both as part of an orderly spiritual scheme.

"She is obviously a tremendously strong person," DePreist said, "and she had to go through a great deal, being a woman, and being a black woman at that time trying to build a career. But her dignity was such a powerful force, and her faith was so strong, that while she obviously was outraged, it would never be her style to be a seething cauldron, and in private, to rant and rave. She was positive. She knew what she wanted to do, she knew that no one should be in her way preventing her from doing it because of her race. And I think she probably felt that she was going to be clearing a path, not just for herself, but for others to follow.

"In both her singing and her presence is an incredible amount of strength that is serene.... It is the kind of serenity that comes from being completely at ease with your faith and your art, so that it is impossible to separate what Aunt Marian is as a human being from what she was as an artist. When people talk about the incredible warmth and power, and almost majesterial and regal bearing, and the poignancy and tenderness with which she can sing in German or the spirituals, it comes from a firmly rooted, wonderful kind of power."

The philosophy that shaped Anderson's life is best characterized in her own words, expressing her reliance on an implacable faith and the simple truths she learned as a child in Philadelphia, the gifted daughter of John and Anna Anderson.

"Mother is a believer," she once said, "and her three children are also believers. It is so necessary in anything that we do, not to feel too complete because you're obliged to come, regardless of whether you like it or not, to your extremity. You cannot leave this world at that point. You've got to see whatever it is through to the end, and although there are many people who seek this help only in extremity, it is nice to be acquainted with it through your whole life, and that is what my mother has taught us. It gives you a peace of mind. It gives you an understanding of your fellow men, even though in some instances they behave so poorly. And you know that if the supreme being were not a just one, the world should long ago have come to an end, and therefore when things happen along the way, which might pull one up rather sharply, through disappointment, you think on your faith and you go back, so to speak, to the well to be replenished.

"There is a Negro spiritual, 'I open my mouth to the Lord and I never will turn back. I *will* go. I *shall* go, to see what the end will be.' And it sums up so much of what so many people need to feel who don't find all those wonderful things around them. I will go and I shall go to see what the end will be. Why? Because I believe in what I find at the end."

# 4

# Harlem's Golden Age: A Musical Awakening

*I*N the mid 1920s and early 1930s, while Marian Anderson set
Europe ablaze and conquered its capitals with her vocal genius, the
streets of Harlem in New York's upper Manhattan hummed to the
rhythm of the Jazz Age. In fact, what was called the Jazz Age by those
who danced to the raspy rapture of Louis Armstrong or the wailings of
Bessie Smith was dubbed the New Negro Movement by the social-
minded, who hailed the advent of a new black consciousness. Organs of
the movement, the NAACP's *The Crisis* and the Urban League's
*Opportunity* magazines, exhibited the genius of the black literati; Langston
Hughes, Jean Toomer, W. E. B. DuBois, and other luminaries painted
vivid portraits of a new black presence—one of intelligence, social
consciousness, and passionate creativity.

Black awareness spawned black themes in serious theater as well.
Minstrelsy had died from lack of interest, and buried with it was the
blackface buffoon. In its place sprang such sophisticated vehicles as
Eugene O'Neill's *The Emperor Jones* in 1920 and *All God's Chillun Got
Wings* in 1923, which starred the young law school graduate Paul

Robeson. Eubie Blake and Noble Sissle's *Shuffle Along* of 1921 (featuring for the first time music, lyrics, and choreography by blacks), ended each evening with its audiences humming "I'm Just Wild about Harry" and "Love Will Find a Way." The legendary Bill "Bojangles" Robinson carried *Blackbirds* (1928) through its two-year run of 500 performances. Dubose Heyward's play *Porgy*, set among the population of Charleston blacks, brought South Carolinian Gullah life to Manhattan sophisticates. Artists Aaron Douglas and Romare Bearden gained recognition for their powerful depictions of black life on canvas, while sculptor Augusta Savage, the *grande dame* of Harlem's artistic community, literally pulled young blacks like Jacob Lawrence off the streets into her storefront studio to discover themselves and their world through art.

Harlem in its heyday was frenetic with creative energy, and it seemed no talent was wasted; singers sang, dancers danced, painters painted, and writers wrote. For nearly fifteen years, the social and cultural milieu that cradled the Harlem Renaissance continued and prospered. It was a high time, an age of black enlightenment—short-lived but intense, as bright and ephemeral as a shooting star.

Late at night, Harlem convulsed to hot, strident jazz and cool blues. Its nightclub scene, according to *Variety*, rivaled anything Broadway had to offer. The Cotton Club was the centerpiece of it all. Originally the property of boxer Jack Johnson, its management later changed hands and complexions to become a white-owned, whites-only observatory of black entertainment. The Cotton Club maintained its blacks-onstage, whites-at-the-door policy for the duration of its existence, while showcasing the talents of Duke Ellington, Cab Calloway, Ethel Waters, Lena Horne, and countless others. Black dancers, singers, and musicians vied for the privilege and prestige of performing for the Cotton Club's stellar patronage. Lady Mountbatten (who hailed the club as the aristocrat of Harlem) and comedian Jimmy Durante were among those who marveled at Duke Ellington's orchestra and the "Tall, Tan and Terrific" line of long-limbed, light brown chorus girls. At the door, the color bar was impenetrable (except for a few fair-skinned blacks who were discreetly given the nod), and black club-goers obediently stayed away. "Racial lines are drawn there to prevent possible trouble," explained Durante. "Nobody wants razors, blackjacks, or fists flying—and the chances of a war are less if there's no mixing..."

The mixing was done elsewhere—and in grand style—at Small's Paradise (an elitist black-owned club), the Clam House, the Nest Club, and a variety of parties. Most of Harlem was poor, but while rent parties fended off eviction notices among Harlemites of lower economic standing, the more fortunate dined and danced in glittery salons. The dapper baritone Jules Bledsoe (star of *Showboat*) played host often to Harlem's upper crust, as did A'Lelia Walker, Harlem's high priestess and heiress to a million-dollar hairdressing enterprise built up by her mother, Madame C. J. Walker.

But it was Carl Van Vechten's parties, where a motley mix of black and white artists, actors, singers, and writers congregated, that were the talk of Manhattan. Van Vechten, once a music critic for the *New York Times*, filled his parlor numerous evenings with Harlem's best and brightest while white Manhattan's social stalwarts, also present, fawned admiration. Theodore Dreiser, Tallulah Bankhead, F. Scott Fitzgerald, and Rudolph Valentino sat transfixed while Paul Robeson sang a spiritual or James Weldon Johnson read from his *God's Trombones*. Sometimes Van Vechten's guests tripped over the invisible social barricade dividing black and white, to great embarrassment. An inebriated Bessie Smith was said to have decked Van Vechten's wife, Fania Marinoff, who had done nothing more than try to kiss the jazz singer goodbye as she was leaving one evening. Langston Hughes, a regular attendee at Van Vechten's soirees, in his autobiography, *The Big Sea*, recalled a much lighter misunderstanding. One evening after black journalist Nora Holt had entertained guests with a robust rendition of "My Daddy Rocks Me with One Steady Roll," Hughes recalled, a white woman approached her with eyes glistening. "My dear," she said, "how lovely you sing the spirituals!"

Van Vechten's fondness for black culture was public knowledge, and his parties became a networking hub and launching platform for black artistic ventures. "Jazz, the blues, Negro spirituals, all stimulate me enormously for the moment," Van Vechten wrote in a letter to H. L. Mencken. "Doubtless, I shall discard them too in time." The classical artists fascinated him as much; it was Van Vechten who introduced Paul Robeson to his accompanist, Lawrence Brown, and arranged for Robeson's first Town Hall recital. His regard for black divas was high—he praised the singing of Mattiwilda Dobbs early in her career ("a warm and brilliant coloratura, and the best Gilda in my experience") and aided soprano Charlotte Holloman's European stint with letters of introduction to prospective vocal coaches. He was fond of the artistry of Marian Anderson, and during his days of dabbling with photography summoned her to his apartment for a lengthy photo session, as he did other black artists down through Leontyne Price.

Surrounding himself with Harlem's finest, Van Vechten studied blacks with scientific scrutiny and wrote about them. When his novel *Nigger Heaven* appeared in 1926, its reviews, among black and white, were as drastically mixed as his parties. The title itself was the cause of much concern—it referred to the balconies of segregated white-owned theaters, where the black patrons were forced to sit. Intended to capture the essence of black life according to Van Vechten's privileged perspective,

*Nigger Heaven* focused on black social extremes, from the primal to the pristine and the bohemian to the bourgeois. True to its roman à clef style, characters were drawn from a roster of Harlem's headliners; prominent blacks like A'Lelia Walker, Nora Holt, James Weldon and Grace Johnson shone vividly through thinly veiled disguises. And while a few blacks appreciated Van Vechten's voyeuristic view of Harlem, many were offended at its caricaturish bent.

Nonetheless, the parties continued and succeeded in pulling together black and white movers and shakers of the age. Two of Van Vechten's most notable guests penned musical works that permanently altered the course of black participation in classical music (specifically opera), and provided work and greatly needed exposure for the black diva and her male counterpart. In 1934 Van Vechten gave a party for composer Virgil Thomson to organize support for his opera *Four Saints in Three Acts*, which, at the composer's insistence, was cast completely with black singers. And George Gershwin, who often entertained Van Vechten's guests with Broadway tunes on the piano, composed *Porgy and Bess* in 1935, an opera based on the Dubose and Dorothy Heyward play of 1927—also for blacks. Both operas were monumentally important. *Four Saints* presented before a large white audience blacks performing serious roles in an opera that had nothing to do with color, thus negating the notion that blacks could play nothing other than blacks. And *Porgy and Bess* provided opera with a black American heroine to rank alongside Carmen, Tosca, and Aida.

To be sure, blacks had been seen in opera before. As early as 1873 the Colored American Opera Company performed in Washington, D.C., to respectable reviews, and in 1938 the Detroit Negro Opera Company was formed. And Mary Cardwell Dawson's brainchild, the National Negro Opera Company, established in 1941, played to audiences in Pittsburgh, Washington, New York, Chicago, and Philadelphia. When Gershwin found his Porgy in Todd Duncan, the young baritone had just performed with the short-lived Aeolian Opera Company in an all-black version of *Cavalleria Rusticana* at New York's Mecca Temple (now called City Center). But for the most part, white American audiences in the early 1930s were unfamiliar with (and perhaps not willing to take seriously) the black singer as opera star until *Four Saints* and *Porgy*. And certainly no approval, either critical or box office, could compete in the long run with the wholesale endorsement of black singers by America's greatest composers. Both Thomson and Gershwin were openly drawn to black culture, black music, and black ethos. And implicit in their works was an undeniable tribute to and respect for the quality of black singers. (The role of Bess is example enough. Gershwin wrote the part feeling sure he could find a black woman who could handle its Verdian level of difficulty.) With *Four Saints in Three Acts* and *Porgy and Bess*, black singers made the most widely witnessed transition from concert work and black musical theater to grand opera, and the image of a black opera singer became not only acceptable, but in some circles desirable.

Virgil Thomson wrote *Four Saints* in collaboration with his good friend Gertrude Stein, with no particular singers in mind. The plotless opera centers around the lives of Spanish saints and depicts them in a series of tableaux engaging in saintly activities: praying, singing, performing miracles, etc. In contrast to Thomson's completely consonant score rich with Western harmony and hymnody, Stein's text is a cryptic mosaic of sounds, where the meaning of words is less important than the sounds and rhythms created by them. Singers were required to sing with total conviction lines like "A saint is one to be for two when three and you make five and two and cover." In notes to a 1981 recording, Maurice Grosser warns, "One should not try to interpret too literally the words of this opera, nor should one fall into the opposite error of thinking that they mean nothing at all."

Thomson felt black singers had the kind of inherent "spirituality" and love for words that would make them ideal saints and thought they would be able to make sense of Stein's illogical libretto. "They came from a heritage in Africa speaking many different languages and practicing many different religions," the ninety-year-old Thomson said in an interview in 1986, "and within one generation they became English-speaking Christians." Thomson's respect and affinity for blacks can be traced to childhood. On an excursion from his native Kansas City to Norfolk, Virginia, he observed with boyish wonder that the "Negro market women in bright bandannas selling highly colored fruits were almost too picturesque to be true." The early 1920s found the Harvard graduate in Paris on the periphery of its cafe society, and the friendship of the notorious Josephine Baker and black nightclub owner Bricktop heightened his fascination even more. His decision to have blacks portray the Spanish saints was the result of late night jaunts to Harlem, where he listened intently to the music of black entertainers. A passage from his autobiography recounts the inspired moment:

> It was on one of these trips uptown, at a small joint where Jimmy Daniels was just starting out as host and entertainer, that I turned to Russell, realizing the impeccable enunciation of Jimmy's speech-in-song, and said, "I think I'll have my opera sung by Negroes." The idea seemed to me a brilliant one; Russell, less impressed, suggested I sleep on it. But next morning I was sure, remembering how proudly the Negroes enunciate and how the whites just hate to move their lips.

Thomson got his wish. He auditioned blacks tirelessly and settled on a cast featuring Edward Matthews as Saint Ignatius, Beatrice Robinson-Wayne as Saint Teresa, Bruce Howard as Saint Teresa II, Embry Bonner as Saint Chavez, Bertha Fitzhugh as Saint Settlement, and Abner Dorsey and Altonell Hines as Compère and Commère. The chorus of black singers was trained by Eva Jessye. As rehearsals progressed, Thomson was elated with his choices. "My singers, as I have wanted, are Negroes," Thomson excitedly wrote to Gertrude Stein in December 1933, "you can't imagine how beautifully they sing." The opera was first performed at the Hartford Atheneum in Hartford, Connecticut, in February 1934. (It was later performed in New York at the 44th Street Theater, where it had the first sustained run of an opera on Broadway.) According to Thomson, museum members were "scared to death" of the black community in Hartford at the time, then later ignited its ire by showing the controversial film *Birth of a Nation*, which portrayed blacks in stereotypically demeaning postures, as part of the museum's film series. "But they cooperated wonderfully on *Four Saints*," Thomson recalled. "They found private houses for the singers to stay in, and they gave us a terrific party after the last performance—one of the best parties I've ever been to."

From the outset, Thomson's all-black cast was received amiably by colleagues and critics; in fact, the *Four Saints* cast was received with more uniform acceptance than the score and libretto, which drew mixed reviews. Thomson was particularly pleased with the singers' ability to articulate Stein's text convincingly and infuse sincerity and meaning into phrases that had no particular meaning. In his autobiography he wrote:

> The Negroes proved in every way rewarding. Not only could they enunciate and sing; they seemed to understand because they sang. They resisted not at all Stein's obscure language, adopted it for theirs, conversed in quotations from it. They moved, sang, spoke with grace and with alacrity, took on roles without self-consciousness, as if they were the saints they said they were. I often marveled at the miracle whereby slavery (and some crossbreeding) had turned them into Christians of an earlier stamp than ours, not analytical or self-pitying or romantic in the nineteenth-century sense, but robust, outgoing, and even in disaster sustained by inner joy, very much as Saint Teresa had been by what she took for true contact with Jesus, Saint Ignatius by dictates from the Holy Ghost. If Beatrice Robinson-Wayne and Edward Matthews, who played these roles, seemed less intensely Spanish and self-tortured than their prototypes, they were, as Baroque saints, in every way as grandly simple and convincing.

With *Four Saints*, many cast and chorus members were earning money as professional singers for the first time. With the exception of a few, they were struggling young artists caught in the middle of the Depression, and were more likely seen at Harlem's rent parties than its posh society gatherings. For some, unemployment was further kept at bay by the appearance of *Porgy and Bess*. But this time the subject of the text was directly related to the ethnicity of the singers.

Gershwin, like Thomson, discovered black music and musicians early on; his love for ragtime, blues, and spirituals began when he was about six years old. On roller-skating excursions through Harlem, he heard the music of Jim Europe's band as it wafted onto the streets from Baron Wilkins' club. Gershwin often stopped outside the door to listen, entranced by the cacophony of music and spirited conversation. He admitted later that the sounds of Harlem would form the rhythmic and harmonic basis for many of his mature compositions. When Gershwin was still in his teens, a black arranger, Will Vodery, found the young Tin Pan Alley song-plugger one of his first real jobs—as a pianist in Fox's City Theater on 14th Street. Even early in his career Gershwin seemed driven by the desire to exploit the wonders of black musical style and employ them in his music. *Porgy and Bess* was not his first attempt at a black theme opera. In 1922 Gershwin and Buddy De Sylva wrote *Blue Monday* (now called *135th Street*), a one-act opera about a love triangle centered in Harlem. It was performed by whites in blackface, and interpolated in the George White Broadway show *Scandals of 1922*. Will Vodery was enlisted to provide the orchestration. The show flopped—its plot was primitive and its characters lacked dimension— but some of its better music survives.

The experience with *Blue Monday* left Gershwin unsatisfied and his commitment to composing a black opera unresolved. Even after enormous successes with *Rhapsody in Blue, An American in Paris*, and a string of Broadway hits, he continued to seek out and study black jazz. "Like everyone in those days, we'd go to Harlem—in ermine and pearls!—where George listened very, very assiduously to the great players of the time," said singer-actress Kitty Carlisle, whom Gershwin squired to Manhattan's upper reaches on evenings away from the theater. His second chance at writing a black opera (this time with real blacks) came when he approached DuBose Heyward, a genteel Charleston-born playwright, about setting his play *Porgy* to music. The story, based on Heyward's memories of colorful characters in Charleston's poor black sector, was set in an imaginary, dilapidated enclave called Catfish Row. After a lengthy correspondence, Gershwin and Heyward agreed to work together on *Porgy and Bess* in 1933.

By this time, Gershwin had acquired the respect and admiration of the music community, and interest in his career escalated with each good review. The Metropolitan Opera was intrigued by the possibility of a Gershwin opera and offered him a $5,000 bonus if he would agree to sign a contract with them. Gershwin politely refused. Though flattered, he felt the Met would have performed his work only a few times, then cast it aside, as it had done with many new American operas. But the prohibitive reason involved the cast for *Porgy and Bess*. Gershwin wanted Catfish Row peopled with black singers and actors, not blackfaced imitations, and in the 1930s the Met would never have permitted such a thing. Instead Gershwin signed with the Theater Guild, which had produced Heyward's original play *Porgy*, and began his search for singers.

The main characters, the crippled beggar Porgy and the wayward Bess, required a baritone and soprano with a high degree of operatic ability and training.

Gershwin's quest for Porgy is now part of opera legend. After the composer had heard more than a hundred baritones and basses, including Paul Robeson, Olin Downes suggested Todd Duncan, a young Howard University teacher he'd heard in a production of *Cavalleria*. Duncan was invited to audition, and showed up at Gershwin's apartment with no accompanist and a repertoire of Lieder and Italian songs—not what Gershwin had expected. The tall, handsome Kentuckian, who exuded breeding and sophistication, sang "Lungi dal caro bene," and Gershwin was floored. "Will you be my Porgy?" he asked, and the search for one title character was over.

Bess was an easier task. A twenty-year-old Juilliard graduate from Baltimore, Anne Brown, wrote Gershwin asking for an audition. She was granted one, and the first Bess was found.

The rest of the cast was filled out with young unknown but well-schooled singers. Carried over from the *Four Saints* cast were Edward Matthews as Jake, and the entire Eva Jessye Chorus. Henry Davis was Robbins, and Warren Coleman, a concert singer discovered by a friend of composer Harold Arlen, was hired as Crown, the rakish stevedore. Ruby Elzy, another talented Juilliard graduate, was cast as Serena, and Abbie Mitchell, who had sung with Duncan in the Mecca Temple production of *Cavalleria*, was given the role of Clara. Georgette Harvey, who played Maria in the theater production of *Porgy*, sang the same role in Gershwin's opera. James Weldon Johnson's brother, J. Rosamund Johnson, was assigned the role of Lawyer Frazier. The only untrained singer in the group, John W. Bubbles, of the vaudeville team of Buck and Bubbles, was signed to play the cynical dope-pusher, Sportin' Life.

The opera opened in Boston on September 30, 1935, and two weeks later had its New York premiere at the Alvin Theater on October 10, 1935. The critics applauded the singers and the chorus. Wrote Olin Downes: "If the Metropolitan chorus could ever put one half the action into the riot scene in the second act of *Meistersinger* that the Negro cast put into the fight that followed the crap game, it would be not merely refreshing but miraculous." But overall, Gershwin's "folk opera" was harshly dismissed as too derivative and showlike, with popular songs instead of genuine arias. The black press found its characters and their use of primitive southern dialect insulting and socially retrogressive. The reviews of the premiere are especially interesting considering the opera's tremendous popularity in the decades since its opening. Thomson, in a review for *Modern Music*, was one of *Porgy*'s biggest detractors: "It is crooked folklore and halfway opera, a strong but crippled work...," he said. "I do not like fake folklore, nor fidgety accompaniment, nor bittersweet harmony, nor six-part choruses, nor gefiltefish orchestration." After a revival a few years later, when it became apparent that he had seriously underrated the opera, Thomson changed his opinion, calling it now "a beautiful piece of music and a deeply moving play for the lyric theater. Its melodic invention is abundant and pretty distinguished. The score has both musical distinction and popular appeal."

Despite the reviews and *Porgy*'s comparatively short Broadway run of 124 performances (although long for an opera), the immodest Gershwin never doubted that *Porgy and Bess* was the work of genius that the wisdom of time and hindsight has since declared it to be. He rationalized that the reviews were, at least in part, the manifestations of professional jealously—a valid point. Not long before Gershwin died in 1937, he invited Todd Duncan to his California home—Gershwin was then performing with the Los Angeles Philharmonic. Duncan remembered the evening in which the pensive composer philosophically reflected on *Porgy*:

> We sat up all night long after the concert and the party he gave, and he told me that his following in Broadway resented the fact that he had written an opera. "We're not going to hear our Georgie in any of that high falutin' music!" And the real opera goers didn't come because they didn't think he could write an opera—to them he was Tin Pan Alley. And he said those same crossed paths of criticism and judgmental action happened with the critics. He said there were some critics, who, whether they liked it or not, weren't going to say they liked it.

Not all of the critics who panned *Porgy and Bess* in 1935 reversed their opinions as Thomson did, but that was not necessary for *Porgy*'s ultimate success. With each revival, and there were many, *Porgy and Bess* became more and more established as an institution in American music. A Scandinavian cast performed the work in Copenhagen in 1943, thus beginning the opera's popularity in Europe. A major revival was undertaken in 1952 with one of the more famous casts in the history of the opera; Leontyne Price as Bess and William Warfield as Porgy toured Europe after an American opening in Dallas. By that time, critics everywhere were ecstatic. After its premiere, producers of the opera pared the work down to a shorter, Broadway-style scale, eliminating lengthy instrumental interludes and recitatives. But in 1976 the Houston Grand Opera restored the opera to its original uncut, three-and-one-half-hour version. And in 1985, a half-century after its opening at the Alvin Theater, the Metropolitan Opera staged *Porgy* for the first time.

The opera's recording history is equally varied. Victor recorded it with Lawrence Tibbett and Helen Jepson under the supervision of Gershwin, and a 1942 Decca version featured Anne Brown and Todd Duncan. Price and Warfield recorded excerpts for RCA, and Camilla Williams sang Bess for Columbia in 1951, creating the first full-length version of the opera on record. Modern versions include Houston's recording for RCA with Clamma Dale and Donnie Ray Albert, and a London recording with Leona Mitchell, Willard White, Barbara Hendricks, and the Cleveland Orchestra and Chorus under Lorin Maazel.

While *Porgy* is finally acknowledged as an opera in the most literal sense of the word, arguments continue as to its social merit. Is DuBose Heyward's dialect of the undereducated black southerner contrived and demeaning? Do the central characters—the servile beggar Porgy, the drug-addicted Bess, and the despicable hustler Sportin' Life—present too negative a statement about the worst aspects of black life? Is the combined perspective of an aristocratic white southern playwright and a New York–born Jewish songwriter viable? The debate is as old and durable as *Porgy* itself. When composer Ned Rorem was asked in the early 1960s to compose an opera based on *Mamba's Daughters*, another DuBose and Dorothy Heyward novel about Gullah blacks (made into a musical in the late 1930s), he tried—and then withdrew from the project. "How could a white artist, however compassionate, presume to depict a black nightmare from inside out?" he asked himself. Gershwin and Heyward apparently were plagued with no such ethical insecurities. But regardless of *Porgy*'s image, it would be impossible to overestimate the profound impact *Porgy* has had on the American black opera scene. The enduring presence and overwhelming popularity of the opera has ensured abundant work for black singers over the decades; rarely has a year gone by since its opening that a production of the work has not been attempted somewhere in the world. And unquestionably, the role of Bess has helped to set in motion the careers of many black divas.

There are other black heroines in the opera repertory—Aida and Selika in *L'Africaine* in particular—but to perform even these roles with major opera companies, black women often had to contend with the competition of white sopranos and hurdle the obstacle of prejudiced opera boards. Through the years Bess has remained, virtually unchallenged, a black woman's domain. (A Gershwin estate stipulation, observed in America but not in Europe, prevents the opera's performance by any but a black cast.) Despite questions raised about the negativity of the role of Catfish Row's fallen woman, it is as vocally complex and dramatically sophisticated as Carmen or Manon. And if Bess is no more virtuous and upright a character than these women, she is at least no less so. Bess is a complicated figure constantly at odds, battling between good (Porgy) and evil (Crown), alienation and acceptance, virtue and immorality. But even in her best moments she remains both drug- and man-dependent. Her fate is predetermined; like the great tragic heroines of classical opera, she enters the play burdened by a past that charts her destiny at its end. Bess does not plummet to her death, Tosca-style, at the conclusion of the opera, but one need not witness Bess's death to realize that despite Porgy's quixotic promise to rescue her ("Oh Lawd, I'm On My Way"), she is heading toward a fall. She is a victim, controlled by circumstances, and the splendor of her woes forms the essence of dramatic theater. "Nobody wants to pay their money to see an angel onstage," said Todd Duncan. "It's always a woman who has fallen from grace. If she's good and angelic...and nothing difficult happens in her life, she's boring."

Anne Brown, the first Bess, was as distant from the street-wise strumpet in character as any actress could be from a role. She was attractive, well educated, and refined, born (in 1915) to a family where learning and culture were high priorities. Her father, Harry F. Brown, was a successful Baltimore physician married to Mary Wiggins, who, according to one press account, was "something of a singer herself." They had three other daughters, Henrietta, Harryette, and Mayme, all of whom became public school teachers.

Brown attended Morgan State College in Baltimore, and later the Institute of Musical Art (now the Juilliard School) on scholarship, as a student of Licia Dunhan. She entered the Juilliard opera department and appeared in *L'Heure Espagnole*. While at the Institute she won a McGill scholarship of $1,000, entitling her to two years of postgraduate study.

Though only twenty years old when she auditioned for Bess (she had in mind that she would be hired for a small role), she was Gershwin's clear choice for the opera's heroine. Olin Downes confirmed the wisdom of Gershwin's casting in his review: "The fresh tone, admirable competent technique, and dramatic delivery of Anne Brown as Bess was a high point of interpretation," he wrote. After *Porgy* closed in the winter of 1936, Brown continued to work in the theater, performing in Broadway productions of Heyward's *Mamba's*

*Daughters* and *La Belle Helene*. Two brief marriages, one to a physician named Floarda Howard and another to New York chiropodist Claudius Petit, ended in divorce.

Brown sang the revival of *Porgy* in 1942 at the Majestic Theater in New York, but resigned after six months, leaving the role to Etta Moten. "I had not wanted to be a one-role woman," she later explained. She was offered the lead in *Carmen Jones*, an urban update of Bizet's *Carmen* with an all-black cast, but turned it down, opting for a career as a concert artist. One theatrical concession was a small part in the Warner Brothers film *Rhapsody in Blue* on the life of Gershwin, in which Brown sang "Summertime." In the 1940s, the lyric soprano became well known as a singer of Brahms and Schubert Lieder, always closing her programs with spirituals such as "City Called Heaven" and "Every Time I Feel the Spirit." After one concert in 1940, a *Washington Star* reporter wrote: "Her voice is large, although she uses its full resources sparingly, and of sweet, if varying, quality. Yet it is in its changing color that a special charm lies and a particular adaptability for the requirement of Lieder singing."

Having created a starring role in the most talked-about opera of the decade by one of the country's greatest composers, Brown enjoyed considerable success as a recitalist in the 1940s. But in the recital world, Brown was not protected by the insular environment of an all-black production, and racial problems, particularly involving the booking of recital halls, were frequent. Even in Baltimore, her hometown, she could not find relief from racial difficulties. Shades of the Anderson–D.A.R. controversy surfaced when she tried to book Baltimore's Lyric Theater a few months after she had been welcomed by the mayor to launch a ship, the S.S. *Frederick Douglass*. Brown was refused and refused again by the management of Ford's Theater. Arrangements were made, finally, to give the recital in a Baltimore church.

In 1946 Brown's agent booked a concert tour in Europe with stops in France, Sweden, Denmark, Switzerland, Norway, Belgium, Portugal, and Italy. In Europe the singer found, as have many other black singers, an alternative to the racial tension in the United States. She fell in love with Norway, with its slow pace and easy-mannered people, and decided to make it her permanent home. She returned to America for four months of concert work, then moved back to Oslo with no concert commitments. She performed for a group of prisoners of war, and within a short time was singing an average of thirty-five concerts a year throughout Europe and Asia.

In 1947 Brown married (and has since divorced) Thorleif Schjelderup, a Norwegian philosopher, journalist, and amateur skier. She continued to perform and became a local favorite among Norwegians. Brown returned to the opera stage to play the role of Bess again in Sweden (in

Anne Brown

1943 and 1948), and appeared in Menotti's *The Medium* and *The Telephone*. She won the Critic's Prize for best performance on the Norwegian stage as the lead in *The Consul* and in 1952 appeared with Kirsten Flagstad in Purcell's *Dido and Aeneas*. She also taught voice, as she had done in the United States, and at one time coached actress Liv Ullmann.

Brown found Norway wholly agreeable, both musically and socially. In 1953 she wrote a lengthy letter-styled article for *Ebony* magazine, describing in detail her life and marriage to Schjelderup. In the piece she explained her preference for Europe, extolling Norway's "lack of race prejudice" and lashing out at American racial injustices:

> My skin is fair—I have low visibility as a Negro...but the fact of the prejudice around me was enough to drive me wild in the United States. It was not just that we, as Negroes, were victims of this prejudice—though that was enough; but it seemed to me incredible— impossible—that I should go on living for the rest of my life, among people so ridiculous as to practice such a stupidity. In Norway...my children and I are simply people who happen to have brown skins. The Norwegians may be curious about these brown skins, but there is no ugliness in the curiosity.

Brown continued to live in Norway. She returned to New York in 1984 as the guest of the management when *Porgy and Bess* premiered, in its original state, at the Metropolitan Opera House.

Interestingly, one of the great Besses never sang the role onstage. Camilla Williams, (1922–    ) who recorded the opera for Columbia, has since been considered a definitive interpreter of the role, but because of her strong feelings against the stereotyped treatment of blacks in *Porgy*, she never agreed to perform Bess in an opera house. Nevertheless, her recording stands as the first document of *Porgy*'s operatic complexity. The sound is unsophisticated and some arias are heavily ad-libbed, but the record's historic value lies in its convincing style and its loyalty, a few minor cuts notwithstanding, to the original score.

Williams' shining hour as an opera singer, however, came the night of May 15, 1946, when she appeared in *Madame Butterfly* with the New York City Opera and made, according to the *New York Times*, "an instant and pronounced success in the title role." Williams also made history. With the Butterfly performance she became the first black artist to receive a contract with a major American opera company. (Though Duncan had preceded her, his contract was not for an entire season.) Williams not only assured her own success as a singer that evening, but also carved a place in opera for black women—the idea of a black Butterfly in a white opera company was revolutionary. But Williams' portrayal of Cio-Cio-San served to prove to opera-goers that a black diva could not only sing the role, but also look the part and act it convincingly. And notions that a black lead performer would be distracting to the viewer's eye were dispelled. The gracefully attractive soprano was trim, petite, and a good actress. With makeup she looked as much like a former Geisha as most singers who have played Butterfly.

Like that of most black singers of the period, Williams' career began humbly. She was born in Danville, Virginia, to Cornelius Booker and Fannie Carey Williams. Her father worked as a chauffeur; her grandfather, Alexander Carey, had been a singer and choir leader. Both her parents were amateur singers, and church activity was central to the lives of the Williams family. Camilla attended Virginia State College, and to aid her career, the Alumni Association contributed funds for further study. Williams went to Philadelphia where she studied with Marion Szekely-Freschl and, to make ends meet, took a job in a local theater as an usher. In 1943 her career advanced significantly when she became the first recipient of the Marian Anderson Award and its prize of $750, and the next year she repeated the achievement. Further recognition came when Williams won the Philadelphia Orchestra Youth Concert Auditions, with as prize an appearance with the orchestra at the Academy of Music.

In the middle 1940s Williams' voice, described as "warm and brilliant," began to attract the attentions of concert managers and recording companies. Even before her debut in opera, she signed with Arthur Judson, Anderson's first manager, and also with RCA Victor. In 1945 her career took another interesting turn when she won the endorsement of the great operatic soprano, Geraldine Farrar. A strange network of acquaintances brought the retired Metropolitan star to a Williams concert in Stamford, Connecticut—Farrar had been invited to the recital, which was arranged by a friend of Lady Astor's niece, who employed Williams' father as a chauffeur. A few days later, Farrar wrote to Arthur Judson: "I was quite unprepared for this young woman's obvious high gifts . . . I should like to voice my unsolicited appreciation and hope that, under careful management and encouragement, the rich promise she shows will mature to even higher artistic endeavors."

Farrar followed Williams' career with interest, and when the young singer debuted with the New York City Opera as Butterfly (her first appearance in any opera), Farrar was there. Williams may have been the most prepared Butterfly ever; three months of hard work with music director Laslo Halasz produced a Butterfly that was vocally and dramatically exceptional. An unqualified success, Williams' performance drew raves from the New York press. And backstage afterwards, Farrar,

Camilla Williams

herself a famous Butterfly, told *Newsweek*, "I would say that already she is one of the great Butterflies of our day."

Williams became, after her remarkable debut, one of the most talked-about singers of the day and, as a black singer of opera in the socially constricted 1940s, enjoyed relative success. In 1948 she appeared again with City Opera, this time as its first Aida. She toured Alaska in 1950, Europe in 1954, and in 1955 sang in the first Viennese performance of Menotti's *Saint of Bleecker Street*. Williams became something of a musical ambassador in the 1960s; at the request of the United States State Department she toured Africa, singing in fourteen countries, and in 1962 sang in Taiwan, Australia, New Zealand, Korea, Japan, the Philippines, Laos, and South Vietnam. In the 1970s she curtailed her performance schedule and directed her musical interests toward teaching. She taught at Brooklyn College, Bronx College, and Queens College and in 1977 accepted a professorship at Indiana University. In 1983, at the invitation of a former Chinese student, she was a guest professor at the Central Conservatory in Beijing.

# 5

## *Dorothy Maynor and the Mid-Century Divas*

*T*HE 1930s, the decade that produced the greatest work of Marian Anderson and two seminal operatic works in *Four Saints* and *Porgy*, yielded another musical revelation of considerable stature. On the heels of Anderson's conquests in America and Europe, soprano Dorothy Maynor arrived on the concert scene, a young unassuming singer with a voice of great beauty and disarming musicality. Her early singing years went by unremarkably—unlike the prodigious Anderson's, Maynor's was a talent slower to develop. When she was fourteen, the seed of the voice that Boston Symphony conductor Serge Koussevitzky later hailed "a miracle" lay buried beneath layers of lesser talent in the Hampton Institute Choir. And were it not for the prescience of chorusmaster Nathaniel Dett and an unexpected vacancy left by a Hampton choir soloist, Maynor might have contributed more to the field of home economics than to music.

Once discovered, though, Maynor's talent was universally acclaimed, and she became a fixture in the elite group of black artists that included Anderson, Roland Hayes, and Paul Robeson. Hers was a supple, multicolored instrument marked by sweetness and yet capable of formidable power, with a floating mezza voce that was magically ethereal. Charpentier's "Depuis le jour" from *Louise* became known as her signature piece, and critic Howard Taubman declared Maynor's singing of it the most beautiful "since the days of glamourous Mary Garden." So associated with the aria was Maynor (and so confident was she that her audience would wait indefinitely for it) that she strategically scheduled the number at the end of her group of encores. Invariably, her admirers left the concert hall with the memory of Maynor's finely spun phrasing of the tour de force still fresh in their minds.

Few disputed Dorothy Maynor's position as one of the great singers of her generation, and among black artists, second only to Anderson. But not everyone agreed on Maynor's level of artistry, especially early in her career. While some critics, groping for the greatest name at the time for comparison, called her an "American Flagstad," others thought such fulsome praise was premature. Many felt her upper register was undeveloped and found her reckless, lacking in control of the full range of her voice. Virgil Thomson, during his second week on the job as critic for the *New York Herald Tribune*, called Maynor "immature vocally and immature emotionally." The statement created a furor and nearly cost him his job; Columbia Artists, angry at the badgering of their newest and most promising star, threatened to pull their advertising from the *Tribune* unless Thomson was fired. Thomson was not fired and no advertising dollars were lost, but the message that Maynor had a strong contingent of backers was abundantly clear.

It was Koussevitzky's public praise of Maynor on hearing her for the first time in 1939 that accelerated her career, and it had the same effect as Toscanini's endorsement of Anderson. An eager press corps followed his lead with extravagant approval: Paul Hume of the *Washington Post* followed her career continuously, calling her voice "glorious," while Olin Downes referred to her as the "consummate artist." Maynor's career, however, was neither long nor particularly varied. Her best years were in the decade following her 1939 debut, and though she learned twenty-three operas, she never sang one—like Anderson, she was ignored by American opera companies. While race was an obvious reason for the slight, Maynor's physiognomy was a more convenient one. A plump, cherubic figure standing less than five feet tall, Maynor, according to critics, had neither the stature nor the commanding presence of a diva. (Howard Taubman, in an otherwise complimentary article for *Collier's* in 1940, tackily referred to her as a "pint-sized and serious Aunt Jemima.") At one time she weighed 206 pounds; a rigorous five-month diet in 1949 eliminated 78 of them, taking the singer from a size 48 to a more svelte size 16. Maynor's physique notwithstanding, her voice captivated four continents, and made many wonder what vocal powers and presence she might have lent to the roles of Mimi or Madam Butterfly, often sung by nonblacks with Maynor-like builds.

The decision to end her recital career in the mid-1960s was her own. After marrying a Presbyterian minister, Maynor made what many felt was her greatest artistic contribution; she founded the Harlem School of the Arts, an educational performing arts facility that provides a student body of mostly indigent black and Hispanic children with what Maynor calls "a cultural oasis in a sea of despair." Established in 1964, the Harlem School was at first a one-woman show, with Maynor assuming the roles of faculty, administrator, and janitorial staff. Since then it has burgeoned from the cramped spaces in the annex of her husband's church where twenty children took piano lessons to a gleaming, modern edifice that contrasts sharply with the unspectacular surroundings of its modest neighborhood and offers an artistic refuge for more than 1,000 students of all ages and races. Today the school is headed by mezzo-soprano Betty Allen.

Maynor's selfless, charitable spirit, an oddity at the top of any profession, is deep-rooted and home-grown. Her grandfather was a Baptist minister; her father, John J. Mainor, was a Methodist clergyman. (Dorothy changed the spelling of her last name to Maynor at the beginning of her professional career.) Music was the social mainstay of the Mainor household. She was born in Norfolk, Virginia, in 1910; her childhood was characterized by group singing of hymns and spirituals in the home and regular appearances with her father's church choir.

At fourteen she was sent to the Hampton Institute in Hampton, Virginia, a preparatory school and college founded in 1868 for freed black slaves. There she studied home economics and fashion design and focused her ambitions on teaching. Maynor joined the Hampton Institute's choir as an obscure alto among its 120 voices. A career in music was a vague, distant thought, and when forty students were chosen for a concert tour, the self-effacing young singer was overlooked. Meanwhile, she kept herself busy during nonacademic hours with tennis, swimming, field hockey, and designing and repairing costumes for the dramatics club. She sang in the chorus for three years before Nathaniel Dett pulled her from the ranks to fill a solo spot made vacant by a departing student. The choir went on tour, and within weeks Maynor was singing, for the first time in public, at Carnegie Hall.

While on tour with the ensemble in Europe, Dett cabled Maynor's father; she was about to enter college classes at Hampton in the fall, and Dett persuaded John Mainor that her major should be changed from home economics and fashion design to music. "I wasn't consulted at all," Maynor later said. "But it didn't matter. I was very happy." After four years at the Hampton Institute, where she studied voice with Dett under the auspices of a patron, Maynor won a scholarship to the Westminster Choir College in Princeton, New Jersey. But the possibility of a career as a singer was still distant; at Princeton she studied choral conducting. At Hampton she had caught the attention of the Dean of Women, Harriett S. Curtis, who raised funds to sponsor private voice lessons for her in New York. So in 1936 Maynor set off for New York City to study and prepare for a performing career.

Once in New York, Maynor approached her new course with zeal and commitment, studying Lieder with Wilfred Klamroth and opera repertory with Alan Haughton. She lived in Harlem and, to support herself, directed the choir of a Brooklyn church. Otherwise, she broke the routine of study with low-paying performing engagements and fruitless singing competitions. Finally, in February 1939, Maynor auditioned for the management company of Evans and Salter and was given a contract. More hard work followed, and a New York debut was planned for the fall.

An event in August, though, marked the true beginning of her career. Friends invited her to the Berkshires, the summer home of the Boston Symphony (now the Tanglewood Festival). A festival patron, Mrs. Gorham Brooks, arranged for the twenty-eight-year-old singer to have an informal audition before a reluctant and skeptical Koussevitzky. Her impromptu performance of Lieder, spirituals, and the impressive "Ho-jo-to-ho" aria from *Die Walküre* inspired him to proclaim her, according to the press, "a musical revelation" that "the world must hear." The next day, at the conductor's annual picnic for members of the orchestra, Maynor was invited to sing again, this time for members of the music press. Her audience was ecstatic. The next day the *New York Times* devoted substantial space to Maynor's performance at the picnic concert, and followed up the story two days later with a Maynor interview. "Miss Maynor sang with a poise worthy of a veteran of the concert stage," wrote *New York Times* critic Noel Straus. "She had but to sing only the opening cadenza of her first offering, the aria, 'O, Sleep, Why Dost Thou Leave Me,' from Handel's *Semele*, to assure all those conversant with the vocal art that a new songstress of startling powers had been discovered."

These were strong words—high praise from the *New York Times*. Talk of Maynor's "startling powers" made the rounds of music circles, and expectations mushroomed in anticipation of her November debut at Town Hall. By then Maynor was ready for the siege of attention. Town Hall was packed the night of the concert. Publicity surrounding the new singer after the Berkshire picnic had made her New York debut the musical event of the 1939 season. As Maynor emerged from the wings in a gown purchased by her Boston patron, a shower of

Dorothy Maynor and Serge Koussevitzky

exploding flashbulbs illuminated the stage. The soprano began with the Bach air "To Thee, Jehovah" and followed with "O Sleep, Why Dost Thou Leave Me," "Tu che invoco con orrore" from Spontini's *La Vestale*, and two Mozart arias—"Ach, ich fühl's" from *The Magic Flute* and "Non mi dir" from *Don Giovanni*. The program was filled out with works by Schumann, Schubert, Strauss, and a group of spirituals. She sang three encores, the last of which was "Depuis le jour."

Maynor's reception from perhaps the most sophisticated audience assembled during the season was spectacular. "The toughness went out of the sophisticates," said Taubman. "By the end of the evening, they were on their feet yelling." The *New York Times* and the *New York Herald Tribune* agreed that Maynor's initial nervousness precluded enjoying full confidence in her opening numbers, and that her upper range needed more development. But both papers also agreed that at particular times in the evening Maynor's singing was matchless in projection of mood, beauty of tone, and sensitivity of phrasing. "She proved that she had virtually everything needed by a great artist," wrote Olin Downes, "—the superb voice, one of the finest that the public can hear today; exceptional musicianship and accuracy of intonation; emotional intensity, communicative power. Her breath control is extraordinary, and it enables her to phrase with wonderful beauty and distinction of melodic line, and to maintain an exquisite pianissimo."

With the blessings of the New York press, Maynor's career was properly launched. Her singing fee, set at $150 the year before her debut, jumped to $1,500 per performance the next. She moved from her Harlem apartment to one on West 57th Street. Within a year she had sung with the country's leading orchestras, including the New York Philharmonic, the Boston Symphony, and the Chicago Symphony. At a rehearsal with the Philadelphia Orchestra, Maynor's run-through of "Depuis le jour" stopped the rehearsal, prompting orchestra players to put down their instruments and reward the singer with a standing ovation. Conductor Eugene Ormandy called Maynor "one of the greatest singers I've ever heard."

Maynor's effect on audiences was equally profound. One especially noteworthy concert took place in Long Beach, California, in 1942. Standing before 4,000 people, Maynor managed to ease wartime tensions by singing during a blackout of the entire area until an all-clear was given. After the blackout was lifted, Maynor's audience remained attentive for several encores.

In a short time, Maynor's career soared, and she became one of the biggest box office attractions of the day. She recorded regularly with RCA, and her voice filled American households via radio broadcasts of "The Firestone Hour" and "The Ford Sunday Evening Hour." But even though she had moved from Harlem and acquired a prestigious midtown address, black life in uppermost Manhattan had impressed her indelibly. As a young woman, Maynor had gone from one cloistered environment to another—the life of a preacher's daughter was no less constricting than that of a hard-working singer. So as an independent adult, Maynor ventured into a new world of jazz in Harlem's popular clubs. It was at the Savoy, "*the* dance club at the time," where Maynor's dream of a music school for young black students took shape. One evening, she noticed that while a group of black performers played intricate rhythms on the bandstand, white musicians stood nearby writing them down. The question of musical literacy among blacks entered her mind. "It occurred to me then," Maynor told *Essence* magazine in 1977, "that if we would only take the time and discipline ourselves to be literate in our work, whatever our gifts, then we would be reaping the rewards."

That happened in the late 1930s, but it would be years later—after countless concerts, world tours, recordings, and marriage to her husband, Reverend Shelby Rooks, in 1942—that the seed of thought would sprout into Maynor's realized vision. Maynor's career separated her from her husband for much of the next twenty years. In 1963 he suffered a heart attack and required a lengthy convalescence. "We discussed our future," Maynor said, and it was decided that her singing career should end. She became active in Rooks' church, St. James Presbyterian, and during the next several months began to put a plan into action for the School of the Arts.

Maynor spent months at PTA meetings, surveying the music situation in Harlem schools, and discovered a glaring void in the area of arts development for young children. Her dream of a school for Harlem's indigent youths was considered little more than that by those she approached for funding—the school board and various foundations. In order to get money, Maynor learned, a school first had to exist. So with modest facilities in the annex of the parish, Maynor began teaching piano. The student body of twenty soon increased. By 1977, with an enrollment of 800 and a faculty of sixty-six, the Harlem School of the Arts had expanded to include instruction in painting, sculpture, and dance.

As the school grew, funding became a matter of survival and future growth. Taking advantage of her standing in the music world, Maynor used her connections unabashedly and with businesslike aplomb. With the dedication and spirit of a Third World missionary, she canvassed the worlds of music and money, winning wealthy souls to the cause and prying open purses with her visionary dream. Few could resist the plea of one of the world's great singers; the Ford, Kresge, and Mellon foundations and the Marion Ascoli Fund came up with $3.5 million for a new building that would include space for theater, photography, ethnic and modern dance, classical ballet instruction, and a library. And even though lesson costs were kept to a bare minimum (a sliding scale was used to accommodate even the lowest family income), a healthy percentage was set aside for scholarships.

Maynor's dream for Harlem now stands next to St. James parish, a 37,000-square-foot brick structure crowding the sidewalk along St. Nicholas Avenue between 141st and 143rd streets. The enrollment has escalated to well above 1,000, and the school's list of patrons, benefactors, guest artists, and well-known well-wishers is impressive: George Balanchine contributed specifications for the ballet stage; Arthur Mitchell, former New York City Ballet principal (and later founder of the Dance Theater of Harlem), taught classes; and Leonard Bernstein, Leontyne Price, Marian Anderson, and others supported the school in one way or another. Pianist Arthur Rubinstein, a Maynor fan, took part in a benefit gala for the school in 1976, and Maynor was honored by Young Audiences for her "incomparable achievement and cultural contribution to the lives of our children." A year earlier she had become the first black to sit on the board of the Metropolitan Opera.

On the grounds of the school, Maynor's presence was as distinctive as the leader of some exotic cult, a diminutive dynamo swathed in dark shroudlike robes of her own design, her cascade of black hair harnessed in twin buns separated by her trademark silver Navajo medallion. As a spokesperson for her mission she was eloquent: "By and large, the springs of song have gone dry in the ghettos," she preached to a gathering of teachers at the 1969 Music Educators National Conference. "I hear many things as I walk through the streets of Harlem, but I do not hear much singing." With evangelical fervor, Maynor made it clear that she would stop at nothing to restore the sound of music to Harlem's streets, starting with the very young. "With our boys and girls in Harlem, life affords them no vista, no ample view of themselves," she said in a 1971 *Sepia* magazine interview. "That is what I want them to have, and I firmly believe the arts are a splendid means of providing this. What I dream of is changing the image held by the children. We have made them believe that everything beautiful is outside this community. I want them to make beauty in this community."

With her wish on the way to fulfillment, Maynor retired to semi-reclusion in 1979, leaving the directorship in the hands of Betty Allen. Had she done nothing more than sing beautifully for more than a decade, Dorothy Maynor would be remembered for her voice. The Harlem School of the Arts, however, stands as a reminder of the magnanimous spirit of a great artist—a shrine to Maynor's uncommon perseverance and a bright, musical fortress against what she called "the dark rubble of our streets."

\*     \*     \*

Like Maynor, Carol Brice, a North Carolina contralto with a voice of arresting richness, was determined to be a concert singer. More significantly, she also had in common with Maynor the supportive interest of Serge Koussevitzky. Though it was actually Pittsburgh Symphony conductor Fritz Reiner who first heard her in 1946, announcing his conviction that she was "destined to be the greatest concert singer of our era," it was Koussevitzky and his enthusiastic endorsement that commanded the attention of the musical world. Koussevitzky, a bass player who also played cello, likened her voice to the smaller instrument. When he presented the young singer in a private concert before a group of Boston Symphony backers, he remarked in Russian-accented English, "Always I try to make the cello play like the human voice and now . . . her voice is like a cello . . . such musicality! Such diction! Never have I heard something like this."

Koussevitzky's excited remarks were not the first public declaration of Brice's talent. Unlike Maynor, Brice came before him with impressive credentials. She had already won the prestigious Naumburg Foundation competition in 1944 (the first black artist to do so), and six months later had sung with the Kansas City Philharmonic under Efrem Kurtz on a national broadcast as part of NBC's "Orchestras of the Nation" series.

Like Reiner, others thought Brice would displace Anderson as the leading contralto of the era, an extraordinary prediction even for someone with Brice's natural gifts. The *Saturday Review* more than hinted at the possibility; in reviewing her 1946 recording of Gustav Mahler's *Songs of a Wayfarer*, that journal called her "equal to Anderson in vocal quality" and boldly suggested she "may well be the greatest Negro voice." Predictions aside, a career can only be evaluated as truly great in retrospect. Brice's career, though an important one, lacked Anderson's longevity and vocal consistency, not to mention her symbolic presence. As with Dorothy Maynor, Brice's career ended sooner than expected. But also like Maynor, Brice stands tall among singers of her genre as an important artist of the period.

Brice, born in 1918 in Indianapolis (she soon moved to Sedalia, North Carolina), came from a musical family. Her father, a Congregational minister, and her mother, a history teacher, both sang. Her brothers, Jonathan (who later became her accompanist) and Eugene, were active musically. A precocious child, she was giving recitations already at the age of three, particularly from the works of black poet Paul Lawrence Dunbar. Even more remarkably, she was said to have been able to hum up to a high C. As a child in North Carolina, she sang an impressive rendition of "There's a Long, Long Trail A-Winding" in a recital. There she was heard by Mrs. Galen S. Stone, a wealthy Beacon Hill Bostonian who later became her benefactor and over a period of several years secretly invested more than $1 million in Brice's career.

While a student at the Palmer Institute, Brice joined a group called the Sedalia Singers and toured with them to earn money for the school. The group traveled from New Hampshire to Alabama with Brice as soloist, and appeared on the stage of Town Hall in New York. Brice attended Talledega College in Alabama, where she worked at becoming a public school music teacher. During the summer of 1939, she joined the chorus of the New York World's Fair all-black production of *The Hot Mikado*. That summer she met her future husband, Neil Scott, also in the cast, and auditioned for the Juilliard graduate school. She won the audition and for the next several years studied with Francis Rogers.

To earn money during her Juilliard days, Brice was employed as a singer at St. George's Episcopal Church in New York (where Harry T. Burleigh had sung) and at Trinity Congregational in East Orange. According to an article in the *Chicago Defender*, hostile feelings at the latter church resulted in racial problems. Opposed to the employment of a black singer, members began to leave the congregation, but not before rebuffing the minister for his liberal leanings. He even delivered an inspired sermon on racial understanding, but to no avail, and eventually left the pulpit to do interracial church work.

Brice was undaunted—soon she would no longer have to depend upon churches for her income. Even as a student recitalist she was becoming known as, in the words of the *Washington Post*, a singer to "keep in mind." In 1941 she was chosen to sing on a program celebrating Roosevelt's third inauguration, and later that year sang in a revival of William Boyce's eighteenth-century opera *The Chaplet*, along with another rising young black singer, Ellabelle Davis. The event was part of the Coffee Concert series held in the Museum of Modern Art, and according to press reports, Brice was the most outstanding performer in an otherwise pedestrian effort. "Carol Brice," reported Thomson in the *Herald Tribune*, "has a rich and round mezzo voice of wide range, accurate pitch and perfect production." He went on: "Her scale is of an equality from bottom to top unequaled by that of any woman singer I have heard on the operatic stage this season."

The year 1944 was a banner one for Brice. In a few months, she had advanced from the black southern college recital circuit to the major recital halls of the country. She had won the Naumburg competition and been selected to sing for a coast-to-coast NBC broadcast with the Kansas City Philharmonic in which the nation heard the twenty-six-year-old singer in "Mura felici" from Rossini's *La Donna del Lago* and two spirituals, "Witness" and "Sometimes I Feel Like a Motherless Child." The Naumburg Foundation gave her a debut recital at Town Hall, held in March 1945. Brice sang three arias from Handel's

Carol Brice

*Hercules*, songs by Schubert and Respighi, and a group of spirituals. Robert A. Hague reported: "Before she had completed the first group on the program...it was evident she had won the admiration and undivided attention of her large audience. Hers is a rich, full, well-trained contralto voice, wide in range and exceptionally pleasing in quality."

When Koussevitzky heard Brice in 1946, he determined to present her privately, as he had done with Maynor, to a group of some 1,000 of the Boston Symphony's biggest contributors. With Symphony Hall curtained off at the halfway point, Koussevitzky first conducted the orchestra in a number of light symphonic excerpts. Then he cleared the stage of musicians and spoke to the audience: "Our Boston Symphony discovered Dorothy Maynor. Today we discover another great singer— Carol Brice. I hope very soon this artist will also be as great as Dorothy Maynor."

Brice repeated her Town Hall recital program, and brought the house down. Koussevitzky's chief ambition for Brice was never realized— he wished to commission a symphony with a contralto obbligato composed for her. But Brice had other opportunities, becoming established as a favorite of the country's best conductors: Reiner helped her to record De Falla's *El amor brujo* and the Mahler songs, and Koussevitzky repeatedly engaged her with the Boston Symphony, including a performance in Stravinsky's *Oedipus Rex* at Tanglewood.

Good press and high praise followed Brice for the next several years. With her brother Jonathan as her accompanist—he was a fine musician in his own right—she won fame in America, Europe, and South America. In the 1950s, Paul Hume of the *Washington Post* called her "one of the remarkable voices of the country," and Noel Straus of the *Times* remarked that Brice "was more than ordinarily equipped with the assets required for success in her chosen field."

But mysteriously, Brice's success waned, and by the 1960s she was seen more often in musical shows such as *Finian's Rainbow* (1960), *Showboat* (1961), and *Gentleman Be Seated* (1963) than in recital. Her only major opera performance was in *Porgy and Bess*, in which she sang the role of Maria in 1961. As a concert contralto, Brice was limited, partly due to the declining popularity of the contralto as a vocal species in recent years, and partly due to the category's small range. Earlier she had confessed that she had never aspired to opera because of lack of opportunities, "so I realistically didn't waste much time on it." Unfortunately, her recording as Maria with the Houston Grand Opera's production of *Porgy and Bess* (1977) displays only a fragment of her former glory.

Brice eventually divorced her first husband and married black baritone Thomas Carey. The two settled in Norman, Oklahoma, in the

1970s, where Brice was appointed to the music faculty of the University of Oklahoma. In addition to teaching and performing in oratorios, she and her husband often sang in joint recitals. She died in Norman in 1985. Though her career ended prematurely, she achieved a considerable measure of success and was one of the foremost singers of her era.

The story of Ellabelle Davis (1907–1960), another important concert singer of the time, has all the requisite charm and naivete of a storybook tale. At the time of her Town Hall debut in 1942, the *New York Times* called her a "refined and sensitive artist with a rare sense of style." But the journey to that point had been long and arduous for the daughter of a New Rochelle grocer, who reportedly "sang herself to sleep at the age of two." Davis' childhood years were filled with church choir performances and joint recitals with her sister Marie, a pianist. From an early age, she desired a singing career, but her family's income precluded private study. To earn money Davis became a seamstress so that, as she put it, "I could sing while I worked."

Once when Davis was stitching a dinner gown for Louise Crane, daughter of a former governor of Massachusetts and United States senator, Crane overheard Davis singing "Depuis le jour." (Charpentier's Louise was also a dressmaker given to song.) Crane was so impressed that she offered to sponsor Davis and immediately arranged for the soprano to sing at the Museum of Modern Art in a revival of the *The Chaplet* with Carol Brice. In his review, Virgil Thomson remarked on Davis' "care and good musicianship" and suggested, "She may well become the next great Negro singer."

Davis' Town Hall debut the next year was a major success; at her third appearance there two years later, the capacity audience overflowed onto the stage. In Mexico City she created excitement worthy of her fairytale beginning. At her first concert there in 1945 she opened before a meager audience, but at intermission the excited concertgoers rushed into the streets with the news of a new star. By the end of the program the hall was filled to standing room, and Davis' next five concerts sold out.

Though she sang Aida with the Opera Nacionale in Mexico City, it is as a recitalist that Davis is chiefly remembered. She followed her 1948 Carnegie Hall recital with a whirlwind tour of Europe, giving twenty-seven concerts in thirteen countries. The League of Composers honored her as its Outstanding American Singer of 1947 and commissioned Lukas Foss to compose a work for her. Davis premiered the solo cantata *The Song of Songs* with the Boston Symphony under Koussevitzky and become identified with the work. The soprano was still performing in concerts up to one month before her death from cancer, at age fifty-three, in New York City.

Inez Matthews (1917–    ), a mezzo-soprano widely known for her work on Broadway in the 1944 production of *Carmen Jones* and Kurt Weill's *Lost in the Stars*, was born in Ossining, New York, to a musical family. The younger sister of baritone Edward Matthews, she grew up singing in the church choir of the Baptist church where her father was minister. Her mother also sang, and her sister taught piano and eventually established her own studio.

Edward Matthews was ten years older than his sister (she was still a small child when he toured Europe as a member of the famed Fisk Jubilee Singers), and Inez Matthews credited his successful career as a major source of inspiration. "My parents encouraged me, as they did my brother," she said. "After noting the experiences that he had, I felt that I could do it, too." Beginning as a lyric soprano and later changing to mezzo, Matthews learned voice exclusively through private study. Among her teachers were Katherine Moran Douglas, Paula Novikova, and Frederick Wilkerson, who later taught the popular singer Roberta Flack.

Matthews attracted the attention of Leonard DePaur, founder and conductor of the highly successful and well-traveled DePaur Infantry Chorus of the war years; one of DePaur's favorite singers, she became a regular soloist with his postwar touring ensemble. She made her Town Hall debut in 1947, and toured Europe and the United States as a recitalist. Matthews and her brother worked together in the 1952 revival of *Four Saints*, with the mezzo performing the role of St. Theresa I and her brother repeating his performance as St. Ignatius. In 1960 Matthews was heard by millions of filmgoers as the voice-over for Serena in the film version of *Porgy and Bess*. From 1965 to 1970 she taught voice at Virginia State College in Petersburg.

In the 1930s and 1940s, many black singers earned a respectable living as concert artists. But even the careers of such recitalists as Marian Anderson, Dorothy Maynor, and Carol Brice offered little consolation to black singers of the day with a yearning for opera. Manager Laslo Halasz had courageously added a few black artists to the roster of his fledgling New York City Opera, but opportunities still were severely limited. In the first half of the century, the black singer who preferred opera had narrow choices—she could perform with all-black opera companies (known to be plagued with financial difficulties), go to Europe, where race was a more subtle issue, or aim at singing roles on Broadway. Fortunately for black artists with theatrical

**Abbie Mitchell**

leanings, musical shows and revues were plentiful during the age of vaudeville and the Harlem Renaissance, and many singers were able to sublimate their desire for opera on the theatrical stage.

Abbie Mitchell (1884–1960), who created the role of Clara in *Porgy and Bess*, was such a singer. The wife of talented composer-violinist Will Marion Cook, the New York–born singer made her debut on Broadway at age fourteen—as early as 1898 she appeared in Cook's hit show, *Clorindy, the Origin of the Cakewalk*. After a brief stint with Black Patti's Troubadours, the young singer-actress found work in vaudeville and minstrelsy. She appeared in Cook's *Jes Lak White Folks* (1899) and the Williams and Walker show *In Dahomey* (1902). In 1905 the soprano joined the Memphis Students, a group of twenty singers, dancers, and instrumentalists who claimed the distinction of being the first group to stage "syncopated music." The group gave 150 performances at Hammerstein's Victoria Theater in New York. Mitchell studied voice in New York with Harry Burleigh and Emilia Serrano, and later in Paris with tenor Jean de Reszke.

Mitchell's varied talents allowed her to make the transition from classical music to vaudeville to theater as time and chance permitted. When singing opportunities slacked, she turned to straight acting roles, and from 1910 serious theater dominated her career. In 1914 she became a member of the original Lafayette Players of Harlem, whose vast repertory included such venerated theatrical works as *Madame X, The Servant in the House, On Trial*, and *Within the Law*. In 1919 Mitchell toured the United States and Europe with Cook's Southern Syncopated Orchestra, and when her husband returned to the states in 1921, the resourceful singer stayed in Europe to tour with a group she named "Abbie Mitchell and Her Full Harmonic Quartet." In Europe Mitchell took part in command performances of *In Dahomey* before King Edward VII and *The Red Moon* before Czar Nicholas of Russia. As a singer, she gave recitals in Paris, Berlin, and Vienna, and as an actress she appeared with Tallulah Bankhead in *The Little Foxes* and with Helen Hayes in *Coquette*. Her portrayals as Santuzza in *Cavalleria Rusticana* at New York's Mecca Temple and as Clara in *Porgy and Bess* were her final operatic performances.

Florence Cole Talbert (1890–1961) opted for a full operatic career, and spent most of her career in small European opera houses. The soprano became known as the first black singer to perform the role of Aida with a European opera company—she essayed the work at the Teatro Comunale in Cosenza, Italy, in 1927. The daughter of a Fisk Jubilee Singer, Talbert was encouraged by Emma Azalia Hackley, who heard her sing early in her career. Born in Detroit, Talbert attended the University of Southern California and the Chicago Music College, and studied with John B. Miller, Oscar Saenger, and Herman DeVries. Between 1925 and 1927 she studied in Rome with Delia Valeri and Vito Carnevale, and in Milan with Julian Quezada. After her successful performance of Aida, she sang throughout southern Italy.

Talbert returned to the United States, and became the first black classical artist to record on the historic "race" label The Black Swan, owned by Harry Pace of the Pace Phonograph Company. Named for Elizabeth Taylor-Greenfield, the label later changed from a classical to popular format to improve its dismal finances and is primarily known for its early recordings of the Broadway singer Ethel Waters. Florence Talbert eventually settled in the United States, where she taught at Bishop College in Marshall, Texas, and served as head of the voice department at the Tuskegee Institute in Alabama.

Talbert's protégée, La Julia Rhea (1908–    ), also became known as one of the early black Aidas, but she pursued an American career. Born in Louisville, she began piano at age five and at sixteen studied at the National University of Music. In addition to Talbert, her teachers included Charles Keep, Victor Chenais, and Herman DeVries. She debuted in 1929 at Kimball Hall in Chicago and in 1931 sang in the Broadway musical *Rhapsody in Black*, featuring Ethel Waters and the Cecil Mack Choir. After her Metropolitan Opera audition in 1934 (she was turned down), Rhea won the Major Bowes radio talent show. She gave a notable performance of Aida in a production of the Chicago Civic Opera Company with black baritone William Franklin as Amonasro. After a much acclaimed all-black production of the opera with the Chicago Negro Opera Guild, a *Chicago Sun* reporter singled Rhea out as "the most arresting of singers," noting that she was "not only in possession of a voice of unusually brilliant quality, but she has learned to use it to the best advantage."

Rhea found great advantage in staying with her signature role, Aida—she starred again as the captive Ethiopian in a 1941 production at the National Association of Negro Musicians convention. The convention was an event of major significance; it became the launching platform for Mary Cardwell Dawson's National Negro Opera Company. The organization's first production was *Aida* in Pittsburgh, starring Rhea.

Dawson's NNOC, formed in response to the exclusion of blacks from a white production of *Aida* at the Boston Opera House, was a major source of work for black singers during the years the financially insecure company struggled to exist. Dawson herself was a musician of considerable merit—the pianist-conductor was a graduate of the New England Conservatory and had done graduate work at the Chicago Musical College. Among NNOC's laureate performers were Carol

**Florence Cole Talbert**

Brice, who had appeared with the company in a production of Clarence Cameron White's opera *Ouanga* in the Metropolitan Opera House, and Robert McFerrin, the first black male artist to be signed by the Met.

But one of the more interesting performers associated with NNOC appeared in perhaps the company's most broadly acclaimed production, *La Traviata*, at the Watergate amphitheater in Washington, D.C. Lillian Evanti (1890–1967), a silver-voiced lyric coloratura, was wildly popular in her native Washington, where the landmark all-black *La Traviata* production was seen by more than 30,000 people. She was a guest of Eleanor Roosevelt at the White House in 1934, where the diva sang Mozart and Verdi arias and spirituals on a program to honor Mary Dawson, then director of the women's division of the Democratic National Committee. Early in her career, Evanti had become the first black artist to sing with an organized European opera company when she bowed as Lakmé with the opera company of Nice, France.

Evanti's colorful lineage is as interesting as her life. She was said to have been a descendant of Nathaniel Green, who fought in the American Revolution, and Evanti's great-uncle Hiram Revels was the first black United States senator, representing Mississippi. Two family members took part in abolitionist John Brown's raid on Harper's Ferry, and her grandfather, Joseph Brooks, served in the D.C. territorial legislature of the 1870s. Evanti's upbringing was more privileged than that of most blacks of the time—her family was cultured, well educated, and middle class. Born Annie Lillian Evans in 1890, she attended Washington's Armstrong Manual Training School, a facility her father, Bruce Evans, helped establish and which he served as its first principal. After graduation from a local teacher's college she taught kindergarten for a while, then enrolled at Howard University and received a Bachelor of Arts degree in music. A few years later she married her voice and piano instructor, Roy Tibbs. When Evans decided on a career in music, she took the advice of Harlem Renaissance poet Jessie Fauset and combined her last name with her husband's to add a touch of distinction. She found the result—Evanti—more befitting as a name for a prima donna.

Friends and relatives of Evanti say the singer had a great sense of style and refinement, including a flair for stylish dress, and maintained an unaffected grandness. In short, she was a born diva. A natural actress with an instinctive temperament for opera, Evanti was determined to have a career on the opera stage. And for a black singer of her time, such a commitment meant travel to Europe. In 1925 she boarded the cruise liner *Homeric*, bound for France. Within months she was singing throughout France and Italy with the Nice Opera and receiving critical raves. At the Mozarteum in Salzburg, the *Salzburger Volksblatt* critic said, "Evanti charmed by her exquisite coloratura, full, rich and

Lillian Evanti

round, as well as by her beauty and grace." She returned to the United States, auditioned for the Metropolitan in 1932, and was refused. Evanti continued to concertize. Of one performance at Washington's John Wesley A.M.E. Church, the *Washington Post*'s Paul Hume said, "Lillian Evanti showed that she still can cast a spell with the beauty of her voice."

The 1943 production of *La Traviata* by the National Negro Opera Company gave Evanti a rare opportunity to display her prowess, theatrical and vocal, before an American audience. Presented on an August evening, the production played to 15,000 people who packed into the amphitheater behind the Lincoln Memorial. The overflow was so great that another performance was scheduled for the next evening. Evanti not only sang the role of Violetta (in English) but provided the translation of the original Italian text. Other cast members included Joseph Lipcomb as Alfredo and Charles Coleman as Germont. The chorus numbered one hundred, and musicians from the National Symphony were enlisted to perform in the pit orchestra under the baton of Frederick Vajda.

The day after the first performance, the *Washington Star* raved. "Poised and elegant in her delineation," wrote Alice Eversman, "she brings out, at the same time, the frivolity of Violetta's life in a way seldom emphasized by other interpreters. Her voice is brilliant with ringing high tones and a sparkling smoothness in florid passages." And the black chorus was commended for its support: "The chorus, 100 strong, was by far the best vocally and dramatically that has been heard in opera performances in this city...." But despite Evanti's obvious operatic talent, encouragement for her singing, at least in the form of opera and concert bookings, did not match her reception in Europe. Not only did she lack a good American manager, but "it was simply too soon in this country," as Paul Hume once remarked. "Doors were not open to her." It is interesting to note that Evanti, a fair-skinned woman with delicate features, could have "passed" for white to benefit her career, but chose not to. Her grandson, Thurlow Tibbs, who remembers his grandmother's pride in her African-American heritage, said: "I think that's significant. I think she drew upon that way of approaching life from...her parents, and her parents' parents, who had perhaps certain physical advantages, but didn't use them in a way that would have negated their background, their heritage." (Tibbs manages the Evans-Tibbs Collection of black visual art in Washington, D.C., dedicated to the memory of his grandmother and grandfather.)

During the war years and afterwards, Evanti remained in the United States. She established her own publishing company, the Columbia Music Bureau, and wrote and published a number of patriotic songs, including "Forward March to Victory," which was performed on a U.S. Army world broadcast. She was politically active; she worked to establish home rule in the District of Columbia, got involved in the Pan-American Movement, and with the blessings of Eleanor Roosevelt, lobbied in Congress for the erection of a national performing arts center in Washington (not achieved until the establishment of the Kennedy Center for the Performing Arts). She also founded the Evanti Chorale, a group of some forty women who sang in local churches. A portrait of Evanti as Rosina in *The Barber of Seville*, painted in the 1940s by well-known artist Lois Mailou Jones, now hangs in Washington's National Portrait Gallery.

Though Evanti's career was successful considering the times, it was tragically premature. Had she been born even ten years later, thus becoming a contemporary of Anderson's, she might have benefitted from the slow, painstaking broadening of horizons for black singers. Hers was the prototypical career of a black artist—a career of great promise truncated by the prejudice of the times and now lost in oblivion. Evanti was perhaps one of the most overlooked singers of the early twentieth century.

Unlike Evanti, who apparently had no interest in Broadway, Caterina Jarboro (1903–1986) benefited from a willingness to delve into popular music. Born Catherine Yarborough in Wilmington, North Carolina, she went to New York to study music at age sixteen and landed a job in the historic Blake and Sissle show *Shuffle Along* in 1921. Later she performed in James P. Johnson's *Running Wild*.

Like her contemporaries, Jarboro set sail for Europe to hone her skills and find work, and in 1930 performed Aida in Milan. Other engagements with small European companies followed, but in 1932 the *Chicago Defender* reported Jarboro's return to the United States after a rocky passage on the *Ile de France*. Still under contract with the San Carlo Opera Company, she presented her Aida in 1933 with the Chicago Civic Opera (becoming the first black to perform with a major opera company in the United States), and gave a widely publicized performance of Selika in *L'Africaine* at the Hippodrome Theater in New York. She had a few good offers in America, among them the opportunity to create the lead role in Clarence Cameron White's *Ouanga* and to perform at Chicago's Ravinia Festival. But Jarboro's American career never gained momentum. She returned to Europe, performed successfully for several more years, and eventually settled in New York.

The distinguished career of Muriel Rahn (1911–1961) was highlighted by her performance in the title role of the 1943 Billy Rose production of the Oscar Hammerstein musical *Carmen Jones*. Thus Rahn's career also entailed a combination of musical theater and opera.

Born in Boston, she was raised at the Tuskegee Institute in Alabama, where both her parents were faculty members. Later she attended Atlanta University and graduated from the Music Conservatory of the University of Nebraska.

The soprano began her career in 1929 with Eva Jessye's Dixie Jubilee Singers and sang in two musicals: Lew Leslie's *Blackbirds* and Connie Inn's *Hot Chocolates*, both in 1929. In the 1940s she turned to opera and sang in productions of the National Orchestral Association in New York, including Mozart's *The Abduction from the Seraglio* and Puccini's *Suor Angelica* and *Gianni Schicchi*. She alternated the title role in *Carmen Jones* with Curtis Institute graduate Muriel Smith. (Smith, better known for her work in musical theater, played a revival of the role in 1956, and that same year sang Bizet's Carmen at London's Covent Garden.)

In the late 1940s, Rahn appeared as Aida in productions staged by the Salmaggi Opera, the San Carlo Opera, and the National Negro Opera Company. Another noteworthy event was Rahn's performance of the lead in *The Barrier*, by Langston Hughes and Jan Meyerowitz, based on Hughes' play *The Mulatto*. She appeared in the show for the first time at Columbia University in 1959 and later costarred in a Broadway production with Lawrence Tibbett. Of the Columbia production, Howard Taubman wrote: "She brings a personal dignity to the part, and her singing is not only accurate and full-blooded, but charged with dramatic cogency." A year before her death of cancer at age fifty, Rahn served as musical director for a German-language production of *Bells are Ringing* at the German State Theater in Frankfurt, Germany.

From Abbie Mitchell to Marian Anderson, the first half of the twentieth century saw a profusion of black divas, with varying degrees of talent and varying styles and levels of success. While the Harlem Renaissance (and its aftermath) might not call to mind black classical singers, the creative spirit of the era is inextricably tied to the successes of the classical artists who thrived during the Jazz Age. If art in any form desires inspiration, not necessarily from its own ilk, then it is difficult to say how many careers might have languished outside the infectious environment of this broadly eclectic age. The musical fever of *Blackbirds* and *Shuffle Along*, the affecting prose of Langston Hughes, the eloquence of W. E. B. Dubois, the physical genius of Bill "Bojangles" Robinson, and the magic of Dorothy Maynor all carried their witnesses along on a wave of contagious creative energy. New York's dizzying blur of black talent—whether visual, literary, jazz, or classical—formed a compelling mix of diverse occupations as legends rubbed shoulders with other legends. If Dorothy Maynor "stomped at the Savoy," the thought is irresistible that on some evening in upper Manhattan Marian

Anderson's taxi, leaving her residence at the 135th Street Y, might have passed Bessie Smith's.

By the end of the 1930s, the Harlem Renaissance was over, the cultural Xanadu had disappeared. But the next era, with its expanding social consciousness and focus on civil rights, promised an even greater time for the black prima donna. Racially, changing times and moods brought giant strides in every area of human achievement; Anderson's Metropolitan debut meant no less to opera than Jackie Robinson's major league initiation did to sports. By the late 1950s the doors, if not fully opened, at least stood enough ajar to permit shafts of light. And the opera world awaited the entrance of the next phenomenon, the modern black diva.

# 6

# Leontyne Price:
# Prima Donna Assoluta

ON January 28, 1961, Langston Hughes wrote to his friend Arna Bontemps and mentioned, among other noteworthy events of the day, a black soprano "busting the walls of the Metropolitan wide open" the night before. It was hyperbole that neared truth. Leontyne Price, just days shy of her thirty-fourth birthday, had debuted before an audience whose standards and expectations were high. She not only lived up to them, but surpassed them beyond even her own imagination. With a stunning performance of Leonora in Verdi's *Il Trovatore*, the Mississippi-born singer inspired one of the most protracted and vociferous ovations in Metropolitan Opera history. At the final E-minor chord, the walls of the old Met vibrated for nearly three-quarters of an hour with noisy appreciation for the voice *Time* magazine described as "like a bright banner unfurling." The soprano had arrived, and American opera would never be the same.

Price's first Met triumph was only a foretaste of future adulation. With star quality, a healthy instrument not yet in its prime, and impeccable training, her promising career had all the earmarks of permanence. This was no untested ingenue singing subordinate roles (major parts in Europe and smaller American houses had affirmed a natural confidence), nor an aging diva teetering on the edge of vocal decline. Price's debut was a marvel of good timing. She appeared, like a nova, with a blinding brilliance that shadowed anyone who stood next to her. Franco Corelli was a case in point. The great tenor co-debuted that evening with Price, but the capacious environs of the Met held room for only one operatic revelation. "I don't want to sing with that soprano again," Corelli told manager Rudolf Bing after Price captured the bulk of press attention. In later years he generously conceded, "The night of our Met debut was a night full of fire and anticipation, a night to remember. Leontyne sang enchantingly and sublimely."

But Price's arrival at the pinnacle of American opera had a dual significance. She was one of few American-trained singers since Rosa Ponselle to establish herself as a truly international star. And as a black artist she dutifully, and with grand style, continued the tradition begun by Marian Anderson—that of trailblazer, barrier-breaker, and door-opener for black performers. Price idolized Anderson, and as a teenager framed a magazine photo of the contralto that still hangs on her studio wall. When she heard Anderson's Met performance, she took it personally, perceiving it as a private challenge to assume the legacy. "I was in the audience and saw my door open for me," Price recounted. "I heard it open. And I said to myself, 'I don't want this night, from you, ever to be wasted.' I'm not trying to sound as if I anointed myself. But then, if it's for a positive reason, carrying something onward in any area is not too bad an ambition to have." Price's ambition to carry the baton led to a list of musical firsts rivaled only by Anderson's. She was the first black artist in a Metropolitan starring role, first to open a season with the company, first to appear in a televised operatic production, and on and on.

While she and Anderson tower like twin giants over black American vocal artists of the twentieth century, their differences are a study in contrasts. Anderson was shy, unaffected, uncommonly humble, and a reluctant star. Price, on the other hand, embraced her superdiva celebrity and reveled in the stardom her position allowed. Regal, imperious, glamorous, and with an unquestionable sense of self-worth, Price became the epitome of the modern prima donna. And though Marian Anderson's debut was a great social triumph for blacks at the Met, Price's was the greater artistic triumph.

Price's art sprang from a seemingly boundless talent, a formidable will, and a single-minded, ascetic drive. But as an impresario once said, "There are three things necessary to produce a great singer: voice, voice, and voice." Price's voice, from the moment she stunned a group of fellow college students on a hazing expedition with a spontaneous performance of "Because," was universally regarded as unique among all singers and destined for greatness. Price herself described the sound as "juicy lyric" or "lyric with a dramatic thrust." Others labeled the voice *lyrico spinto*, a term for voices that can sing comfortably dramatic roles of roughly medium weight.

Price found her niche in the heroines of Verdi—Aida and both Leonoras—as well as in the repertories of Mozart, Puccini, and Strauss. Clearly, Verdi roles were her favorites—her Metropolitan career was launched on one and ended dramatically with Aida in 1985. "Verdi and Mozart are the best vocal pals I have," the diva said once. "They like me and I like them." With a wealth of color, texture, and nuance, Price's voice traversed the musical spectrum, from dark, spiritual depths to effervescent, floating heights, with a buoyant lightness at the top that belied the burgundy-colored richness at the bottom. In her prime, Harold Schonberg's description, "the Stradivarius of singers," seemed entirely fitting.

Significantly, as Price's career soared to its inevitable extremes, so did the civil rights movement in America; the prima donna was the first to admit that—"My career was simultaneous with the opening up of civil rights. Whenever there was any copy about me, what I was as an artist, what I had as ability, got shoveled under because all the attention was on racial connotations." The connotations might have been un-avoidable. Race was the hot topic of the day, as a dynamic movement for black equality, spurred by intolerable incidents in southern pockets of racial repression, reached a bloody, fevered pitch in the 1950s and 1960s.

For the ascending black star, musical milestones were matched with racial watersheds. Months before Price became the first black to appear in an opera on television, the United States Supreme Court issued its epochal decision in *Brown* vs. *Topeka Board of Education* denouncing school segregation as unconstitutional. And in Montgomery, Alabama, black citizens led by the young Martin Luther King, Jr., fought against segregation in public transportation with a bus boycott that lasted a year. In 1957, when Price first sang to admiring opera audiences in San Francisco, federal troops struggled daily to restrain jeering mobs as nine black students integrated Little Rock's Central High School. And in the year of her Metropolitan debut, and of her appearance as the first black artist to sing before a mixed audience in her hometown in Mississippi, rioting broke out at nearby Oxford after James Meredith, flanked by federal guards, entered the University of Mississippi as its first black student.

The paradox was vivid; while white insurgents violently challenged the human rights of blacks on one hand, Price, with her irresistible purity of sound, lulled nonbelievers into submission on the other.

In the late sixties, when the American ethnic consciousness focused on black pride and power, Price sported a flattering Afro hairstyle and, while admittedly no spokesman for the cause, voiced her admiration for such activist groups as the Black Panthers. With feet in two different worlds, the diva became a bicultural phenomenon. Journalists were often perplexed at the seemingly divided personality. On stage, she had the dignified comportment of a typical European diva. Price could assume grandeur with the best of them, whether gazing icily before singing an aria as if to summon some recalcitrant muse, or sprinkling her responses to interviewers' questions with foreign phrases. At other times the true southerner shone through as Price effused earth-motherly warmth, her voice slipping comfortably into the patois of blacks from the deep South.

The fact that the first true black prima donna of grand opera of the century emerged from the race-sensitive South seemed ironically appropriate. Price's roots ran deep in the Mississippi soil and stretched like an umbilical cord, tethering the soprano to her homeland even while she performed in the music capitals of the world. As Price herself admitted, the bond of family love and the southerner's natural homing instinct reeled her in whenever she strayed too far from the familiar.

Mary Violet Leontyne was born to James Anthony and Katherine Baker Price on February 10, 1927, in Laurel, a town known for its flowering shrubs of laurel, its canopied oak-lined streets, and its burgeoning timber business. A sturdy yet slight man with ruggedly chiseled features, James Price earned a spartan living in the sawmills. Kate Price, a sternly compassionate woman, achieved local fame as Jones County's favorite midwife, delivering some nine hundred children in her career. In Price's words, Kate was "the lighthouse of her community... all things to all people and all ages." Leontyne was born fourteen years after the couple married, and two years later a son, George, was born.

As the unwritten law of the 1920s South decreed, Laurel's 27,000 citizens were geographically divided according to race. The small frame houses of South Fifth Street, where the Prices lived, bore no resemblance to the mansions of North Fifth, where the town's successful whites lived. The inhabitants of those separate worlds rarely mingled but they coexisted civilly; the laws of social separation in Laurel were implicit and unchallenged. Price's aunt Everlina Greer, her mother's sister, straddled the diverse cultures with ease and élan; she lived with the Prices and traveled daily to her job as a domestic for the Alexander Chisholms, often with her young niece in tow. The Chisholms were cultured, prominent Laurelites who figured in Leontyne's future, grooming her for the life for which she seemed destined. Elizabeth was the daughter of a wealthy lumber magnate and had married her husband, a banker, after attending college in New England. Everlina was working

Leontyne Price
*Photo by Metropolitan Opera Association, Inc.*

for Elizabeth Wisner Chisholm's family already before the marriage and served both families for nearly forty-five years. Leontyne and George befriended the Chisholm children as the two families practically became one extended family, and Leontyne often was called upon to sing at the Chisholms' musical soirees. In the Price household at the other end of town, James and Kate ruled firmly but "with love and care," teaching their children, as George Price, later a Brigadier General, said, "to judge people as individuals, not on the pigment of their skin."

If the Price children were not hard-pushed to be successful, neither were they taught to fear the possibility. "[Our parents] never told us we couldn't succeed," remembered Leontyne. "The word failure never entered their conversations with us. The words 'do your best' was the constant echo we heard, and that was all we did." A close-knit, sheltering black community of concerned neighbors played its part too: "You had many parents in my community," Price added. "If you . . . goofed, you know? If the teacher didn't get you, your mother would get you or your father would get you, or a neighbor. It worked."

Like her mother, Kate, whose lyric soprano voice easily filled the spaces of St. Paul's Methodist Church, where she sang in the choir, Leontyne demonstrated an unusual vocal talent and affinity for music early. Formal training began when she was three and a half years old; she studied piano with Hattie McInnis, a local black pianist, and when she was five the family phonograph was traded for a piano. In elementary school she penned a poem about her hometown: "I know on my laurels I'll never rest," wrote the precocious child at eleven, already showing a seriousness of purpose and an eye for success. Later, at Oak Park Vocational High School, Leontyne was popular, studious, and active. She was a cheerleader, salutatorian of her graduating class, and sang for nearly every musical event in town, specializing in weddings and funerals.

At seventeen, with a scholarship in hand, she boarded a bus bound northward to enter Central State University in Wilberforce, Ohio. "I'm worried about the future," she wrote on her college application, "because I want so much to be a success." She majored in music education, later changing to voice at the advice of the college president. When her stint at Central State neared its end, Price eyed the Juilliard School for graduate work. In 1948 she sang at Antioch College and met Paul Robeson; the bass was impressed with Leontyne's voice and offered to help raise money for the Juilliard tuition. With the help of Central State administrators, a benefit concert was arranged and $1,000 was raised for Price's further studies.

The Chisholms, ardent music lovers, took an active interest in Price's education as well, and volunteered to assume the brunt of financial responsibility for her Juilliard education. Price took up residence at International House and worked at the information desk after classes. Florence Page Kimball, her voice teacher, listened to her "heavy molasses mezzo" and began shaping the raw talent into a refined soprano.

While still a student, Price got the "opera bug"; a performance of *Turandot* at City Center sparked a budding interest, but "the second performance I went to did it for me," she told a reporter for *Holiday* magazine. "I stood up at the Met to see *Salome*. I was completely gone on it and said to myself, 'I have got to be an opera singer.'" In her first major role in the Juilliard opera theatre as Alice Ford in Verdi's *Falstaff*, Price caught the attention of Olin Downes, who forecast a bright future for the young singer. Kimball became her mentor and friend, plying her with confidence and good advice: "Sing on your interest and not your principal," she told her students. "What she meant was, as in any walk of life, there should be something more to give," Price later explained to an *Opera News* reporter. "I wouldn't say necessarily in reserve, in the technical sound of singing, but in your attitude."

For the soprano, New York was a gold mine of exposure and opportunity. Planned revivals of Gershwin's *Porgy and Bess* and Virgil Thomson's *Four Saints in Three Acts* meant work for young black singers. Thomson and Robert Breen, producer of the new *Porgy* production, heard Leontyne at Juilliard. She impressed them both, and the young student was hired for both productions. The new *Four Saints* featured Edward Matthews (St. Ignatius), Altonell Hines (Commère), Inez Matthews (St. Teresa I), Betty Allen (St. Teresa II), and Rawn Spearman (St. Chavez). Price sang in the chorus along with Martha Flowers, Gloria Davy, Olga James, and Billie Daniel. Eventually, she was pulled from the chorus to replace Matthews as St. Teresa. Thomson was elated at the discovery. "Leontyne...was at her peak," said the composer. "I don't think she has ever sounded or looked more lovely."

As Bess in the *Porgy* revival, Price sang opposite William Warfield, who played the Catfish Row cripple. The cast was filled out with Lorenzo Fuller (Sportin' Life), John McCurry (Crown), Helen Thigpen (Serena), and Helen Colbert (Clara). The tour began with performances in Dallas in June 1952, and the southwestern city remained true to the code of the South in the fifties—cast members had trouble with discrimination in hotels, restaurants, and car rental agencies. But the audiences at Fair Park were exuberant, and *Porgy and Bess* became, according to the *Dallas Times Herald*, "the box office champion in the history of summer musicals in Dallas." Price captured the fancy of the Dallas press with her portrayal of Bess: "There was dramatic genius in her range, an incisive detailing meant for the audience, not the wings," said the *Morning News*. "Her voice has purity, power and impact."

The production triumphed as the company went to Chicago, Pittsburgh, Washington, D.C., and on to the major European capitals, including London, Paris, Vienna, and Berlin. Warfield was a vocally and physically imposing Porgy, well known for his role in the MGM film *Showboat* and a stalwart presence in the black music theater circles of New York. Price had heard him perform but never met him until *Porgy*. She and the baritone began a relationship that would take them to the altar in the middle of *Porgy*'s run; they became engaged, and were married at Harlem's Abyssinian Baptist Church on August 31, 1952. The next morning, they left with the company for Berlin. The marriage eventually succumbed to the pressures of two colliding careers; the couple separated after two years and eventually divorced.

In 1955, when Price was still an aspiring diva showing flashes of incipient greatness, the Metropolitan Opera grabbed the lion's share of press coverage with its announcement of Marian Anderson's debut. But months before Rudolf Bing shook the opera world with the desegregation of the Metropolitan, the National Broadcasting Corporation was busy planning its own casting adventure. NBC Orchestra conductor Peter Herman Adler heard Price in *Porgy and Bess* and was taken with her performance, particularly her ethereal, diminishing high A as Bess says goodbye to Porgy at the end of Act Two. Price, he decided, was the ideal choice for a televised production of *Tosca*. In a way, the selection of the twenty-six-year-old soprano to play Puccini's charismatic heroine on national television was even more controversial than Anderson's debut. Anderson's role was safely couched in mysticism—as defined in the libretto, Ulrica was a dark-skinned sorceress, and her impact on the opera was anything but sexual. Also, Anderson's *Un Ballo* played only in eastern cities. Price would play the provocative Floria Tosca in love with a white Cavarodossi before an audience of millions, including a large contingent of diehard southern segregationists.

If NBC expected trouble from its southern affiliates, it wasn't disappointed. Conservative markets found the idea untenable; eleven cities refused to broadcast the interracial performance. But Price vocally vindicated NBC's executives for their courageous experiment. "At first sight her striking features looked rather exotic," wrote *Time* magazine, "although the TV screen virtually wiped out the color contrast between her and the other singers." But as the reviewer observed, Price was as unlike her colleagues in talent as she was in appearance. "Vocally she was head and shoulders above the others, crooning pearly high notes here, dropping into gutty dramatic tones there. She sang the great second act aria 'Vissi d'arte' with a flair worthy of the Met."

Any doubts about whether Price could bridge the musical chasm between the street-wise Bess and the pious Tosca were dispelled by the NBC broadcast. Price demonstrated dramatic presence and a flair for movement in addition to voice, and she was hired for televised versions of *The Magic Flute, Dialogues of the Carmelites,* and *Don Giovanni*. And soon opera companies began to take notice. San Francisco Opera audiences cheered her first opera performance on stage when Price appeared in *Dialogues of the Carmelites* under Kurt Herbert Adler. Later, luck intervened, as two unlikely coincidences produced opportunities to sing Aida. When soprano Antonietta Stella contracted appendicitis before a 1957 production in San Francisco, Price was called to replace her; at Covent Garden she substituted for Anita Cerquetti, who was similarly disabled.

Price always felt at home with Aida. The Verdi heroine suited her voice, temperament, and complexion. "In *Aida*, my skin is my costume," she said. As a black woman of the 1950s, she envisioned herself the embodiment of the Ethiopian slave-princess—dignified in captivity, powerful even in her powerlessness. And because she had performed white roles before Aida (typically the black diva's visa into grand opera), she escaped the trap of typecasting and was free to enjoy herself in the Verdi role. "Real freedom is when you can be bored with typecasting," Price said. "Not emotional about it, not upset, but bored, because someone continues to insist to pinpoint you or to keep an image of you which is passé.... You've gone so far beyond it, that sometimes I wonder if it is their own mental way of being able to handle how much more you have done." In a 1985 interview with *Opera News,* Robert Jacobson, Price defined her feelings for her favorite character:

Aida is a very personal role for me. She is where I am, often, as a woman. That makes her more facile to present. Not for the obvious reason—the color of the skin is a luxury in *Aida*....It's a luxury because you are there, and if you've taken good care of it, it is the costume. You just drape something over it! And I actually luxuriate in that idea. You are presenting a woman as you would yourself. And the thing I've always known about Aida is what I always thought—that there must be a reason this person is in captivity. Why, with all the ladies-in-waiting for a noble young princess like Amneris, does she choose this captive person to be her handmaiden? There's something about her that is provocative, and on that kernel of feeling I build my character of Aida. She is a noblewoman in captivity, which makes the elasticity of the role extend to its...farthest width and height, because something about that fact bothers Amneris. She wants it close at hand so she can observe it. And when she finds out that Aida's personality is provocative to her, in that she cannot make her bend—she is not automatically subservient—there is something about her carriage that reminds her of herself.

Even in 1958, Price's immersive identity with Aida translated into success after success. She took her signature role to Vienna at conductor Herbert von Karajan's invitation—"She gave me goosepimples," said the conductor on hearing her—and to La Scala two years later. Her performance at the Italian house brought unprecedented applause after the opening trio, with shouts of "Brava, Leonessa!" from the audience. *Time* magazine called her portrayal "at once feline and tender, sweet and aggressive." And from one Italian critic came the highest accolade: "Our great Verdi would have found her the ideal Aida."

Price's triumphs accumulated quickly, each adding a layer of confidence onto a career that surged with increasing speed. Her strengths tested and approved by the critics and audiences of America and Europe, she was ready for the ultimate American challenge, the Metropolitan. In 1958 she was offered a contract, but declined. "It was the wrong contract and the wrong time," she told Samuel Chotzinoff in an article for *Holiday*. "I was doing something else. I was crying and getting advice from two or three people, and I forgot all about being the first Negro to be a Tosca at NBC, the first to be Pamina at NBC, all that went out the window...And I just thought, 'Oh well, I can't go now, so I'll never make the Met.'"

But in 1961 the offer came again, this time to Price's satisfaction. "I'm better prepared now," she said. "My La Scala triumph made me deliciously sure of myself—and being sure of myself was the only way I could go to the Met." The decision to wait paid off. Price's debut, one of opera's historic events, showed her to be a star of the first rank. Her Leonora was the work of a seasoned artist with an absorbing sense of drama and an uninhibited, soaring musicality. And the audience, sensing the weight of the moment, applauded for a reported forty-two minutes, a record in Metropolitan history. "She has matured into a beautiful singer," wrote Harold C. Schonberg. "She moves well and is a complete actress. But no soprano makes a career of acting. Voice is what counts. And voice is what Miss Price has." *Time* magazine echoed the praise of the *Times* and other dailies. "Her Leonora proved to be a remarkable portrayal of a woman in whom dignity struggled with desperation, and in whom grief somehow shone more moving through a profound sense of repose."

Despite all the attention on her, Price still found time to return to Laurel and her southern roots. The St. Paul Methodist Church, her first public forum, needed financial help to build a new church, and Price gave a benefit concert for the fund, attended by 2,000. Even there she made history; it was the first time blacks and whites in Laurel had sat together in the same auditorium. Though they sat in separate sections, according to the *New York Times*, "the ovation was spontaneously integrated."

Even when she later toured the South with the Met, Price could not escape the issue of racism. As with Anderson, Price's presence forced a moral commitment from the Metropolitan. It was not enough that blacks were allowed on the New York stage; the spring tour, which normally traveled to southern cities, had to be considered. Rudolf Bing made his policy clear; the Met would not sing before segregated audiences nor stay in hotels that discriminated. Price handled the situation with wry wit. Before a trip with the Met to Atlanta to perform *The Girl of the Golden West*, Price, aware of hotel policy in the South, told Bing, "I am sure you will find room for the horse and me." Wary that she might be mistreated, Bing made a point of taking her to dinner at his hotel the night the company arrived in Atlanta. "As we walked in," remembered Bing, "there was a sudden hush, which I greatly enjoyed."

After her Met debut Price was sought by every major house and immediately contracted by the Metropolitan to do four more roles: Aida, Madam Butterfly, Donna Anna in *Don Giovanni*, and Liù in *Turandot*. And with her performance as Minnie in *The Girl of the Golden West*, she became the first black artist to open a Metropolitan season. But even during the heady times in her career, when many singers are most distracted by what Price called the "noise around success," she was guided by a firm fusion of intelligence and instinct. Though hardly acrophobic, she knew the awesome heights of international stardom could have dizzying, even perilous effects. "I've never been very good at doing anything anyone else has told me to do," Price admitted. "The one or two times that I did were the only few—one or two—off-the-wall crises that I've had."

She learned self-dependence the hard way. An early vocal mishap left her a wiser artist with resolve to take full control of her career. On a night well into the run of *The Girl of the Golden West*, an overworked Price stepped onstage to sing Minnie, the scourge of many a lyric soprano. In the middle of the second act, her voice faltered, then failed completely. In what a Met spokesman later called "a heroic gesture on the part of a great artist," the diva marked her lines until Dorothy Kirsten could replace her in the third act. The illness—a viral infection—required a long rest. Price took the experience to heart. "It's stupid to repeat mistakes," she said. And she never did.

From that point on, whenever Price needed guidance she confidently consulted her own intuition and native intelligence. She mastered the art of saying no, to the frustration of many conductors and opera managers worldwide. If she said yes, she committed herself wholly, to the extent of months of preparation, rigid discipline, and monastic seclusion.

One of the greatest honors of her career required such commitment. When the Metropolitan Opera finally outgrew its home on 39th Street and replaced it with a $45-million structure in Lincoln Center in 1966, Rudolf Bing looked to America's most celebrated composer and its "diva *assoluta*" to grace the inaugural performance. The Met commissioned Samuel Barber to compose an opera based on Shakespeare's *Antony and Cleopatra* and chose Leontyne Price to sing the title role. Thus came the American opera establishment's tacit endorsement of the Mississippi soprano as the country's first lady of opera. Price, keenly aware of the great honor, severely pared down her schedule for an entire year to prepare for the event, needing, she said, "to find a quietness within myself." She spent the time working with Florence Page Kimball and even delved into Egyptian history to create the role of the Nile queen. "I have read every book I can find—novels, pictures, reproductions of paintings," said Price. "I want to see how she carried herself." Her routine became even more ascetic than usual; socializing was out, and getting into "fine fettle" was her first priority. "You can't say 'I don't feel well this morning,'" Price said. "This is one time you can't say that. You have to be there with everything you've got. I am not going to have this chance again."

Nor did Price underestimate the social significance of the event, yet another landmark in the career of the pioneering black diva. "I pioneer every time I open my mouth," she said. The soprano took her share of heat from the black community, who often considered her music "too esoteric to relate to" and criticized her distance from the civil rights movement. But Price, preferring to speak through her music, said, "This is the only way I can speak for them, my people, to let them know that I am a part of what they feel, that I am not away from it, that this is the way I have to help." Looking back years later she said, "My involvement was *being* black, not talking about it. Why should I sit around chatting, when I'm busy getting things done?"

The furor of inaugurating the new Met came to an anticlimactic conclusion on the opening night of *Antony and Cleopatra*. The company pulled out all the stops for Barber's big new opera. While Price survived the opulent, menagerie-like spectacle with her usual artistic dignity, the production collapsed in excess. Franco Zeffirelli's ostentatious sets, critics agreed, achieved a glittery gaudiness that suffocated any hint of musical and dramatic integrity. It was lavish beyond believability, overproduced beyond reason, and, as critic Schonberg said, was "unselfconsciously exhibitionistic." Zeffirelli's 950 costumes, including Price's, were overwhelming and unflattering, and the high-tech sets, Schonberg added, were handled "with the enthusiasm of a group of children around a big, new Erector set." Lost in the welter of whirling platforms, ponderous pyramids, and live, strutting animals were Barber's interesting score and excellent performances by Price,

Justino Diaz as Antony, and the rest of the cast. Early on, Rudolf Bing knew the company had overextended itself with the production. Price's mother met Bing for the first time just before the performance. "Mr. Bing," she said, "I had envisioned you a much larger man." Bing replied, "Until a week ago, I was."

But despite the mayhem and mishaps in *Antony and Cleopatra* (Price even got stuck in a faulty pyramid during rehearsal), the honor of selection cemented Price's position as one of the world's most respected singers. Among the other great divas of the time—Sutherland, Nilsson, Callas, Tebaldi—Price held her own, and in the opinion of many, her artistry surpassed the others'. As a successful diva will do, she began to revel in the luxury of choice, carefully selecting roles and companies—resting after an opera's run, singing, then resting again. When she cut back on her opera schedule in the 1970s to sing more recitals, rumors circulated among opera cognoscenti that Price was angry with the Met. Some said a rift was sparked by a lack of premieres and new productions, and Price even admitted (during a return to do *Butterfly* in 1973) that it was no fun "just to keep doing one *Aida* and *Forza* after another, with never any real impact." Whatever the reasons for her lengthy absences from opera, Price's longevity as an artist may be owed in part to those languorous, fortifying periods of silence— "Sing on your interest, never your principal." Florence Kimball's greatest student lived her teacher's favorite axiom, and it served her well.

It was Price's nearly miserly sense of vocal economy as well as her common sense that allowed her career to continue well into her sixties. Long after other singers of her generation had shouted and overworked themselves into vocal oblivion, Price endured. Even Anderson, who at fifty showed the effects of too many ninety-concert seasons, gave in to the demands of a management and public who unwittingly hastened her decline. But as Price entered her sixth decade, it must be said that she and Sutherland were the fittest sexagenarian singers of the day.

By the mid-1980s *Opera News* was able to say, without fear of contradiction, "No native born singer of her era has been so honored as Leontyne Price." In fact, no one came close. As was the case with Anderson, it seemed no American awards ceremony was complete without some tribute to Price. She was the first opera singer to receive the Presidential Medal of Freedom, presented by Lyndon Johnson in 1965. The Republic of Italy honored her with its highest award, the Order of Merit. Three Emmy awards were given to her for two White House performances and a New York Philharmonic broadcast of "Live From Lincoln Center." *Life* magazine listed her among its "Remarkable American Women—1776–1976," and a library was named for her in Holly Springs, Mississippi.

In her recording years, Price amassed a considerable discography and received eighteen Grammy awards. One of her favorites served as a tribute to her longtime affinity for the music of Samuel Barber—as a Juilliard student, Price had premiered Barber's Hermit Songs at the Library of Congress. Her recording of his *Knoxville: Summer of 1915* stands out among her recorded works. As a southerner, Price brought a special pathos to the music of Barber and the words of James Agee's prose masterpiece, taken from *A Death in the Family*. "I recorded that the same month that my father had died," said Price. "And I think it has an extra poignancy, because instead of disintegrating, I sang through that poem, everything that he meant to me—and he was not gone from me, he was extremely alive—and everything I knew about being his daughter, about being a southerner... I think that's the height of artistic expression; because you don't waste that strength that has been given to you. Courage is to overcome things when they are difficult, to ride through them."

In 1985 Price rode through another emotional test. After twenty-five years with the Metropolitan, she took her last bow as an opera diva in the house she had opened. Broadcast on PBS's "Live from the Met," Price's final Aida played to a television audience of millions. And during a lengthy, sentimental ovation following "O patria mia," Price fought back tears of mixed emotion. Retirement from opera had been her own decision; her voice had lost little of its power and glory, but timing, to the diva, is as important at the end of a career as at the beginning. And Price's ever vigilant inner voice told her the time was right to leave. "I'm trying to exhibit good taste," she said. "I want to leave standing up, like a well-mannered guest at a party." And the wise words of Katherine Price rang in her memory: "My mother told me and my brother always to leave a piece of dessert and not to stay too late, and that's how I'm going to handle this." Aida, her operatic alter-ego, was the perfect exit vehicle. "I left her on the crest of a wave, my best friend," said Price. "I think that through her I made my niche. I will always love her as I do me, because she is me, and my last performances were of me, I think, as a human being who is more at peace with herself."

Peace, for Leontyne Price, meant a relaxation of pace, a transition from the high drama of grand opera to concert-singing and finding more time for family and friends. There was time to work the soil in her small city garden ("I've had some of my best rehearsals there," she said) and to try her hand at teaching master classes in the San Francisco Opera's Merola Program. "It was my latest challenge," she said. "I wanted to see if I could teach one week, and do what I asked my students to do the following week, and I got away with it."

There was also time for encouraging her musical progeny. She invited younger sopranos to her house on Van Dam Street in New York, entertaining them with tea and sisterly chats, and when asked, delivering sage advice. "The kids have dubbed me 'mother' behind my back," Price slyly admitted. The "kids" are some of the world's most talented singers: Leona Mitchell, Marvis Martin, and other gifted blacks rising to stardom in the 1980s. The younger singers regard the diva as an exemplary model, a living lesson in how to conduct one's life and career. And to them no one could offer better counsel than the Mississippi-born soprano on the exigencies of the black American artist, who must walk the line between loyalty to her history and devotion to her art.

"If you are going to think black, think positive about it," Price insisted. "Don't think down on it, or think it is something in your way. And this way, when you really do want to stretch out, and express how beautiful black is, everybody will hear you. It is overwhelming, because it is so honest, so total, and so unapologetic. So...*strong*. It has focus, because you are taking a column of what is wonderful about you to express with. You don't apologize for it—you like it. You *love* it. It's the time when you can feel there can't be a negative vibration. How can you not stand tall?—because you are saying who you are."

# 7

# Martina Arroyo and a New Firmament of Stars

*E*VEN before the 1960s, musical America was poised for change. Like the mantra of some eastern religion, the words "civil rights" took on the power of a spiritual catchphrase, resonating through the country's conscience. It was an idea whose time had come, and blacks in opera, as in every other aspect of American life, made the slow transition from tolerance to acceptance to vogue. The modern black prima donna had evolved almost unrecognizably from her nineteenth-century sister—now she exuded confidence, sophistication, and artistic savvy. The transformation that had begun with Greenfield, Jones, and Selika accelerated with Anderson and Price, and opera companies began to dismantle barriers of prejudice.

As arguments against a black artist's performing European operatic roles were exposed as weak and illogical, American audiences began to realize what many Europeans already knew—that if opera, any opera, requires of its audience a certain leap of faith to accept the implausible, a black Pamina or Tosca is no less convincing than a white Aida or Othello, a fifty-year-old Salome, or even a female in the "trouser" roles of Octavian or Cherubino. And as more and more black artists made their presence and talent known, the inclusion of the greatest of them on the rosters of major companies became a point of pride, and omission of the talented black artist because of race betrayed the mood and spirit of the times.

While black opera companies and operas such as *Porgy and Bess*, *Four Saints in Three Acts*, and Clarence Cameron White's *Ouanga* offered employment, the amount of work generated by them could hardly sustain an entire career. And in terms of artistic integrity, to many American eyes and ears even *Porgy* was still considered déclassé— too popular, too accessible and commonly appealing for serious art. It took performances of standard European opera roles in established white companies before the black artist was perceived as a worthy member of the international opera community.

The sixties marked the first time black artists could make a living principally as singers of opera in America, without compromise in the form of musical theater or recital work. The New York City Opera (then at City Center) laid the groundwork in the mid-1940s; Todd Duncan's performance of Tonio in *Pagliacci* with the company in 1945, making him the first black artist to sing with a white company, signaled the beginning of a new epoch. And Camilla Williams' Butterfly and Aida further staked the claim of black singers in mainstream opera. (In an even more daring move, City Opera, a young company with progressive ideas, premiered black composer William Grant Still's opera *The Troubled Island* in 1949.) Precedents were established, if not enthusiastically followed, and the press reported each breakthrough performance by a "first black." But it was not until Anderson's appearance at the Metropolitan, when the most celebrated bastion of segregated opera finally relented, that the feasibility of an American opera career for blacks became real.

Price's debut was the final landmark, ushering out—or at least beginning to close the door on—the hidebound, race-conscious casting traditions of the old guard. As a compelling Leonora, she became a colorless, raceless singing voice, quelling preoccupations with skin color and ethnic physiognomy. Once it was clear that a black singer could create such excitement solely through her artistry, other debuts were anticlimactic. It was enough to place in shadow other black artists who followed her—and those who preceded her as well. After Price, the second most noteworthy addition to the Met's roster of black stars was Martina Arroyo. Her debut actually preceded Price's by three years (she was the offstage Celestial Voice in *Don Carlos* in 1958), but it was Price, the newer member of the company, who first caught the opera world's attention. Yet Arroyo's career, a major one by any standard, was not without its own sense of contour, drama, and impact on the American opera scene.

Arroyo's dramatic arrival at the top of opera was the stuff of dreams—hopeful ingenue replaces star and becomes one herself. Until she filled in for an indisposed Birgit Nilsson at the Met in 1965, her career had a workaday, journeyman quality—the Harlem-born singer trekked across Europe singing low-budget one-nighters, flew home now and again for a concert, then flew back to Europe again. And interspersed between American engagements were concerts at small colleges, mostly black and in the South. Her first appearance at the Met (years before she subbed for Nilsson) was unaccompanied by fanfare or praise. In fact, a humbler unveiling of a new talent would be hard to imagine. Fairly well known in American music circles, having won the Metropolitan Auditions of the Air (the same year as Grace Bumbry), she sang her debut in street clothes, perched high on a ladder outside of audience view. Critics ignored her, and her fine singing of the inglorious role did not engender much respect from the Met management. Small parts, mostly blonde-haired Wagnerian Valkyries or Rhinemaidens, were doled out to her thereafter. But on February 6, 1965, when she substituted for Nilsson, the Metropolitan realized it had one of the great Aidas of the day. Arroyo gave an exceptional performance before the downcast Nilsson fans, and by the end of the evening had turned their groans to cheers. The next day Arroyo was able to retire her Valkyrie's helmet and braided wig, replacing them with a contract for leading roles.

Arroyo ably fulfilled her star status. Excellent reviews followed performances of Elvira in Verdi's *Ernani*, Leonora in *Il Trovatore*, and Donna Anna in *Don Giovanni*. A Metropolitan favorite in the early seventies, she held the record for number of season-opening performances. (She was Elvira in *Ernani* to open the 1970-71 season, Elizabeth in *Don Carlos* for the first night of the 1971-72 season, Amelia in *Un Ballo* the opening week of the 1972-73 season, and Leonora in *Il Trovatore* at the beginning of the 1973-74 season.) Unlike a lot of singers, Arroyo lent her talent to the promotion of new music; she was an exemplary exponent of the works of contemporary composers such as Varèse and Dallapiccola, and sang the world premiere of Stockhausen's *Momente* to critical acclaim.

In the early sixties Arroyo married an Italian violist named Emilio Poggioni and acquired a bicontinental lifestyle; shuttling between a home in Zurich and a New York apartment, Arroyo epitomized the diva of the Jet Age. Once, in a remarkably comedic (not to mention expensive) mishap, she and her husband, each lonely for the other on the opposite continent, decided to surprise the other with a visit.

Arroyo boarded a plane in New York for Europe, while Poggioni left Europe for New York, and the next morning the ocean still separated them.

Arroyo's image countered the popular stereotype of the preening, mannered prima donna; hers was that of a down-to-earth unpretentious star, an "anti-diva" characterized by jovial wit, warmth, and self-deprecating humor. She was not above engaging in good-natured antics to lend comic relief to serious situations. Once at a rehearsal of *Un Ballo in Maschera* she came onstage in the conventional costume as Amelia, but wearing a full beard. When she turned to face the chorus, it dissolved into hysterics. ("You couldn't do that with every group of singers," Arroyo explained. "You have to know what kind of group you can pull something like that on.") Arroyo was so ebullient and gracious in receiving guests backstage after one performance that a television executive standing in line to meet her decided she would be a natural talk show guest; their meeting resulted in Arroyo's twenty appearances on NBC's "The Tonight Show" with Johnny Carson. Arroyo proved a scintillating conversationalist with a screen presence to match, and helped demystify opera and its personalities through television. Once she even appeared in an acting role on the hit television comedy "The Odd Couple," singing an aria from *Il Trovatore* and the popular tune "For Once in My Life."

In spite of Arroyo's amiable personality, the press in the 1960s alluded to a tense rivalry between herself and Price. "Hard feelings," caused by sharing the same repertory, were said to have created a gulf between the two divas. Arroyo, insisting the rivalry was contrived by the press, claimed her respect for the elder diva approached a school girl's adulation: "I have admired Leontyne Price from the moment I heard that lady open her mouth. She knows that, I hope. She's a very great artist, and a beautiful, beautiful voice. There is nothing you can say about her work that is not superlative."

Superlative is also how critics described Arroyo's liquid, creamily textured spinto soprano voice. With Price she shared the Verdi heroines, and though Price was the dominant Verdian, Arroyo maintained a considerable following, evoking generous press tributes such as the "reigning queen of Verdi opera" and "one of the most gorgeous voices before the public today." Yet Arroyo's urban, lower middle-class background—centered on Harlem's 111th Street, where she grew up—was an unlikely training ground for a world class soprano.

Her father, Demetrio Arroyo, earned an adequate living by black Harlem standards as a mechanical engineer at the Brooklyn Navy Yard. Her mother, Lucille Washington, occasionally did domestic work. Both her parents sang, though not professionally, and her mother played

**Martina Arroyo in *Aida***
*Photo by Winnie Klotz, Metropolitan Opera Association, Inc.*

piano "by ear." "When you spoke to my mother or father," said Arroyo, "either one would say 'she got her voice from me.'"

The singer described her immediate and extended family as "closely knit" and musical during childhood, with relatives congregating regularly at the Arroyo household for informal group sings. Martina divided her religious loyalties between Catholic and Baptist denominations; her brother, sixteen years older than she, was a minister at St. Augustine's Baptist Church, where Arroyo often sang for spending money. Her afternoon tea specialties, "Inflammatus" and "Indian Love Call," brought in as much as five dollars from an appreciative congregation. Other childhood activities included Girl Scout meetings and dance lessons at the Harlem studio of Mary Bruce, a former dancer and friend of Bill Robinson. Arroyo studied ballet "until I found out I was bigger than the biggest boy in the class," but lessons in dance and basic movement were good practice for the future opera singer. "It was very valuable—not just the technical part of ballet, but being with people, learning ensemble work. I was never going to be a ballet dancer, I wouldn't even say that I'm a graceful person, but all these elements can help a total performance."

Arroyo passed an entrance examination for Hunter High School and there discovered what would become her life's work. The Hunter College Opera Workshop, directed by Joseph Turnau, fascinated her. Arroyo wandered in one day and sang an informal audition—a phonetically learned yet musically impressive rendering of the "Jewel Song" from *Faust*, memorized from a recording. Not only was she accepted by Turnau, but he introduced her to Thea Dispeker, her future manager, and Marinka Gurewich, who became her voice teacher for the next thirty years. After her first opera role, a charwoman in an opera called *Bad Boys in School*, Arroyo was resolutely career-bound. Though her parents initially associated professional singing with "show business" and therefore found it a career of questionable respectability and security, they encouraged her. Arroyo became a serious opera buff, standing at the Met to hear Renata Tebaldi, taking voice lessons, studying Romance languages, and efficiently juggling schoolwork with opera rehearsals.

Arroyo entered Hunter College and finished in three years, studying voice and the languages of opera. After graduation she taught at P.S. 45 in the Bronx and later joined the staff of the East End Welfare Center as a social worker. As an investigator, Arroyo came into contact with Harlem's struggling poor and handled a case load of more than a hundred clients. It was a job requiring patience, compassion, and judgment; Arroyo worked hard to supply her clients with essential household items, triumphantly extracting funds from the system for a badly needed ironing board or a new graduation dress for a poorly clothed high school senior. "My whole life has been geared toward dealing with other people," Arroyo said. "Whether in church, as a school teacher, or social worker, it's always been involved with people, and I like that."

Throughout her years with the New York City welfare system, Arroyo continued her lessons regularly with Gurewich, who, Arroyo says, "refined my voice without taking away its freedom." In 1957 she auditioned for the Met; she was told to come back in a year. She returned in 1958 when the Met invited her to compete in its annual Auditions of the Air. She chose the difficult "O patria mia" from *Aida* and, with her new friend Grace Bumbry, won a top prize. Her award included a "guest" contract, $1,000 in cash, and a scholarship to the Met's Kathryn Long School, where she would study drama, English diction, French, German, and fencing. If Arroyo had any thoughts about allowing her success to go to her head, her environment wouldn't have allowed it. When she returned to work at the welfare office the Monday after the audition, she was met by a phone call from a client. The welfare recipient wanted to congratulate his case worker on her Met triumph—"and I need some pants," he added.

At home, too, things were kept in perspective. "In my family, if you came in with a swelled head, my mother would bring it down to size very quickly. There was only one diva in that house—my mother. It was very difficult to grow up with too much of any ego. Security, yes, and self-confidence. But special, unique? My parents said you're special, but special in a very small pond, not the world's special. You know, 'You're special, now go clean your room.' I'm very grateful for that."

Though Arroyo's start at the Met was humble, it produced steady work for the next several years. After the offstage debut in *Don Carlos*, she was offered roles in Europe. In Perugia, Italy, she met Poggioni during a production of Handel's *Solomon* and began a trans-Atlantic correspondence with him. He became her husband five years later (the marriage eventually ended in divorce). Throughout Europe, Arroyo was an accommodating, versatile singer, taking part in an oratorio here, a recital there, and an occasional opera. Her efforts brought an abundance of accolades and good wishes, but very little money. It was dues-paying time for the young singer: "I remember a concert in Dubrovnik where I got a grand total of forty dollars for the recital. Not only did I enjoy that forty dollars, but I had a great time [singing]. It was a wonderful experience, and the audience just applauded and applauded—I think I did about seven encores. You're not counting the dollars when that happens."

Arroyo good-naturedly tolerated the rigorous schedule of one-night stands heaped one upon the other—"Once we hit forty-five cities in forty-nine days," she said of a barnstorming tour across the Continent sponsored by the United States Information Service—and patiently waited for better times. She saw those slimly paid peripatetic days as a learning experience, "that wonderful period when you are young, they recognize that you are good . . . you are at your best, and you are cheap! A lot of the little companies who cannot afford the Pavarottis grab onto the young people, and they are right to do that."

Meanwhile her American bookings were not much more prestigious— her biggest payday in 1960 was a $250 Bach B-minor Mass at Carnegie Hall. But the southern black college circuit, a testing ground in more ways than one, proved a social revelation for the singer whose knowledge of the world was basically limited to the city of New York and the opera-loving towns of Europe. Racial tension in the South was at an all-time high in 1961 when Arroyo, escorted by her accompanist, Jonathan Brice, landed in Alabama for a concert. It was the summer of the Freedom Riders, an integrated group of civil rights volunteers charged by the Congress of Racial Equality with the task of riding by bus from the North to the deep South to test racial fairness in public transportation. In Alabama the riders were beaten by angry mobs, and a terrified Arroyo witnessed violent animosity and bloodshed. "I saw prejudice for the first time. I had to go to bed—I was sick. I hadn't seen it like that. I saw a young blonde girl come in, and the officers beat her until her head turned red. At first I wanted to run to her, but Jonathan grabbed me and said, 'You stay here. You'll do more by singing better.'"

The southern tour continued as scheduled, but hotel accommodations were arranged with secrecy and discretion: "Very private, very carefully. We stayed often at the university in their guest house. I wasn't allowed to go out and experience what it was really like. We were extremely fortunate, not only because we were graced with exceptional talent—the man who would say, 'I'm not taking you because you are black,' would have been an idiot—but there is also the element of our being different, like the uniqueness of having an Aida who looked like Aida or having a Butterfly who is Japanese."

Arroyo's career fulfilled the cliche of stardom when a phone call from the Met thrust her to national prominence overnight. Birgit Nilsson, overextended by a schedule that had her juggling the title roles in *Salome* and *Aida*, asked to be excused from the second performance of the latter, and the Met had no one on hand to perform the role. Arroyo, of course, was on intimate terms with *Aida* from her days in Europe and agreed to fill in, with only a run-through rehearsal. Though the public had been warned of the replacement by an article in the *New York Times*, hundreds of uninformed Nilsson followers showed up expecting the Swedish star. "When they announced that she wasn't going to sing," Arroyo said, "I think you could have stayed home, opened your windows and heard the groans. But audiences are for you—they want to see something happen."

Something did happen. Arroyo knew that, given such an opportunity, success was mandatory. Nervous but confident, she rose above her anxiety to produce an Aida worthy of the great practitioners of Verdian singing. "You don't have the time to enjoy the luxury of fainting," she said. "You've got to figure what you are doing. You've got to think about where you are, and singing. You've got to be in character, which doesn't allow you to be distracted. But in the triumphal scene when she's standing there holding the crown, I realized I was on the Met stage—I looked down and my knees were knocking."

But the audience heard only the sound of a newcomer making a success out of less than ideal circumstances; her Nile aria brought cheers and eased any disappointment over Nilsson's nonappearance. At the end there were still more cheers, and a standing ovation. No one was more pleased than Rudolf Bing, who waited backstage afterwards. Without looking beyond its own roster, his company had acquired a soprano who could handily fill repertorial gaps. Good Verdi singers are always at a premium, and Arroyo, with her lyric sweetness and dramatic power, was more than equal to the demands of Verdi's heroines.

Over the next decade, Arroyo became one of the Met's favored singers and was given only leading parts, particularly the great roles of the Italian repertory—*Il Trovatore, Don Carlos, Ernani*, and occasionally a Puccini or Mozart role. She made a brief foray into Wagner as Elsa in *Lohengrin*. Her recording career over the next several years was enviable, including a *Don Giovanni* and Handel's *Samson* on Deutsche Grammophon, *La Forza del Destino* on Angel, and the difficult Stockhausen piece *Momente* on Nonesuch. She was constantly in demand in both America and Europe to do recitals, oratorios, and opera. But despite her popularity at the Met and her long-held record of opening nights, new productions for her were scarce and rehearsal time was a major point of friction. Adamant on the subject of the cavalier attitudes of management toward rehearsals and the resulting ill-prepared performances, Arroyo recalled productions that were so underrehearsed as to be laughable. Even in Europe it had been a problem. Once during a Frankfurt production she went onstage as Aida, not knowing which of the assembled prisoners was her father, Amonasro. Arroyo had to feign recognition until the baritone, frozen in an actor's pose, began to sing. "When you come through that kind of school of hard knocks, you learn to survive, but it's not what you want for the public," Arroyo said.

Arroyo invokes the name of Maria Callas as a model performer. "There is no such thing as making the miracle happen spontaneously and on the spot," Arroyo said. "You've got to work. The great actresses were hardworking—workaholics. Callas used to stand on that stage a long time—for hours, working out movements. People don't realize that. They think she just walked out there and made it happen. She didn't. She worked. And you cannot do that when you have a half-hour rehearsal saying, 'Go left, go right—by the way, if you run into something it could be a tree or it could be a super.' That is not giving your audience the best."

In the late 1970s, unfortunate circumstances prevented Arroyo from giving her best, particularly in America, where she was conspicuously absent from the New York opera and concert scene between 1978 and 1983. It was a "grim" time, according to Arroyo, a time of emotional upheaval and change. A shift in power at the Met (after Bing's regime) resulted in a shuffling about of singers, and space on the roster was made for newer talents. Rehearsal time, many singers felt, became a lost priority, and casting complications became commonplace. Also the death of Arroyo's mother was a crushing blow, leaving the soprano emotionally shaken and despondent. Lucille Washington Arroyo had been her daughter's constant companion, a lively, mothering presence around the Met, beloved by stage hands as well as singers. "I was very, very close to my mother and her death proved quite traumatic," Arroyo told the *New York Times*. "Still I forced myself to go out and sing, because if I hadn't, I might never have gone back to singing at all."

But the most debilitating circumstance involved Arroyo's health. Small tumors pressing against her spine caused her much pain and restricted her movement onstage. After an Avery Fisher Hall recital in 1976, the *Times* reported that Arroyo was "gallantly performing with a painful back condition that necessitated the use of a cane and a curtailment of the scheduled program," but added that her voice "functioned wonderfully well, the registers seamlessly knit, the quality full and even at every dynamic level." For the next several months, the back trouble severely limited Arroyo's choice of characters—parts requiring bending and kneeling, such as Butterfly, were out. And when she could perform, couches had to be placed offstage for her to rest on during rehearsal breaks. Finally the problem became unbearable—performances had to be cancelled, and surgery was scheduled. After a five-year recuperative period during which she sang only a few times in New York, Arroyo, who had not been seen at the Met since a 1978 *Cavalleria*, returned for the Met's one-hundredth anniversary "Gala of Stars." With a well-received Carnegie Hall recital in April 1983, her American career regained its momentum.

Her health problems finally behind her, Arroyo's career recaptured the consistency, if not the fast pace, of her younger years. She began to ease her schedule and divide time between performances and teaching at Louisiana State University—advising young singers on their careers in a "sort of a master class on a one-to-one basis," said Arroyo. With her voice still strong at fifty and still closely monitored by her friend and coach Gurewich, Arroyo conceded her position at the zenith of opera to younger singers: "You know yourself when you are getting a little bit tired of packing that bag and getting on that plane. Secondly, you know that the young singers are coming along and getting ready to take their place in life. This is very real, this must be. This is how I got started, this is how the next group has gotten started, and there will be a group after that, and after them. Its the natural cycle, whether it's your own life or your professional life. It should be. And therefore, it comes as no surprise that at seventy years old, they are not going to want to hear me, when they could hear a young Aprile Millo, or whomever. Then, you also get to a certain level economically where organizations are looking for talent as good as yours, and they don't have to pay as much. That is also right. I didn't start earning what I earn now—I started out earning one hundred fifty dollars, one hundred eighty dollars, and at that time that was still good, but it was down on the ladder. Now, they know that there are people who are just as talented—they are going to be the great ones tomorrow. That's the way it is supposed to be, and I like the idea. That's why we should help them get their right. Life doesn't end when I sing my last note; neither does it end for the public, nor for me, or for music."

After Anderson's barrier-breaking Ulrica undammed the flow of black talent into America's foremost opera company, the new singers entered one by one. Bing, backed half-heartedly by the Metropolitan board, flaunted both his power and his principles to admit a veritable parade of black divas. Mattiwilda Dobbs (1925– ), the attractive Georgia-born coloratura was actually second in line, though she didn't create the impact of the next major stars, Price and Arroyo. After desegregating the San Francisco Opera with her performance of the Queen of Shemakhan in Rimsky-Korsakoff's *Coq d'Or*, Dobbs won over Met audiences with her impressive Gilda (in *Rigoletto*) in 1956. In 1953 she had been the first black performer at La Scala, portraying Elvira in *The Italian Woman in Algiers*. In London she was a favorite; when the Queen and King of Sweden visited the British royal family, Dobbs was summoned from the Glyndebourne Festival to perform at a gala production honoring their visit. Dobbs' voice was silver-coated, flexible and brilliant; as a well-schooled coloratura, she could toss off the Queen of the Night's arias from Mozart's *Magic Flute*, hitting its high F's with confidence and assurance. As Zerbinetta in a Town Hall concert performance of Strauss's *Ariadne auf Naxos*, Dobbs "was not only...a musician with a remarkable voice," wrote *Newsweek*, "but she was also a performer who could command the stage." By the middle 1950s, she was in demand at major houses and had won a sizeable following.

Dobbs was born in Atlanta, the second youngest of six girls, to a railroad mail clerk, John Wesley Dobbs, and his wife. Mattiwilda studied piano from the age of seven, and at eight the shy child sang her first solo when her sister June, with whom she'd been rehearsing a duet, became ill. Timid and self-effacing throughout most of her childhood, she sang often for family and in the choir of the First Congregational Church. She entered Spelman College (her father and mother somehow managed to put all six daughters through college) and studied voice with Naomi Maise and Wilis James. After graduating valedictorian, Dobbs was taken to New York by her father, who wanted the best musical instruction for her. There she attended Columbia University and studied voice with Lotte Leonard.

In her early years in New York, Dobbs won the Marian Anderson Award and also won scholarships to study at Mannes Music School and at the Berkshire Music Center. As a John Hay Whitney Opportunity Fellow, she traveled to Paris to coach with Pierre Bernac. Her hard work and training led to the top prize in an international contest in Geneva, where she sang her finals while enduring the pain of a badly sprained ankle. She later sang in Paris, was heard by Sol Hurok, and upon signing with him began her career as a professional singer.

Dobbs started out in Europe, singing recitals and orchestral appearances in France, Sweden, Holland, and Luxembourg. After her La Scala performance, she sang the role of Queen of the Night at the opera house in Genoa, and then undertook a tour of Scandinavian cities. It was while she was performing at Glyndebourne, in the role of Zerbinetta, that she heard her services were required by the royal family. Quickly, another soprano was hired to replace her so that Dobbs might appear in a revival of *Le Coq d'Or* before Queen Elizabeth, Princess Margaret, and their guests. Complete with scarlet-uniformed Yeomen of the Guard, a lavishly decorated royal box, and silver-plated heraldic trumpets, the event was a spectacle with pomp and pageantry befitting a royal wedding. For Dobbs it was an honor that mixed drama with tragedy, coming as it did just four days after the death of her husband of one year, a Spanish radio script writer named Luiz Rodriguez. Much to her credit, Dobbs did not cancel, and after the performance she was called to the royal box to be decorated by King Gustav with the Order of the North Star.

The event caught the fancy of the American press. Returning home, Dobbs made headlines with her San Francisco Opera debut and speculation abounded as to whether she would become the first black to sing at the Met. "Mattiwilda Dobbs became a member of the San

**Mattiwilda Dobbs**

Francisco Opera in good standing last night," wrote Taubman of the *New York Times*, "and the fact that she happened to be the first Negro to sing with this group was taken in stride by nearly everyone in the audience." In New York the following year her Town Hall recital debut was equally well received, as was her Metropolitan performance of Gilda. Dobbs became a Met regular, tackling the most difficult coloratura roles, and eventually moved back to Europe, where she continued to tour as a recitalist and opera singer. In the 1970s she returned to the United States and accepted a teaching post at Howard University in Washington, D.C.

Though Brooklyn-born soprano Gloria Davy (1931–   ) is remembered as Leontyne Price's replacement for the role of Bess during the famed 1952 *Porgy and Bess* revival, she was also well known for her winning portrayal of Aida in Europe and America. She provided the Metropolitan with its first black Aida at her debut in 1958, and Carl Van Vechten was so taken with her performance that he insisted on photographing the diva in costume. In Europe she was widely acclaimed, and after she played the Ethiopian princess for the first time in Nice, the news of her success spread across the Continent. She took the role to Covent Garden and to the Vienna State Opera at the invitation of von Karajan. *The Times* of London wrote, "Vocally and physically, she is a striking Aida." At the Deutsche Oper in Berlin, where she performed the role under the direction of Wieland Wagner, she was equally popular.

Davy was born to West Indian parents (who had moved from Saint Vincent in the Windward Islands to settle in New York) and described her family as "the most unmusical you'd ever want to see." When she was a child, a music teacher at P.S. 129 recognized her talent and recommended the High School of Music and Art. Davy enrolled there and after graduation attended the Juilliard School, where she studied with Belle Julie Soudant. She remained at Juilliard a year after receiving her degree to study opera, and was given the role of the Countess in the United States premiere of Strauss' opera *Capriccio*. She sang in a production of *Four Saints* in 1952 in Paris, and made her professional debut at Town Hall in 1954. Shortly afterwards Davy replaced Price as Bess in the Breen-Davis production of *Porgy*, which toured Europe for fourteen months. When the company returned to America, Davy stayed in Milan, where she was a regular at La Scala, and later settled in Geneva. Her lyric voice allowed her an expansive repertory, including the roles of Butterfly, Leonora in *Il Trovatore*, Pamina in *The Magic Flute*, Nedda in *Pagliacci*, and Donna Anna and Donna Elvira in *Don Giovanni*. Of her Lieder singing, for which she was also highly praised, the German journal *Die Welt* wrote: "Her

**Gloria Davy**

velvety, beautiful soprano voice, with its lovely timbre, is a highly trained instrument of innate intelligence. When combined with the personal charm of this artist, it presents a rare harmony." Throughout the 1980s, Davy maintained a home in Geneva, and like Camilla Williams, taught at Indiana University in Bloomington.

Like Dobbs and Davy, Felicia Weathers (1937– ) also began her professional career in Europe. The soprano's roles varied, but it was her interpretation of Salome that brought her stardom. The part called for youthful agility and vocal power, and Weathers had both. She debuted as Salome in Kiel, Germany, in 1961, and the news of her portrayal swept the Continent. When she finally brought the role to America at Chicago's Lyric Opera, the *Daily News* wrote: "Miss Weathers makes something genuinely inflammatory of the Dance of the Seven Veils. At the same time, her gyrations have a slightly innocent, amateurish quality that is exactly right for the role."

Rudolf Bing heard Weathers at a private audition in Milan in 1965 and was so impressed he hired her on the spot to debut in Tchaikovsky's *Queen of Spades* in 1965. Weathers brought considerable experience to the Met stage. She had toured Europe's opera houses singing her varied repertory of sixty-three roles, among them Aida, Nedda, the Countess in *The Marriage of Figaro*, and heroines of the more contemporary works of Hans Werner Henze and Kurt Weill. The European press was generous with praise. The British magazine *Opera* called her performance of Elisabeth in a production of *Don Carlos* in Cologne "beautifully controlled and sensitively shaped." And a few months later, Harold Rosenthal, *Opera*'s editor, called her Butterfly "one of the most fragile and convincing Cio-Cio-Sans I have ever seen or heard. The voice, anything but fragile, was used with infinite taste, and her impersonation was most touching."

Born in St. Louis, the daughter of Frank and Nettie Fairchild Weathers, Felicia showed singing talent at age four. Her father was an attorney, and her parents prescribed a medical career for their daughter. After high school she was enrolled at St. Louis University. Weathers, however, had other plans. Wanting a chance to develop her voice to its full potential, she chose to study music and transferred to Lincoln University, a black college in Jefferson City, Missouri. She was only nineteen years old when she competed in and won the regional Met auditions, and she took second place in the New York finals. Her showing there led to a scholarship to study voice at Indiana University. Later she traveled to Sofia, Bulgaria, to compete in an international vocal competition and, with her interpretation of the vision scene from Menotti's *The Saint of Bleecker Street*, inspired the audience to break the contest's no applause rule with an enthusiastic ovation. Weathers was

Felicia Weathers
*Photo by David H. Fishman*

declared a "laureate" of the contest and was immediately engaged to tour the country.

After Weathers' first Salome, she was invited to sing the role at the Bavarian State Opera and again at the Vienna State Opera under von Karajan. In 1965 she returned to the United States for her long-awaited Met debut. The return home enabled Weathers to bring her acclaimed Salome to American companies. But like many other singers of her generation, Weathers preferred singing in Europe, with its almost limitless supply of opera houses and opportunities for black singers, and continued to sing Lieder and opera throughout the Continent.

Few artists have been able to make a more successful transition from Broadway to grand opera than Reri Grist (1932– ). As Cindy Lou (the Micaela counterpart) in a City Center revival of *Carmen Jones* in 1956 and as an engaging Consuelo in Bernstein's *West Side Story* the next year, Grist combined the power and stamina of a theater singer with a coloratura voice of unusual facility and clarity. Once the singer set opera as her goal, she became a definitive interpreter of such roles as Gilda, Zerbinetta, and the Mozart opera soubrette roles of Despina, Zerlina, and Susanna. Her light lyric voice of burnished copper appealed to audiences in both Europe and America. In her San Francisco debut in 1963 the audience found her a charming Rosina in *The Barber of Seville*. And *Time* magazine tagged her "a coloratura to the heart," declaring that "the last time a new singer so captured the San Francisco season the object of affections was Leontyne Price." She had an impressive following among conductors: Stravinsky admired her work enough to invite her to perform his *Le Rossignol* in Washington, D.C., and Bernstein, recalling her Broadway performance, invited her to appear as soloist with him and the New York Philharmonic in a performance of Mahler's Fourth Symphony. Grist joined the Metropolitan in 1966 and debuted as Rosina.

Grist was born in New York City and began her initiation into theater and show business at an early age. Not only did her mother name all three of her children after film stars (Reri was named for an actress in a film called *Tabu*), but at age three little Reri was already performing in amateur plays, and soon after she was acting in Broadway bit parts. Like Davy, she was a student at the High School of Music and Art, and she thereafter attended Queens College, where she studied music, psychology, and Romance languages. After *West Side Story*, she played Blondchen in Mozart's *The Abduction from the Seraglio*, with the Santa Fe Opera. In New York she sang oratorios and operas, notably Mozart's seldom-performed work *The Impresario* in Washington Square, a City Center production of *Carmina Burana*, and the Bernstein performance of Mahler's Fourth. The next year she went to Europe and appeared as the Queen of the Night in Cologne and played Zerbinetta as a permanent member of the Zurich Opera. More success followed, with engagements at La Scala and on British television. In the early seventies she traveled between Europe and America, fulfilling opera and concert commitments, and made as many as seventeen appearances in one Met season.

Grist gained a reputation as a demanding, no-nonsense artist for whom musical integrity was a high priority. Like Arroyo, she was adamant about getting adequate rehearsal time. Once, in Vienna, she was told the schedule did not allow a stage rehearsal for *Figaro*. (Grist was Susanna, the busiest character in the entire opera in terms of stage

**Reri Grist**

movement.) "That's all right," she replied. "Then I don't sing." Somehow management found time for a rehearsal onstage. Grist's principles paid off—not only was her stage career successful, but her singing of Gilda in a full-length recording of *Rigoletto* was called by critic Martin Mayer "to my taste the best full-length recording of the role since the beginning of the LP era. Vocally, her production is clean and (save for one moment) accurate, and her phrasing is both girlish and Verdian, which is a difficult combination." Like Weathers, Grist felt a fondness for Europe ("I feel less pressured," she told *Look* magazine) and doubtless found its abundance of opera houses appealing. In the late sixties she married Ulf Thomson, a musicologist, and settled in Berlin.

Though mezzo-soprano Betty Allen (1930–  ) is best known in recent years as Dorothy Maynor's successor to the directorship of the Harlem School of the Arts, her thirty-five-year singing career was distinguished and varied. When Leonard Bernstein ended his ten-year stay at the New York Philharmonic in 1969, Allen was the conductor's choice to sing his final performances of the Mahler Third Symphony. Bernstein himself could take credit for discovering the talented mezzo; he had heard Allen at Tanglewood in 1952 and asked her to sing in his *Jeremiah* Symphony. Also that year Virgil Thomson, equally impressed, recruited her for the role of St. Teresa II in the revival of his *Four Saints*. She remained a favorite of both men for years. In fact, when she was awarded a $5,000 Ford Foundation grant for concert singers, Thomson was commissioned to compose "Praise and Prayers" in her honor.

Allen's singing was marked by a rich fullness of tone and impeccable diction (owing to her fascination for linguistics). Her stage presence was commanding. When Harold Schonberg heard her in performance at the peak of her career, he wrote: "When she was on stage, everything came to life, and everything around her dimmed. She was marvelous. When is she not?"

Except for the Mini-Met's *Four Saints*, Allen never sang at the Metropolitan, though some feel the omission was more a reflection on the Met management's sometimes capricious taste during the height of her career than on the singer's level of talent and ability.

Born in Campbell, Ohio, a small industrial town populated with Middle European immigrants, Allen was the daughter of a steel mill worker who had graduated from the Tuskegee Institute in Alabama. Her mother was a champion washerwoman, pulling in the impressive sum of $30 per week doing laundry during the Depression. ("She had two Maytags going all the time, from six o'clock in the morning 'till midnight.") Before dying of cancer when Betty was twelve, she instilled in her daughter a desire to achieve. When her father was unable to care

**Betty Allen**
*Photo by Bolaños*

for her after her mother's death, Allen lived in a succession of foster homes until she entered Wilberforce College, where she and Leontyne Price were classmates. Later she attended the Hartford School of Music, where she studied with Sarah Peck More. In addition to More, Allen credits two other pedagogues, Carolina Segrera and Zinka Milanov, with the training of her voice.

The years after college were highlighted by winning the Marian Anderson competition twice; a summer at Tanglewood, where Allen performed a Honegger piece at the request of conductor Charles Munch; the Bernstein *Jeremiah* Symphony concert; the *Four Saints* revival; and her recital debut at Town Hall in 1958. By this time, Allen was touring the world, with concert and oratorio performances in Europe, North Africa, and Asia. She made her opera debut as Jocasta in *Oedipus Rex* in Buenos Aires.

Teaching was always Allen's passion. Besides her work overseeing the Harlem School, in 1973 she directed a program of gifted inner city youths at the Marlboro Festival (conceived by pianist Rudolf Serkin), taught at the Curtis Institute in Philadelphia, and was a faculty member of the North Carolina School of the Arts.

Another great Salome of the period was Virginia-born soprano Margaret Tynes (1929– ). When she performed the role of the Strauss heroine at the Spoleto Festival in 1961 under director Luchino Visconti, critics were ecstatic in witnessing a Salome who, like Weathers, was equally convincing vocally and physically. *Time* magazine called her "the sexiest Salome since red-haired Ljuba Welitch" and praised her interpretation of the role as a "kind of cannibalistic sex kitten. Moving about the stage with cat-like grace, her rich, ringing voice zooming with ease through the high, precarious lines, Tynes was by turns willful, vindictive, enraged."

For Tynes it was overnight stardom—after years of hard work. Born the daughter of a minister and mathematician, she began singing early and won a talent contest at age five. After attending North Carolina A & T State University at Greensboro, and the Juilliard School, Tynes studied at Columbia University Teacher's College. Among her teachers were Emil Cooper, Lola Hayes, Tullio Serafin, and Giuseppe Pais. She worked for a while in the chorus at City Center and then made her debut in opera as Lady Macbeth in 1952. That year also brought worldwide recognition—the soprano sang on "The Ed Sullivan Show" and so impressed Sullivan that he invited her to accompany the cast of the show to Russia to perform during the Moscow Trade Fair.

Tynes was studying in Milan when conductor Thomas Schippers invited her to New York for an audition. He listened to her and announced, "This is Salome." Her success at the Spoleto Festival of Two Worlds, which drew some 120,000 tourists each summer, was immediate and unqualified. Later she gained a reputation as an exponent of Verdi heroines, and was once the subject of a BBC television special called "Tynes' Dark Pilgrimage." Her Metropolitan debut, in 1974, was the result of last-minute casting; she was called upon to sub for an ailing Teresa Kubiak in the role of Janáček's Jenufa. Other roles for which the soprano was well known include Dido, Jenny (in Weill's *Mahagonny*), Norma, Tosca, and Bess, and in Europe she was a popular Lieder singer. Tynes married a Czech-born businessman, Hans von Klier, and remained a resident of Europe.

When she returned to New York after a successful recital tour of five Russian cities in the early 1960s, Adele Addison (1925–  ) told a *Musical America* reporter, "The Russian people don't need journalistic persuasion to go to concerts.... Word spreads quickly through the grapevine, not morning newspaper reviews." Her words proved to be true. Addison's first concert in Moscow attracted an audience of considerable size, but tickets for the second performance sold out within a half hour.

Addison's immense popularity in Europe was due to her reputation, in the words of one critic, as "a truly great interpreter of song." She was a master of the long line, the legato phrase. A confirmed recitalist, Addison was respected as one of the foremost Lieder singers for her sensitivity and projection of mood in the songs of Schubert and Wolf, as well as in the works of Handel, Mozart, Haydn, and contemporary composers. Wrote one critic of her Town Hall recital in 1964: "One has to note that Miss Addison's voice seemed a limited one, limited in volume and limited above the staff... But what a wealth of miracles she accomplished within the boundaries of her voice through the range of coloration and nuance at her beck and call."

Addison was born in New York and grew up in Springfield, Massachusetts. Dorothy Maynor recognized her talent, and encouraged her to attend Westminster Choir College in Princeton. In 1948 she made her recital debut in Boston, and she gave her first New York recital at Town Hall in 1952. Thereafter she toured the United States and Canada, then Russia as part of a cultural exchange program.

Though she was best known for her recitals, she sang a number of operas, among them *La Bohème* with the New York City Opera and, as a member of the New England Opera Company, *Carmen*, *Rigoletto*, and *Il Turco in Italia*. Notably, she was the voice of Bess on the soundtrack of the film version of the Gershwin opera. Other highlights of Addison's career include a number of world premieres: John La Montaine's *Fragments from Song of Songs* with the New Haven Symphony (1959),

**Adele Addison**

Poulenc's *Gloria* with the Boston Symphony (1961), and Foss' *Time Cycle* with the New York Philharmonic (1960). She also sang the American premiere of Berlioz's *Beatrice and Benedict*.

At her first Town Hall recital in 1954, lyric soprano Charlotte Holloman was described by the *New York Times* as "an extraordinarily gifted young soprano" who demonstrated "a vocal range and a facility nothing short of phenomenal." The talented light lyric soprano emerged from a well-educated and musical family. Born in Washington, D.C., she was the daughter of Charles Wesley, a former president of Central State Teacher's College in Wilberforce, Ohio, who once sang with the Fisk Jubilee Singers, along with his classmate Roland Hayes. When her father received a Guggenheim Fellowship to observe and study educational institutions in England, Charlotte accompanied her parents and studied at the Guildhall School of Music and Drama in London. Later she attended college at Howard University in Washington, where she graduated cum laude. During her early career years, Holloman was inspired and advised by another Washingtonian, Todd Duncan.

Holloman traveled to Europe, where a letter of introduction from Carl Van Vechten allowed her entree into the musical circles of Europe. She studied in Germany with Charlotte Busch and toured the Continent, giving recitals and performing in operas and oratorios, accumulating a repertory of twenty-two roles (including the Queen of the Night, Klytemnestra in Gluck's *Iphigenia in Aulis*, Butterfly, and Tosca). Among her career highlights were performances with the Boston Symphony Orchestra under Lucas Foss in Tanglewood and with the Basel Opera in Switzerland, and a performance of Langston Hughes' *The Barrier* at the Square Theater in New York. Her 1961 recital in London's Wigmore Hall inspired a London *Times* reviewer to write, "She has intelligence, character, and charm as well as a voice...and she was clever in sustaining the atmosphere of each song...."

There is no question that black singers' achievements in the 1960s reflected the mood of the times. Opera house managers were in large part responsible for the new acceptance—Rudolf Bing at the Met, Laslo Halasz at City Opera, and Kurt Herbert Adler at San Francisco were forceful in promoting music and talent above racial consider-ations. Composers and conductors, too, had a hand in determining the mood of this new age. Leonard Bernstein, Thomas Schippers, and Virgil Thomson, among others, insisted on using their favorite singers for particular works, and for them color was a nonexistent priority. Opera and symphony boards, who often had wielded narrow-minded power in the past, now deferred to the wishes of the artists at the helm of their organizations. Musical quality was beginning to become more important than satisfying popular prejudices.

Of course, the major force behind the dawning of the modern black diva was the profusion of talent, now too obvious and abundant to be ignored. Things were far from perfect, and Europe was still, by some divas' accounts, a better place. Though there they may have been regarded as curiosities, they were well-respected curiosities. But in America, though many social problems still remained unresolved, the changing times brought forth a musical revolution as well as an evolution of the black artist.

# 8

# Grace Bumbry:
# Modern Diva

IF Leontyne Price defined the essence of the black prima donna, Grace Bumbry, a singer who combined talent with dramatic flair, further shaped its meaning. For Price, the distance from grass roots to grand opera was long enough, but Bumbry, emerging from a similarly modest, hard-working, church-centered background in St. Louis' inner city, took the journey a step further. While Price remains one of the leading artists of her generation—in Bumbry's own words "the most beautiful voice I've ever heard"—Bumbry represented the quintessence of "diva," fulfilling the word's most stylistic, theatrical applications.

Bumbry once said of Maria Callas, the incendiary, enigmatic diva whose real life matched the complexity of her roles, "She is the epitome of prima donna." As with Callas, Bumbry's flamboyance, intercontinental lifestyle, and unfettered candor lent credence to the title. At the height of her career, she left the United States and settled abroad. A European husband and logistical practicality—Bumbry was performing often at the Basel opera house—led to a permanent residence in

Lugano, Switzerland. Critics quickly labeled her an expatriate. "I hate that word," she said, bristling at the epithet. "I'm certainly patriotic, that's for sure, but I live in Switzerland." About her drastic transformation from unassuming midwesterner to exuberant, internationally known singing actress, Bumbry was as bemused as anyone. "I think many times about having traveled from St. Louis to where I am now, because I used to be a very, very shy girl—very timid—and here I am flailing my arms all about the place. I just don't know how I got from there to here."

Bumbry's claims to childhood shyness and inhibition might have surprised even her closest colleagues, but, as with many artists whose talents force upon them the ability to rise to certain occasions, Bumbry's adult personality dutifully followed the lead of her aggressive, uninhibited talent. At her Covent Garden debut, the once-shy singer's sultry Salome, aided by a svelte figure, a seductive ease of movement, and some fetching choreography by Arthur Mitchell, set British tongues wagging about the most provocative "Dance of the Seven Veils" that country had ever seen. To the role of Carmen, not a vehicle for the faint-hearted, Bumbry brought a primal energy both dramatically and vocally, so that she came to be touted as an exemplary interpreter of Bizet's Spanish heroine. After an early Carnegie Hall recital, Winthrop Sargent, writing for *The New Yorker*, said: "Her stage presence suggests a combination of an urchin and a leopard, with a lot of smoldering heat held resolutely in check—an array of God-given physical and temperamental attributes that reminded me slightly of the movie actress Sophia Loren."

Comparing the black diva with the Italian actress was not so farfetched. Bumbry, doe-eyed, and evenly brown-skinned with pronounced cheekbones, had an exotic appeal marked by a quiet sensuality. Doubtless, her physiognomy as well as her voice caused Richard Wagner's grandson to engage Bumbry as the Bayreuth Festival's controversial black Venus in a 1961 production of *Tannhäuser*. Wieland Wagner's search for an "elemental erotic quality" saw Bumbry breaking Bayreuth's long-held tradition of blonde, blue-eyed Nordic goddesses, and in the process creating headlines around the world. Aryan chauvinists were outraged at Wagner's audacious casting, and Bumbry was catapulted to opera's upper echelon amid a maelstrom of controversy.

After the Bayreuth sensation, deemed an artistic success even by German reviewers and eliciting the kind of press coverage that many artists only dream of, Bumbry became the consummate diva, flaunting a penchant for high fashion, fast cars, and sleek horses. Though a self-defined "disciplined" artist, she played as hard as she worked. The paparazzi in Europe and America trailed her doggedly, photographing her astride a thoroughbred, behind the wheel of her Lamborghini

Grace Bumbry in *Porgy and Bess*
*Photo by Winnie Klotz, Metropolitan Opera Association, Inc.*

sports car, or wearing her latest Ungaro gown. And a fondness for motorcycles further epitomized the risk-taking, caution-to-the-wind philosophy of this true diva.

But if Bumbry's varied lifestyle reflected flexibility as well as the ability to cope with risk, her career displayed even more. "If you really want to make a serious career, and also have an exciting career, you've got to take chances," Bumbry insisted. A soprano in her career's fledgling stages, the singer became a mezzo-soprano, then a soprano again in the early 1970s. A confusingly broad and multi-colored range left her with both the luxury and the burden of choice that took years to reconcile. The voice itself (which even in youth, she said, allowed her to vocalize to a top C) was a dramatic sound of dark, molten bronze with an evenness of power throughout, from voluptuous depths to gleaming heights. As a mezzo, Bumbry favored the roles of Carmen, Eboli in *Don Carlos*, Amneris in *Aida*, Azucena in *Il Trovatore*, and Adalgisa in *Norma*, while as a soprano her tastes ran to the likes of Norma, Salome, Aida, and Lady Macbeth. But even when she finally declared herself a soprano, Bumbry retained a few mezzo roles—notably Amneris and Eboli.

Bumbry's transition from mezzo to soprano left her open to criticism from those who claimed switching back and forth would lead to vocal damage. But the singer refused to be bound by categories, preferring to choose her roles according to range, color, temperament, and vocal demands. "One has to sing what fits her voice," she said, "no matter what labels are put on it. Those labels were not put on by the composers." Bumbry's risky ventures even extended as far as her choice of opera houses. While most singers preferred to try out large, demanding roles in a small house, Bumbry performed her first Salome at Covent Garden, her first Amneris at the Paris Opera, her first Venus at Bayreuth, and her first Tosca at the Metropolitan. The gambles paid off, as each role brought considerable critical approval.

Bumbry's artistic self-assurance may be traced to her childhood in St. Louis, where, as the youngest child of three born to Benjamin and Melzia Bumbry (in 1937), she led the protected life of the fragile, gifted child. Melzia, a proud, devout woman, was a transplanted school teacher from the Mississippi delta. Her husband worked the Cotton Belt as a railroad freight handler. Aware of Grace's talent and its implications, Melzia and Benjamin taught their daughter early that special talent deserved special care, that hard work paid rich rewards.

Melzia, herself a talented singer but "born too soon" for the opportunities that expanding social consciousness and racial tolerance afforded young Grace, found vicarious satisfaction in her daughter's musical possibilities. She remembered dreamily anticipating her daughter's career: "Even before Grace was born, I used to dream about parties, where music would be playing—big affairs. I liked all those things." Even Grace may have had a prescient inkling of the glamorous life—Melzia recalled her daughter "dressing up in my clothes and shoes, and covering her face with talcum powder."

From the age of seven, Grace studied piano with her mother. Thursday evenings the entire Bumbry family engaged in church musical activities—mother and father sang in adult choirs, and their sons, Benjamin and Charles, filled out the youth chorus. Grace, too young for the youth choir and too young to stay at home, sat idly until her brothers' plea to the youth choir director gained her admittance before the required age. By eleven, she was the pride of Union Memorial United Methodist, singing "This Little Light of Mine" and "O Holy Night" before an admiring congregation.

Bumbry describes her childhood in St. Louis' West End as falling somewhere between poor and middle class. "We had everything we needed—and with a few luxuries as well—but my father had to work very hard." During Grace's teenage years, the Bumbry household resounded with music and became a magnet for the neighborhood's young and musically inclined. "There was always a lot of activity," Bumbry said. "The kids on the block were always at our house. The boys played instruments, I played the piano, and the kids would congregate there whenever they wanted to rehearse. There was always something going on. I found it to be just a great time."

For the most part, Bumbry's social life centered around home and music-filled evenings around an upright piano. Otherwise, she spent her time studying, practicing, singing. "She was very shy, and a loner," Melzia said. Though an occasional outing to a basketball game was permitted—her brother Charles was Sumner High's starring player—football games, because of the chilling, voice-threatening night air, were off limits. (Melzia Bumbry had permanently lost her own voice to an unheated church auditorium during a Christmas program.)

At school, Bumbry was a conscientious student, active in vocal ensembles and a popular soloist. She was "crestfallen" at being rejected by the Girls' Glee Club, but the disappointment was assuaged when she was accepted by the more prestigious A Capella Choir. She studied voice with Kenneth Billups, a no-nonsense taskmaster. As a student of voice, Bumbry was diligent, self-critical, and impatient. Her lessons often ended with Bumbry, annoyed at her sluggish progress, walking home through a fog of tears. On those evenings, a phone call from Billups prepared Melzia Bumbry. "She's all right," he would say. "She just had another voice lesson today."

At seventeen, Bumbry sang for her idol, Marian Anderson, and was awe-struck. "I had seen her many times at Kiel Auditorium, and when I finally got to meet her, it was as if a dream was coming true.

She was such a larger-than-life figure, and you just really couldn't talk to her, not because she was not receptive or not at all conversant, but because you just didn't talk to deity." Anderson was impressed enough with Bumbry's "O don fatale" from *Don Carlos* to report the find to her manager, Sol Hurok. "She has a magnificent voice of great beauty," Anderson declared. Hurok, with characteristic vigilance, kept a watchful eye on the young singer's growth and years later recruited her into his high-profile stable of performing artists.

As Bumbry's talent bloomed and attention was lavished on her by the likes of Anderson and Hurok, she became singlemindedly career-bound. When local radio station KMOX sponsored a teenage talent contest, Bumbry won the event. The prize was a $1,000 war bond, a trip to New York, and a $1,000 scholarship to the St. Louis Institute of Music. But the institute, then run by southern-born "old boy" trustees, wouldn't admit blacks to the student body. Instead, they offered Grace segregated student status with a few private lessons. "I would not subject my daughter to those indignities," said Bumbry's mother. In a meeting with the administrators, Melzia, her indignation rising, said, "It may be *your* school, but it's *my* daughter." She thanked them and walked out.

KMOX executive Robert Hyland, embarrassed at the outcome, arranged for Bumbry to appear on Arthur Godfrey's "Talent Scouts," a popular forum for undiscovered talent. Bumbry's "O don fatale" moved Godfrey to predict, "Her name will be one of the most famous in the music world one day." After the broadcast, scholarship offers poured in from major schools, and Grace chose Boston University. Later she transferred to Northwestern University, because "something wasn't forthcoming that I was looking for. I didn't know what it was, but I knew I wasn't getting it there [at Boston]. I was always an impatient person. I wanted to have it done already—like yesterday—so I told my mother and father that I would like to transfer to Northwestern. Don't ask me why Northwestern—I don't know why. I've always said that I've been led by a higher being—I really do believe this. My father just couldn't understand. He thought, 'This girl is completely mad.'"

But the move to Northwestern proved propitious, as there Bumbry met the woman who would shape her career and profoundly affect her life. Bumbry's attendance at Lotte Lehmann's master classes at Northwestern was the beginning of one of the great mentor-protégée collaborations in opera. Born in Perlberg, Germany, in 1888, Lehmann had been a star soprano at the Vienna Hofoper from 1916 to 1938 and was particularly famous for her interpretation of the Marschallin in Strauss' *Der Rosenkavalier*. She made her American debut with the Chicago Opera Company as Sieglinde in Wagner's *Die Walküre*, and sang at the Metropolitan until 1945. After retirement, she moved to Santa Barbara, where she became one of the most venerated pedagogues of opera interpretation in the world. Taken with Bumbry's talent, Lehmann arranged for the young singer to spend a summer under her tutelage at the Music Academy of the West in Santa Barbara. What was to be a three-month summer stint lasted three-and-a-half years.

Lehmann acknowledged Bumbry's musical gifts, but the girl's shyness posed an artistic obstacle—her stilted movements left her singing sorely lacking in interpretation and dramatic projection. So Lehmann coaxed, scolded, and cajoled Bumbry to be more demonstrative, to project her feelings and become more physically responsive to the music.

"She had a goal," Bumbry said. "That was to bring Grace Bumbry about—to give her a rebirth. I couldn't do the things she wanted me to do. I could feel the music like nobody else could, and the sound would come out, but the movement would not come. I see myself today and think, 'How on earth could I be the same person I was then—that shy little mouse who couldn't get her hands above her head?'"

For that "shy little mouse" personality—the bane of Bumbry's early musical life—Lehmann prescribed opera classes. But while Lehmann envisioned an opera career for her student, Bumbry had other ideas—inspired by Anderson, she set her sights on a recital career and fought Lehmann's push toward opera. Lehmann won by using dramatically demanding scenes to release Bumbry's ability to act. "We had been doing a scene from *Aida*," Bumbry said, "and she had a way of repeating until you got it right, until it became second nature. We had done this scene I don't know how many times, and she wanted me to make this larger than life gesture, and I couldn't! I just couldn't get my arms way up there in the air. It was dreadful, it was just awful." Frustrated, Bumbry finally resorted to desperate measures. "I got in front of the mirror at home and made all these crazy gestures." She was ready for Lehmann the next time, and "this personality came out, that evidently had been lying dormant. All of a sudden Grace was there, and there was no stopping me."

Bumbry's relationship with Lehmann extended beyond the usual realm of teacher and student—it became symbiotic. To Bumbry, Lehmann was a sage spirit, a guiding force who welcomed her discipleship. And for Lehmann, Bumbry served as an extension of her own artistic life. "When we hear a special sound," Bumbry said, "when you've been in this business and you sing all the time, you know what is good, what is bad, and what is exceptional. When somebody exceptional comes along, of course, you want to nurture it, you want to further that talent. It's like extending your own career, and I think that's what she was doing." So great was Lehmann's faith in Bumbry's musical promise that, on her seventieth birthday, she presented her gifted student in recital at the Little Theatre of the California Palace of the Legion of Honor—the diva emerita passing the torch to the incipient star before an audience of respected peers. Bumbry sang the songs of Schubert, Brahms, and Schumann, Lehmann's own forte during her singing days, to enthusiastic response from audience and critics. Lehmann instilled a respect and affinity for Lieder in the twenty-one-year-old singer that would last throughout her career.

> Lehmann was very, very precise and she had an analytical mind. She wanted to instill in us the importance of analyzing a piece of music before you sing it, even while you're learning it—you have to analyze it to find out what's behind all those different key signatures, rhythm changes, dynamic markings and what the composer was trying to say in a certain phrase, the turn of a phrase, and what the part wants to say. So all those things went into my studies with Lehmann, and I can tell you they were absolutely priceless. You can't get that kind of study today. There are no teachers that I know of that go into the inside of a piece of music, the structure of a piece of music, like Lehmann did.

But Bumbry's time with Lehmann was not completely free from friction. In California Lehmann shared Bumbry's attention with the student's voice teacher, Armand Tokatyan. The two pedagogues, both with imposing personalities, had considerable rifts over whether Bumbry was a soprano or a mezzo-soprano. "She thought I was a mezzo, but Tokatyan said, 'I believe this is a dramatic soprano voice.' There was a fight between Madame Lehmann and Tokatyan, because Lehmann liked that dark, rich sound, that black velvet sound, and he thought there was more to the voice than just A to A, the two octaves. She heard something she had never heard before. She was European, and this black voice, this black quality, this velvety sound—you couldn't hear it in Europe. It fascinated her." Bumbry, caught in the middle of this musical tug-of-war, voiced no preference. "All I wanted to do was sing," she said. "They gave me the music; I studied it and just fit it to my voice."

But when Tokatyan died in the spring of 1960, and "there was no one left who believed in the soprano," the dispute ended—for a while. And Bumbry, the mezzo-soprano, began her steady rise to recognition. She won the Kimber Foundation Award in San Francisco, the Marian Anderson Award, and the Metropolitan Opera Auditions of the Air, which carried a $1,000 prize. Bumbry used the money for her first trip abroad, to study the French art song with Pierre Bernac. In 1960 she made her operatic debut as Amneris in *Aida* at the Paris Opéra, receiving a standing ovation at the end of the Judgment scene. Afterwards the Opéra re-engaged her for Carmen, a role that helped define her artistic identity.

In 1961, just months after Leontyne Price's Met debut, Bumbry's career suddenly jolted forward. Circumstances, though, were as much the reason as her talent and ability. An air of notoriety can be damaging, but in Bumbry's case it spotlighted a talent that, at her young age, might otherwise have gone unnoticed. Shortly after signing a two-year contract with the Opera House of Basel, Switzerland, Bumbry sang for Wolfgang Sawallisch in Cologne. As conductor at the annual Bayreuth Festival in Bavaria, Sawallisch was aiding Wieland Wagner's search for a Venus to fill out a new production of *Tannhäuser* at the Wagner shrine. In the opera, Venus, goddess of love, tempts the wandering Tannhäuser into her Venusberg, a garden of erotic, otherworldly delights. He leaves, longing to return to the world, but is forever haunted by her great beauty and allure. For the new production, Wagner scanned the opera world for his ideal Venus, one who could convey a sense of mythological deity while maintaining a harnessed, yet commanding sexuality.

What was to become "Die schwarze Venus" (the black Venus) affair began when Bumbry, at Wieland Wagner's invitation, appeared at Bayreuth to audition for the role, along with a half dozen other singers. With no German repertory under her belt, she sang her good-luck aria, "O don fatale." Bumbry heard the other singers and even had her favorite among them, a blonde German with a "beautiful voice and a wonderful manner of presentation. I just knew she was going to get it." But Bumbry was Wagner's clear choice. "That was the beginning of it all," Bumbry said. "As things got closer and closer to the time of the opera, there came the controversy about this black person singing in the hallowed halls of Wagner."

Upon announcement of the cast, the German press exploded with sensational headlines about the black intruder in the sacred Aryan shrine, fanning the flames of controversy to bonfire proportion. Bayreuth was inundated with more than 200 letters of protest ("a Negro singing Venus did not conform with the intentions of Wagner," one letter read) and angry phone calls declaring the casting a shameful affront to the composer. *Reichsruf*, the organ of the neo-Nazi German Reich Party, called it "a cultural disgrace." One correspondent demanded, "Keep the blacks out of Bayreuth," while another penned his disgust: "If Richard Wagner knew this he'd be turning in his grave. Why does Venus have to be black? We've always known her to be pink."

But Wieland Wagner stood steadfastly by his choice. "Venus," Wagner said, "must convey eroticism without resorting to the clichés of a Hollywood sex bomb, yet she cannot personify the classic passive idea. Venus must find the middle ground between two extremes, and no European singer I know has thus far succeeded.

"Has Richard Wagner ever said that any role should be sung only by the possessor of a certain skin color?" Wagner asked. His confidence in the matter bordered on truculence. "I shall bring in black, yellow, and brown artists if I feel them appropriate for productions. I require no ideal Nordic specimens. When I heard Grace Bumbry, I knew she was the perfect Venus. Grandfather would have been delighted."

But Wieland Wagner may have spoken a bit too hastily and hopefully about his grandfather's racial bent. Richard Wagner, whose reputation is that of an avowed anti-Semite and champion of Aryan purity, might have been less than sympathetic with Wieland's choice. His operas were steeped in Nordic legend and mythology. And during the Nazi period the Wagner stories, subject to loose interpretation like other monumental works, were used as fodder for propagandists who exploited them for their doctrines of racial superiority. Hitler himself had attended the Bayreuth Festival regularly. But after World War II, when the black American GIs liberating Bayreuth sarcastically paraded down its streets in the costumes of Wagner heroes Wotan, Siegfried, and Parsifal, Wieland Wagner committed himself to the quelling of Nazi overtones.

Grace Bumbry, oblivious to the storm, concentrated on the musical task at hand. Her reaction to the situation was marked by coolness and a sense of artistic purpose. Not until a friend who worked for a German newspaper asked for her reaction to the stir did she consider the controversy her presence inspired. To the query, she replied, "I heard about it, but I haven't gotten involved with it. He said, 'How could you not?' I said, 'You know, I have a job to do.' I can't let myself down, I can't let Wieland Wagner down, who certainly hired me for a reason, and he had already gone on record as saying 'My grandfather did not write for skin colors, he wrote for vocal colors.' So at least I had that as my support. Then I had my mother and father and all the people in St. Louis who had helped me up to that point—and Madame Lehmann—I couldn't let anybody down. I really believe that we as black people have had so many problems put in front of us as we grow up, that you don't let things like that bother you."

There were no protesters among the audience the night of July 24, 1961, when Wagner's *Tannhäuser* opened at Bayreuth. And at the production's end, a jubilant audience commanded forty-two curtain calls during the thirty-minute ovation, the most rousing demonstrations taking place during Bumbry's bows. While Harold C. Schonberg, writing for the *New York Times*, deemed Bumbry's twenty-four-year-old voice one that "has not yet set," the European press was ecstatic with her performance. Berlin's *Der Tagesspiegel* called Bumbry "an authentic goddess with a radiant, noble voice," while *Die Welt* called the voice "brilliant, precise as crystal." Ronald Eyer, writer for the *New York Herald Tribune*, said, "The voice is ravishing. It is brilliant at the top, full bodied in the best German tradition in the middle range and well supported throughout. She is a dramatic soprano of the first quality." Though many thought Bumbry's appearance might herald a new era for black voices at Bayreuth, it would be a long time before another would be heard. The next black to sing there was bass baritone Simon Estes, in a production of *The Flying Dutchman* in 1978.

Meanwhile, sparks from the "schwarze Venus" controversy drifted across the Atlantic, as Americans got wind of the protests that had been silenced by Bumbry's performance. If Sol Hurok had been impressed with her before, the notoriety of her Bayreuth debut played right into his managerial hand. Three weeks after the Bayreuth production opened he summoned Bumbry to London to offer her a contract, eager to capitalize on the excitement. In the 1960s major contracts made headlines, and Bumbry's five-year, $250,000 deal with Hurok was no exception. Though Bumbry was booked for the rest of the year in Europe, Hurok immediately announced plans to bring her back to America for a Carnegie Hall recital in 1962. Meanwhile, despite the residual hostility of a few German purists suffering from what one journalist called the "Teutonic plague," Bumbry toured throughout Germany as the conquering heroine; her Berlin recitals drew splashy accolades such as "sumptuous," "astounding," and "bewitching." Ironically, the country where her blackness proved such an issue became her most receptive terrain. "I give enormous allegiance to Germany," she said. "They were the first ones to really give me my enormous chance. They have been so supportive to me that every year I go back to Germany to sing."

If ever a career was launched on a single event, Bumbry's began with Bayreuth. But as with Marian Anderson's return to the United States after her European successes in 1935, Americans lay in wait to see what substance backed the noise and fury. Upon Bumbry's return, First Lady Jacqueline Kennedy immediately invited her to perform in the East Room of the White House before an audience that included the President, Vice President, the Speaker of the House, and the Chief Justice. After the performance, the *Washington Star*'s Irving Lowens concluded: "Americans can take pride in . . . the fact that musicians such as Grace Bumbry can feel comfortable and at home in the President's house."

The success of Bumbry's Carnegie Hall recital in the fall of 1962 assured the singer a place in opera's upper strata. "A superbly gifted artist . . . a gorgeous, clear, ringing voice," effused the *New York Times*. On the program were Bumbry's tour de force, "O don fatale," "Mon coeur s'ouvre à ta voix" from Saint-Saëns' *Samson and Delilah*, songs by Wolf, Schubert, and Brahms, and a group of spirituals. "She is . . . a refined singer, with a cultivated sense of phrase," wrote Winthrop Sargent for *The New Yorker*, "and she has a feeling for delicate elements of shading and inflection that arise from intelligence as well as natural instinct." And after her Metropolitan debut as Amneris in 1965, Alan Rich, in the *New York Herald Tribune*, proclaimed Bumbry "an exciting, magnetic, dynamic singer."

The early 1960s were magical for Bumbry: "Very exciting," she said. "Everything was going off like a rocket—there were just too many great things happening at once." And if her professional life was going well, her personal life also took on another dimension. In 1963 Bumbry married Erwin Jaeckel, a blond, blue-eyed Polish-German tenor she had met during her days with the Basel Opera. When the inevitable strain of two careers in one household proved threatening, Jaeckel abandoned his career to manage his wife's. But a few years into the marriage, when Bumbry showed interest in exploring the soprano repertory, Jaeckel, her self-appointed adviser, disagreed vehemently with the proposed transition. Arguments ensued—the old dispute between Lehmann and Tokatyan was reborn between Bumbry and her husband. "My husband and I had this problem," she said. "He thought I had to be a mezzo, and I felt I couldn't force my voice to do one thing or the other. I go where it wants to go, and these two little [vocal cords] in here said you've got to follow the soprano way." So the transition was twofold—Bumbry became a soprano, and once again a single woman.

Others' belief in Bumbry as a soprano had not died with her voice teacher, Tokatyan. Even after his death, Bumbry was offered major soprano roles, partly because she had sung the Venus at Bayreuth in the soprano version. Encouraging responses to a performance of Lady Macbeth with the Basel Opera Company as early as 1963 helped her realize "the high voice was really there." Offers to sing soprano from such conductors as Karl Böhm, Sir Georg Solti, and Herbert von Karajan tempted her, but she shied away because "I had not studied the repertory."

In 1970, however, Bumbry accepted the role of Salome for a new production with Covent Garden, her "first unambiguous venture into the soprano repertoire." Even then she admitted to a reporter, "I don't know whether I am soprano or mezzo. I must decide where I want to put myself. I can't go back and forth forever; in years to come it might damage the voice. I must decide very soon where I am going."

If Bumbry had lingering doubts about committing herself to the soprano repertory, they were dispelled with the Covent Garden *Salome*. Strauss himself had prescribed "a sixteen-year-old princess with an Isolde voice," an order Bumbry—thirty-three years old but still convincingly nubile—could fill. She tantalized the London press with the promise of a "sexy" Dance of the Seven Veils—one in which she would shed all seven diaphanous layers, stripping down to "jewels and perfume." Arthur Mitchell was brought in to choreograph the provocative bid to Herod for the head of John the Baptist, and Bumbry did not disappoint. She stripped to a bikini-shaped cluster of jewels and performed what the *New York Times* called a "hip-rolling dance," to the delight of the audience. ("They never sold so many binoculars," Bumbry chuckled later.) But the applause was equally due to her vocal security. Of her official soprano debut, Andrew Porter wrote: "It is rare to find a Salome so splendidly worked, so admirably sung, so lustrously played. Miss Bumbry has the compass and the power for the role." And William Mann of the *Times* of London wrote: "Her German is clear, her voice usually as lovely as her figure. And hers is a finely conceived and elaborated dramatic portrayal in stillness as in motion."

The success of *Salome* brought Bumbry acceptance as a soprano. Even Lehmann, who had urged against the switch, afterwards admitted, "You were absolutely right." Bumbry took the role to the Met in 1973; there her performance was greeted with the same enthusiastic approval. Lehmann even became carried away and suggested to Bumbry a heavy diet of German soprano roles—particularly the three Brünnhildes of Wagner's *Ring*. Bumbry declined, but added to her repertory Tosca, Norma, Lady Macbeth, and others. She never completely forsook mezzo roles and even alternated compatible combinations; in one Herculean effort, she performed both the soprano and mezzo-soprano roles of Bellini's *Norma* in a span of eight days.

Further confirmation of Bumbry's new identity came from the Paris Opéra, which in 1975 revived Paul Dukas' *Ariane and Bluebeard* especially for her. The opera, based on Maeterlinck's version of the Bluebeard story, had been absent from the repertory for twenty years. The Paris audience, normally a reserved group, greeted the performance with a standing ovation. "The revival promises to go down as one of the milestones of the Liebermann era in Paris," wrote George Movshon of the *New York Times*, "not least for the quality that Bumbry brings to it." "She revels in Dukas' long, impassioned, soaring vocal lines and in Ariane's warm heroism," wrote William Mann.

By the mid-1970s Bumbry was firmly established as a soprano. In America, though, her career slowed noticeably after the repertory change. Her preference for continental living might have been a factor, not to mention the fact that European employment was more lucrative, due to the weakness of the dollar against European currency. But there were other reasons as well. Even though a number of good reviews certified Bumbry's new position as soprano, in America resistance to the switch extended from her fans to opera company managers. Renata

Scotto reigned at the Met, edging Bumbry out of contention for many major roles. And while Bumbry's 1973 Lady Macbeth at the Met received good reviews with minor reservations (and in 1977 she alternated Tosca and Salome effectively), soprano offers from America's leading house became scarce.

In 1981, shortly after City Opera's newly appointed general manager Beverly Sills announced plans to shore up her company's roster with big-name artists, Bumbry signed on to play Abigaille in *Nabucco* and Medea. The results were commendable; according to Donal Henahan's *New York Times* account, she "made an exciting night of it." But as the decade progressed, Bumbry's transatlantic treks to perform opera in the U.S. became few. Her allegiance to her native country notwithstanding, Europe clearly was her most successful turf, her musical home. European critics found her charismatic and imposing, while the American press remained more cautious and critical. But when Bumbry returned to the U.S. to perform the mezzo roles that made her famous (such as Eboli and Amneris, which she performed successfully at the Met in 1986), American reviewers were supportive.

In 1985, when the Metropolitan needed a well-known artist for its production of *Porgy and Bess*, general manager James Levine and director Nathaniel Merrill called on Bumbry to play Bess. She was not the first offered the part—Leona Mitchell had turned it down. Bumbry had misgivings as well. By this time Bess was not the role of choice for the most successful black sopranos, many of whom had suffered through typecasting and "Bess-burnout" in their younger singing years. They wondered if opera managers would be as eager to hire them for non-black roles like Leonora and Donna Anna. Even Leontyne Price admitted she had tired of Bess: "I will never go back to Catfish Row again," she announced a few years after her *Porgy* tour in the fifties. But Bumbry's hesitation had to do with the opera itself. "It's a negative story about blacks," she said, "and in view of the fact that we have worked so hard to erase all that, we don't need to be reminded of it." But Bumbry reconsidered. "It is a part of American history, and whether we are ashamed of it or not is immaterial; it still happened, and it still happens," she reasoned. "They are going to do the opera whether I do it or not—they didn't ask for my permission. So I said, 'fine, I'll do it.'"

The Met's *Porgy*, as lavish and spectacular as any Wagner production, was a hit of the 1985 season. With Simon Estes in the title role, Florence Quivar as Serena, Barbara Conrad as Maria, Myra Merritt as Clara, Gregg Baker as Crown and Bruce Hubbard as Jake (as well as a host of alternates in lead roles), it played to packed houses for three years. There were more than a dozen blacks debuting, and the impact of Levine's controversial all-black casting will be discussed in a later chapter.

Basically, the production was a critical success, but many critics complained that with *Porgy*'s transition to grand opera, the simplicity and humility Gershwin intended was lost. Todd Duncan, a guest of the management opening night, was disappointed. "They sang as if they had swords and spears," he complained. Bumbry's Bess inspired divided reactions. Her severest critics dismissed her singing as too dramatic and aggressive, while others welcomed her heroic interpretation. "After a few rough moments in the first act, her singing opening night was of the opulent major-voiced sort this score has cried out for and rarely received," wrote the *Christian Science Monitor*. "Miss Bumbry's blazing diva presence puts this evening squarely in an opera house."

Bumbry's "blazing diva presence," a characterization of her personal as well as her professional life in the early part of her career, toned down considerably in later years. She trimmed the accoutrements of success—the European sports cars, the furs—to a modest few reminders. "I'm past all that now," she said of her once famed flamboyant style. Maturity brought a shift in priorities; childless, she developed an interest in helping disadvantaged youths. At Harlem's Inwood House in New York, Bumbry counseled pregnant teenagers. "I try to be a role model to them, to let them see what can be done. It's very good for me, because I never had any children...it's a wonderful outlet to have somebody that I care for as well, and that I can give something to."

Visits to St. Louis accentuated the distance between Bumbry's lofty perch at the top of opera and her contrasting background in St. Louis—her Swiss villa lies far afield from the house on Goode Street in the all-black neighborhood of the city's West End. Returning home posed its problems—sometimes the distance was too great, the contrast too sharp. "On the surface, being black in this profession is no great problem, not really. Once you've gotten your foot in the door, that's not the big problem. Being black, and going back to this early childhood in St. Louis, Missouri—it's not easy, because so many of your early friends don't really understand what you're about. Oftentimes they tend to think you are putting on airs. I went through that period where they thought, 'Oh well, she's speaking all these languages, she's being snooty, she's being arrogant, you can't reach her.' But what they fail to remember is that Grace made certain sacrifices to get there, and those same sacrifices hold true, and hold through to today. There are certain things you cannot do. They don't understand that. They expect you to be the same sweet Grace of 1950, or whatever. The problem was in trying to keep the contact, the friendships, but at the same time, to be able to do what you have to do when you have to do it."

Beneath the surface glamor of Bumbry's life, besides an unquestioning knowledge of her worth there is also a resignation to the inevitable sacrifices of the artist's life. "I get great joy out of singing," Bumbry once said. "For me it's a kind of opium. I enjoy making that sound." And if the sacrifices involved in making that sound exceeded the expectations of the youngster from St. Louis, Bumbry seems not to mind. Ultimately, she says, "It's a lonely life ... but it's worth it. At this point it's what I need. I can't do it any other way."

# 9

# Shirley Verrett:
# Artist and Maverick

"*I*'M a maverick," Shirley Verrett stated with pride. "I've had a career that, if someone else had tried it, wouldn't have worked." Whereas Bumbry's career spiraled steadily upward, Verrett's rise to success was more circuitous, marked by an occasional detour. But her unconventional path to success yielded a career that shines as a model of durability and a testament to persistence. She weathered a late, tentative start, as her ties since childhood with the Seventh Day Adventist Church, a denomination that disdains opera as well as a number of Verrett's favorite pastimes, had to be severed slowly and gingerly. Her youthful uncertainty about a career in music (as a young adult she sold real estate for her living), a vocal coach whose advice often opposed the singer's natural inclinations, and chronic sinus ailments were additional obstacles. Yet Shirley Verrett, whose music-making brims with an uncompromising commitment to art, loyalty, and instinct, survives as a singer who has inspired the respect of colleagues, critics, and audiences for decades.

Born in the pre–civil rights South of 1931, a time when racism stymied ambition in many blacks, Verrett was uprooted from her birthplace by a father whose hatred for the South fueled his determination to seek a better life for his family. And Verrett more than lived up to her father's legacy of pride and sense of self-worth. Her self-perceived role of maverick was born of a rebellious spirit, an exploring, analytical mind, and an obstinate refusal to live her musical life according to the limitations of others. Simply stated, Verrett took chances and, more often than not, won.

A *New York Times* headline in 1973 neatly summed up her career maxim. "Verrett Takes Up the Challenge," it read, announcing her performance of both the mezzo and soprano roles in Berlioz's *Les Troyens* in a single evening. Such an event in opera is as rare as it is difficult. But Verrett, who switched from mezzo to soprano in midcareer and, like Bumbry, retained a few favored mezzo roles, balanced her reputation on the edge of a precipice, unafraid to test the limits of her musical and artistic elasticity. And if at times the results fell short of her standards, Verrett was first to admit an error in judgment.

The comparison with Grace Bumbry has dogged both singers for years. Members of the same generation and sharing the same repertory, both dislike the pigeonholes and customs of tradition. But even more than Bumbry, Verrett seemed to pride herself on mastery of the calculated risk. "I don't mind taking chances," she said. "I don't mind saying 'I·did this—I made the decision to do this and I will stand by my decision.' If I make a mistake, I will say, 'I made a mistake.' I'm not afraid to fall flat on my face, and I'm not afraid to take the risk—to get out there and say, 'Look, I think this is what I'm about at this particular moment.' I don't really care who else thinks it, because I'm the one who has to live with me—I live with Shirley Verrett.

"I always tell students, you have a guideline," she continued. "You see what the singers did in the past; you see what they're doing now in your own time. You have a voice that's similar to that one or the other. But in the end it is your own voice. God has given you your own set of vocal cords, and you have to work with that. And then you take the responsibility upon your own two shoulders and you go out and do it—you go for the gold. And if you fail, you say, 'Okay, I learned something from it. I won't do that again.' But if you never try, you'll never know whether you were going to fail or not."

Verrett's voice—with a lower range of great strength and muscular intensity, extending securely into soprano territory with the flexibility of a coloratura—lends itself to a variety of roles that makes categorizing her a futile task. Over the years her repertoire has included the contralto roles of Delilah and Orfeo; the mezzo roles of Amneris, Princess Eboli, Azucena, and Carmen; and the soprano roles of Elisabetta in *Maria Stuarda*, Lady Macbeth, and Norma. The career of this one singer suggests the musical expanse of two or three careers.

But Verrett's roles were not lightly chosen. Timing was a particular consideration. After winning a vocal competition in the early 1960s, she turned down a chance to study with Lotte Lehmann because she felt she "wasn't ready yet." And during the Bing regime at the Metropolitan she said "no, thank you" to two opportunities for her debut before accepting Carmen. The first offers, she felt, were small, uninspiring roles and did not suit her voice and temperament. "I got the impression they were interested only in putting bodies on the stage, without regard to the human beings inside them," Verrett explained to a *New Yorker* reporter. "They didn't take the time to find out what Shirley Verrett was all about."

What Verrett was about was the pure and simple business of music-making, on her own terms. It was a business that began when she was a child learning songs from her mother and father, barely old enough to remember the words to "Jesus Loves Me," the first solo she sang in the Ephesus Seventh Day Adventist Church in New Orleans. "At five years old I sounded as if I could have been ten or twelve," she said. "My voice was always more mature than the other children's voices, 'with a warmth to it,' as my father says." Leon Verrett worked in the construction business and conducted the church choir, while his wife, Elvira, possessed what her daughter called "a very beautiful soprano voice." Shirley remembered being enthralled by her father's natural acting ability in church cantatas, and particularly as Old Black Joe in a local amateur production of *Heaven Bound*. Leon and Elvira's devotion to the Adventist faith was unshakable, and on Friday evenings when the Sabbath began, mother, father, and their six children congregated at home to sing hymns, anthems, and spirituals.

The segregated South was anathema to Leon Verrett, and the 1930s found him embittered by the daily battle of raising a family amid such social oppression. Before Shirley finished elementary school, he moved the family from New Orleans to California, where construction opportunities abounded and blacks moved about with a freedom seldom seen in the South. "He did not want us to have to go through the same humiliation he had to go through to take care of his family," Verrett said. "He traveled because of his work, and he said, 'Look, I have seen wonderful places. I want you out of the South.' The South was just a bad word to him."

The family lived in Oxnard, north of Los Angeles, and Leon Verrett started the Verrett Construction Company. Shirley and her four brothers and sister went to Adventist schools. But even at a young age, she began to squirm within the tight morality of the faith. Certain foods were forbidden, as were dancing, jazz, self-adorning makeup and jewelry, and any form of secular theater. "I didn't agree with many of the things when I was a child, and I rebelled," Verrett recalled. When she could, she sneaked over to the house of less devout relatives to listen to jazz. The provocative rhythms and the earthiness of the music intrigued her. "I listened to all these recordings, and I fell in love with Billie Holiday. I loved listening to my uncles play jazz on the piano. A cousin of mine—Sammy Lee—is a fantastic saxophonist. He records in Europe, and I loved to hear him play when I was a child."

Though Verrett grew increasingly impatient with the discipline of the Adventist Church, she held loosely to the faith for years. She attended an Adventist school, the Los Angeles Union Academy, and later Ventura Junior College. For a short period, she even studied at an Adventist college in Huntsville, Alabama. Meanwhile, her maturing voice raised the possibility of further developing her musical talent.

When she was seventeen her father suggested she enter a local competition for a John Charles Thomas Scholarship. "It was on a dare, because my father thought I could do anything," Verrett said. "He thought I could even climb over the barriers of not having studied Latin and so forth. I said, 'Okay, Dad, I'll enter it.' So I went up to Santa Barbara. The first round of the auditions was held at a beautiful ranch house up there—I never will forget that. It was the first competition I had been in, and these girls were all talking about their studies in Italy, and Madame this and Madame that, and I thought, Oh my God, what am I doing here? My dad knew what was in my mind...and he took me aside right before they called me. He said, 'Shirley, don't ever listen to what people do when they're bragging on themselves—really, it doesn't mean anything. Maybe they are good, but nine times out of ten, the ones who talk the loudest about what they can do, can't do it.'"

When her turn came, Verrett, buoyed by her father's good words and wishes, sang "little songs I had learned from my little anthologies." John Charles Thomas himself had been listening from a hallway and was about to walk away when Verrett began a homemade arrangement of a song from *The Chocolate Soldier*. "It was a duet, but I made an aria out of it," Verrett recalled. Thomas halted in his tracks and listened with rapt attention. Verrett won the round, and Thomas was so impressed that he offered to pay her studies with Lotte Lehmann at the Music Academy of the West. The seventeen-year-old Verrett, intimidated by the possibility of intense study with the legendary Lehmann, refused the scholarship. The timing wasn't right, and she wasn't ready. She told Thomas, "I would really be doing myself an injustice—and Madame Lehmann and you—because to tell you the truth, I'm not ready to study yet, and until I'm ready to study I think it would be a waste of time."

**Shirley Verrett in *Don Carlos***
*Photo by Winnie Klotz, Metropolitan Opera Association, Inc.*

As a student at Los Angeles State College, Verrett tabled music to study real estate law. At eighteen, she met a black real estate businessman fourteen years her senior and married him. The marriage was short-lived, lasting only a few years. Divorce was "inevitable almost from the first week I was married to him," Verrett said. "But because of the church, I stayed married." Music was sidelined even further after college, when Verrett began to sell real estate, a lucrative occupation during the southern California building boom days of the 1950s. "It was fun, and I must say I sold a lot of homes," Verrett remembered. But one day, sitting alone in her sterile office, she realized something was missing. Ennui had crept insidiously into her life as a business-woman and filled her with doubts about her career choice. It made her realize she just might be wasting a great talent, and she began to reconsider her musical alternatives.

The confidence, absent when she was seventeen, suddenly appeared. With the same urgency and calculation one might devote to finding the right dentist, Verrett thumbed through the Los Angles Yellow Pages to find a music teacher. Her eyes fell upon a likely name—a Madame Consoli. She called and lessons were arranged, but it didn't take Consoli long to realize Verrett's talents exceeded her own ability as a teacher. She sent Shirley to a teacher more qualified for her level of talent—Anna Fitziu.

For five intensive months, Verrett studied music by total immer-sion; lessons with Fitziu were a full-time job, spanning hours each day for five days each week. "It was like being in a European study program," Verrett said. "I felt quite close to the old tradition, because of being at home with her all day, where she only spoke of musical things. We used to sit down and mend tablecloths, and we talked about music."

Fitziu's accompanist, a German, encouraged Verrett to study Lieder, and her curiosity about singing became insatiable. She wanted more knowledge about spirituals, so she sought help from black arranger and chorus director Hall Johnson. He advised her on the spirituals, but like Fitziu's accompanist, sensed a quality in her voice that suggested other possibilities. "You are going to be a Lieder singer," he told her. Johnson himself was well schooled in the genre and became both her German teacher and her guide into the world of Brahms and Schubert.

In 1955 Verrett won two competitions given by the Young Musicians Foundation, a California organization with Jascha Heifetz and Gregor Piatigorsky on its supervisory board. That year Arthur Godfrey began his West coast search for young performers to appear on "Talent Scouts," and Verrett was invited to audition. When the singer won that audition and found herself for the first time in New York, it soon became apparent that she was there to stay. She sang for the Godfrey show and with her performance of "Mon coeur s'ouvre à ta voix" attracted the attention of Marian Szekely-Freschl, who invited her to become her student at Juilliard.

Szekely-Freschl, a strong-willed woman with an imposing personality, decided Verrett's was a mezzo voice, even though she had been doing soprano exercises. "We had a fight, and I gave in," Verrett said. "In the long run it was a wonderful thing to me because it gave me time to find out what the voice was all about. And it did me no harm—in fact, it helped me, singing as a mezzo all those years."

But Verrett found Szekely-Freschl's personality at times overbearing and intractable and felt the older woman often overstepped her bounds as a teacher of music. Lessons became confrontations as the two women locked horns over Verrett's personal and professional life. "She was like a mother to me, which is good and it's bad. Eventually, we pulled apart because I'm a very independent person, and I don't like to be smothered. She gave me what she could give me, and it was a good, solid foundation on which I could build afterwards on my own. This is what teaching should be all about anyway."

At Juilliard Verrett worked compulsively, entering and winning a handful of vocal competitions. Estranged from her husband as well as the Adventist faith, it was only a matter of time before the break with both was complete. Indeed, it was Szekely-Freschl who convinced Verrett to end her marriage. "In that way she was very helpful to me, because she said, 'Listen, God did not put you into this world, give you the voice that you have and the talent that you have to suffer the way you are suffering because of this marriage and the mistake you made. Okay, so your parents told you you were going to make a mistake—you made the mistake, but you don't have to stay there.' I mean, she was marvelous, because she would tell me things that my parents would like to have told me, but they couldn't because of the church."

Verrett divorced her husband, but her tenuous bond with the church was not so easily severed. It involved disentangling a web of emotions connected to the teachings of her parents and their plans for her life. She grappled daily with the dilemma. Meanwhile, New York living allowed her the freedom to try some aberrations; she began to wear makeup, lipstick, and jewelry and ate foods not sanctioned by the church. But the final break was presaged when Verrett, out of mild curiosity, decided to enter Juilliard's opera department. Growing up with the music of Marian Anderson, she had decided to model her career after the great recitalist. But entering the world of opera, an undesirable art form according to Adventists, required Verrett to forswear completely the tenets of the faith. "God gave me a voice—he gave me a talent, like the parable of talents in the Bible," Verrett reasoned, "and he didn't expect for me to take this talent and hide it.

He thought that I would take this talent and multiply it, and I am multiplying it in very beautiful music. You can't get greater music than the music I sing both in recital—which they [my parents] love—and in opera. Those men who composed this music were inspired, I feel, by the same God that I believe in. And in that case I had to make up my mind whether God wanted me to use my talent to the fullest or to bury a part of it, and this is what made me make the change.

"It's a very curious thing about my parents, because they were my greatest fans. . . . They were very, very precise in most things about the religion, but when I made this decision, they were proud of the fact that for the first time in their lives they broke a rule of the church, and they came to my performances. My parents have stood behind me, even though it is, as they say, 'against the religion,' and other people in the church have followed them, wanting to hear me sing. So they have mixed emotions about it, deep down where it really counts in themselves, but as parents who were always pushing me forward, they still do that. I think my father got pleasure out of telling people that I'm an opera singer, yet the church doesn't believe in it. It's as if they are sort of split in two, but still giving me all the love and all the encouragement.

"I feel that my religion today is within me. I don't need to have an assemblage of people, I feel, because I feel so much deeply inside of myself. And I love going to churches. I might be in a Baptist church one week, or two months from now, if I'm in Italy, I'm in a Catholic church, just to visit, just to sit down and kneel and pray. In other words, I feel that God is everywhere, and therefore I have not chosen at this point to belong to any particular denomination. But with my parents knowing all this about me, they still were my biggest fans."

For Verrett, fulfillment and inspiration as an opera singer did not come from the Juilliard School. Rather, a scholarship-funded summer at Tanglewood under opera coach Boris Goldovsky was the catalytic experience. "That summer I really learned, I think, more from him in that six weeks at Tanglewood about what opera was all about than I did in the years at Juilliard." Her debut in opera came in 1957 with the title role in Britten's *The Rape of Lucretia*, and the next year she portrayed Irina in Kurt Weill's *Lost in the Stars* at the New York City Opera. "That showed me how I could change characters, being a virgin one night and two nights later a dance hall girl coming down the stairs with a split in my skirt. Everything I had learned in church went right down the drain!"

Another summer between semesters was spent in Cologne, where Verrett was engaged to sing in the premiere of Nicolas Nabokov's opera *Rasputin's Death*. Through that she met and sang for Leopold Stokowski, then conductor of the Houston Symphony, who invited her to sing Schoenberg's *Gurrelieder* with his orchestra. That performance, however, never took place—Houston's symphony board in the late fifties did not welcome black singers. Stokowski, who took the Houston post after a fiery departure from the Philadelphia Orchestra, was embarrassed and appalled at the board's attitude. His liberal stance on race and music was public knowledge; several times he had gone on record as a crusader against discrimination. But this time the aging conductor told Verrett, "I'm too old to be fighting battles...I've fought enough battles in my life." A few months later amends were made; when Stokowski made his triumphant return to Philadelphia after a nineteen-year absence, his first concert featured Verrett as soloist, performing (and later recording) Falla's *El Amor Brujo*.

By the time Verrett graduated from Juilliard in 1961, she had become known as a singer to watch. The Metropolitan Opera came calling with offers of roles: Erda, the earth mother in Wagner's *Ring*, and the Priestess in *Aida*, among others. Verrett turned them down, twice. However vague her ties with the church, she could not yet renounce the faith wholly through defining herself as a singer of opera. And there were other factors. The parts were small and vocally inappropriate, and for the aspiring recitalist the image of the regal Marian Anderson still loomed large in her mind. Instead, Verrett signed with the Herbert Barrett management office in New York, and recitals were booked.

Nineteen sixty-one marked the year of Shirley Verrett's reacquaintance with the South she had left as a child. Three decades had passed, and significant gains for blacks had been made. When Barrett's office booked the young recitalist on a tour of southern cities, she pondered the possibility and consequences of returning. "I had a very deep hate of the South when we left," Verrett said. "And it wasn't because of the stories my father told, but the stories I read in the newspapers that made me so upset with the South. There was one time I was so violent I wished that it could have been absolutely eradicated from the earth."

Verrett asked her parents for advice. "My father said, 'You go.' My mother said, 'Shirley, you are just like your dad; whatever you feel, that's what you are going to do, and I don't want them putting you in jail.' And I said, 'No, mother, I might be very outspoken, but I'm also sensible.' I went, and I was very happy, because most of the colleges I went to were black campuses. It was a good time for me to begin and for them to see me as a young singer coming out, and to let them know that no matter what their ambitions, it could work. It was wonderful seeing the black kids in colleges. . . . They were beginning to have such great pride in what they were doing and what they could accomplish."

But Verrett would not enter the South without the guarantee of proper treatment from her management and the colleges where she would be performing. She refused to tolerate segregation at her concerts—"If I see it, I will walk off the stage," she promised—and demanded a private car to meet her at airports. "I will not be mistreated," she said. "I've come down here to give of my talent and to give of my love of my music, and not to be humiliated." Verrett's outspokenness marked her as a young firebrand among her colleagues, one who refused to allow her blackness to mitigate the respect she deserved as an artist. "This is why Leontyne, when I talked like this in the late sixties, said to me, 'This is the new wave, you are the new wave.' And I feel that Grace Bumbry had the same kind of attitude that I did—that we were on the scene, we knew we were qualified, and we were not going to take a back seat."

Despite her vehemence toward racial injustice, Verrett moved among white social circles as one of Herbert Barrett's artists. At about the same time she signed with Barrett, Verrett met Louis LoMonaco, a white Brooklyn-born artist of Italian descent. The two began a relationship that culminated in marriage three years later. "I was involved in the white world," said Verrett. "I was surrounded by this, and my friends were white, mostly. I had lots of black friends, but the people I saw all the time were of another race. It just goes to show, you fall in love with the people that you know and who you are around all the time...Had it not been so, had I been a blues singer or a jazz singer...I probably would have met another black man and married him."

Verrett found in LoMonaco a friend and protector against subtle slights, even from her own management. Being white, he was privy to the indiscreet racist slips from some of Verrett's so-called liberal friends. And some management parties held to entertain southern clients did not include Verrett. "They showed me off at certain parties, but other parties I was not invited to, and I wouldn't have known that I was not invited to them had I not been married to my husband," she said. "They would tell him things that they wouldn't tell me—it was so *stupid*. So many people were cut completely out of my life because they would say something to him, thinking that he is white like them, and he wouldn't come back and tell me. He protected me. He'd say, 'You're not that person's friend. That person doesn't come to the house anymore.'"

Now happily married and steadily winning more acceptance as a major artist, Verrett reached full flower by the late 1960s. She had broken from the church, to her parents' dismay, and her operatic performances had gained her a considerable following. Critics were united in praise of her innate musicality and her regal bearing on stage, and gushed over her "unbelievable beauty." At Covent Garden she became a house favorite, with performances of Ulrica, Amneris, Azucena, and Eboli. Word of her memorable performances as Carmen at the

Spoleto Festival in 1962, at the Bolshoi Opera in 1963, at City Opera in 1964, and at La Scala in 1966 had reached the offices of the Metropolitan.

Once again Bing approached Verrett with an offer, this time to do Carmen and Eboli. Verrett was not delighted—she had grown weary of Carmen and had been frequently disappointed with directors' over-blown concepts of what she considered to be a "chamber opera." But "I had to debut in something," Verrett said, and finally accepted the contract for the 1968 season. "I had some friends . . . who happened to be involved with the Met to a great extent. One friend said to me, 'Shirley, if I were you I would not turn this down, because it may be years before they ask you again.'" But Verrett seconded Bumbry's opinion on the role of the Spanish temptress. "Carmen," Bumbry had complained, "is the same sickness for black mezzos as Aida is for black sopranos."

"I have been, all of my life, since I was a student at Juilliard, pushed into Carmen," said Verrett. "I was very thin in those days . . . and I was very curvaceous. It was marvelous—the body was lovely, and I had a lovely voice. They looked at me the same way they looked at black sopranos in that day and said, 'You're a soprano—Aida!' They said, 'Oh, she's so sexy-looking, it has to be Carmen.' And that's how I started doing Carmen, because they thought I looked the part. I never had the feeling that I had for Delilah—that role I like so much better for myself." Typecast or not, reviews of the performance were mixed. Verrett deplored the production and was as disappointed with Jean-Louis Barrault's staging as her tougher critics were with her uninspired performance of the role in such a lifeless context. Nevertheless, for most in the audience, Shirley Verrett was physically, dramatically, and vocally convincing and held forth for a time as one of opera's favorite Carmens.

It might have been the "Carmen syndrome" that quelled the mezzo in Verrett and released the latent soprano. In 1964 *McCall's* magazine announced that at year's end Verrett would have performed the role of the Sevillian siren more than any other U.S. singer (although a strong case could have been made for Risë Stevens' record). Clearly, Verrett tired of traipsing from one lackluster, ill-conceived production to another. She contended she had become a mezzo by circumstance anyway: If she'd sung her planned soprano aria instead of "Mon coeur s'ouvre à ta voix," Szekely-Freschl would have heard her soprano potential on Godfrey's "Talent Scouts." Instinctively, Verrett felt she was a soprano from the beginning. But after many heated arguments with her teacher she acquiesced, partly to be agreeable and partly out of disappointment in her own ability to produce a high pianissimo.

But the arguments never really stopped, and Verrett stubbornly insisted on singing soprano exercises. Eventually, Verrett parted with Szekely-Freschl and became her own teacher, reading copiously about the voice and analyzing her own. A year before her Metropolitan debut, she had sung the soprano role of Queen Elizabeth in Donizetti's *Maria Stuarda* and incited a tumultuous ovation. Though establishing herself as a soprano in the collective eye of the opera world was a painstaking process, gradually she got her way. Later, stunning performances of Selika in Meyerbeer's *L'Africaine* and Norma in the late seventies helped certify her position.

Her decision to turn soprano was not entirely popular, and like Bumbry she was criticized for the switch. "All the prophets of doom came out of the woodwork," Verrett recalled, "and they began to say, 'Oh, she's going to ruin her voice.'" One doomsayer, British record producer Walter Legge, lambasted Verrett as if she were a willful child. "I wish Verrett would listen to plain common sense," he wrote. "She is by achievement the best mezzo in the world. She should be forbidden to sing Norma...I adore her as an artist, her application, natural acting ability, lovely velvety timbre, agility and brilliance. These particular qualities are so rare in one beautiful young woman that someone should lay down the law."

What most didn't know was that Verrett was just as frustrated with the label of soprano. She didn't like labels, period. "I would like for them to just put my name up—Shirley Verrett, singer," she often said. On an evening in New York in 1973, she came as close as ever to getting her wish. When Verrett was hired to sing Cassandra in a new Metropolitan production of Berlioz's *Les Troyens*, rumor had it that Christa Ludwig, who had been given the role of Dido, was ill and might not be up for opening night. As performance time drew nearer and the rumors increased (Ludwig marked the part for every rehearsal) friends of Verrett encouraged her to learn Dido's part, "just in case." A week before opening night, the Met's new general manager, Schuyler Chapin, asked her to learn Dido for a dress rehearsal. Verrett preferred that role anyway—she had sung it unmemorized years before on Italian radio, and she found the prospect of singing the two roles in one evening a tantalizing challenge. But she insisted, "I can't do this unless I *know* I'm going to sing one of those performances." Chapin complied, and on October 22, 1973, Verrett stepped onstage in Act One of Berlioz's four-and-a-half-hour opera to sing the prophetess Cassandra, and came back after intermission to perform as Dido, Queen of Carthage. Triumphant as both, Verrett made Metropolitan history that night as the first singer to sing both roles in *Troyens* with virtually no cuts. The next day she dominated musical conversations and had clearly quieted the skeptical rumblings of those who had been quick to forecast failure. "I found out later that Miss Ludwig didn't think I would do it. A lot of people didn't—everybody was shocked. They didn't think that one singer would be able to do that and two nights later do it again. When I looked back on it, I said, 'You know, that was fun.'" But she resisted the temptation to repeat the feat at other houses and in other productions. "My husband said, 'When you do a grand slam—leave it. Let history build it up.'"

What critics found most appealing about Verrett's dual achievement was her ability to create two distinctly different personalities, not only vocally but dramatically. In the *New Yorker*, Winthrop Sargent applauded her "unforgettable stage presence, tigerlike and intense in its movements as Cassandra, yielding and sorrowful in its appearance as Dido." Verrett's acting ability, grounded in keen intellect and hard work, allowed her to dissolve into each role to the point of total self-effacement. As Warren Wilson, Verrett's accompanist for more than twenty years, remarked, "Shirley is a very dramatic person with an inquisitive mind—a born student. She's a great believer in separating the words from the music. It's not as if Shirley Verrett is playing Lady Macbeth, she *is* Lady Macbeth. There is such total artistic involvement in what she is doing that Shirley Verrett goes out the window."

That fluid, easy grace onstage and Verrett's naturally dramatic presence prompted offers to do feature films. Actor Sidney Poitier at one time showed interest in casting Verrett for his *Buck and the Preacher* and *A Warm December*. From France came the offer to play the lead in *Diva*, a pop-culture film of mystery and intrigue set against the backdrop of Paris's opera world. Verrett turned it down, and the part was played by Wilhelminia Fernandez. It went on to become a cult classic. "I went to see the film, and I had some regrets about not being able to do it," Verrett admitted. She did star in director Claude D'Anna's film version of Verdi's *Macbeth*, set in a tenth-century Belgian castle, which closed the 1987 Cannes Film Festival with good reviews. "These films are in my horoscope," Verrett said. "They are something else I was not taught to believe in." In France, the singer became a favorite; LoMonaco, Verrett, and their daughter, Francesca, spent three years in Paris in the mid-1980s before making their home in New York. Verrett performed *Médéa* and *Iphigénie en Tauride* at the Paris Opéra to critical acclaim, and an admiring French government honored her with the distinction Chevalier des Arts et Lettres, and later Commandeur des Arts et Lettres.

Despite Verrett's successes and ardent following, at various times in her career she was plagued by health problems—colds were aggravated by chronic sinus ailments and interfered with her performance schedule. Protracted stretches of vocal fitness became rare, and Verrett, battling health problems, was accused of altering her schedule capriciously. It was even reported that she had walked out on engagements in Italy after being reviled by a heckler during a recital. In truth, failing health was the reason for her abrupt exit. Once Verrett remarked, "I catch a cold or flu at the drop of a hat, and it seems there has rarely been a long, sustained period during my career when I have been one hundred percent well." In Italy, Verrett was likened to Maria Callas, whose health problems also were misunderstood by a maligning press. Comparison with Callas, however, was an unwitting compliment. Verrett had always admired Callas, and it was the latter's performance of Norma that had inspired her to sing opera. "Whatever they said about Callas, she was a professional to her fingertips," Verrett said. Both singers were considered willfully independent, headstrong, and led by instinct. For Verrett, Callas was the consummate singer-actress, one for whom art was all-important and risk represented an opportunity to learn and grow. In separate ways, both were mavericks—both had the kind of career that "if someone else had tried it, it wouldn't have worked."

But at the heart of Verrett's personal pantheon of divas was Marian Anderson. During her childhood in New Orleans, and later California, she attended Anderson recitals with religious regularity. Like Bumbry and Price, Verrett is one of a small group of black divas who bridge the distance between Anderson, the first twentieth-century diva, and the many talented black singers on opera company rosters today. Verrett's generation remembers the inspiring presence of the Philadelphia-born contralto and can recall the powerfully poignant voice that opened a new era for the modern black artist.

"We all need heroines and heroes," said Verrett, "and for us, I just feel that here was this beacon of light, here was someone who not only sang beautifully, but who carried herself beautifully—like a queen. And you couldn't have a better role model than this. A lot of the younger singers did not get a chance to hear her, unfortunately, but then we never got to hear some of the older singers like Sissieretta Jones, which is a pity. The biographies that I've read on Miss Anderson's life, I mean the things that she went through, to be able to sing in those little towns in the South...I suppose if I had been born at that time I would have done it too, if I had had the same love and desire and burning ambition inside. Taking myself apart from that time, standing off from it, sometimes I wonder—and I've talked to other blacks about it—would we have had that kind of courage? Maybe we would have."

# 10

# My Soul Is a Witness: A Digression on the Black Church and the Spiritual

*J*UST south of downtown Philadelphia stands the Union Baptist Church, a formidable mass of stone and wood hovering imposingly over the neat rows of modest houses that line Martin and Fitzwater streets. Inside, polished, crescent-shaped benches arranged beneath an intricately carved wood-beam ceiling seat about 2,600 people—as many as any respectable American concert hall. Union Baptist Church is an outstanding building in a city of outstanding buildings, but apart from its ruggedly elegant exterior and cavernous auditorium, it has a singular distinction. One of the oldest black churches in the country, its congregation was the first audience to witness, and nourish, the promising artistry of the young Marian Anderson.

If music is a time-honored tradition in black churches, Union Baptist did its part to foster it. Few churches boast a history of world-class music that is longer or more richly endowed. Founded in 1832 (and occupying its present location since 1916), the church was known during Anderson's youth for its annual gala concerts, where the music was of the highest level and the oak pews filled to overflowing with blacks from every corner of Philadelphia. With the encouragement of Union's music-minded minister, Reverend Wesley G. Parks, the church's musical reputation grew. In addition to Anderson's, performances were given in the church sanctuary by the violinist Clarence Cameron White, the soprano Florence Cole Talbert, and the young tenor Roland Hayes. Anderson's sister, Ethel DePreist, recalled the glory days of Union Baptist: "It was always one of the most popular churches," she said. "Everyone knew to come there. It was a church where music was very important."

The function of the black church as concert hall is, historically, not unusual. In previous decades, with few public venues open to blacks, the church was, in the words of James Weldon Johnson, "much more than a place of worship. It is a social centre, it is a club, it is an arena for the exercise of one's capabilities and powers, a world in which one may achieve self-realization and preferment." When black artists, in need of performance space, were turned away from white theaters and auditoriums, they found artistic refuge in the church. It was an eager, ever friendly forum—a place where gifted young performers could display their talent, develop self-confidence, hone their performance skills, and gain unqualified acceptance in a congenial environment.

The bond between the black singing artist and the church is legendary, and many singers of opera and concert music credit their success, at least in part, to early experiences before a church congregation. It may be no more than a coincidence that a number of well-known artists were the daughters of ministers—Sissieretta Jones, Dorothy Maynor, Carol Brice, Inez Matthews, Margaret Tynes, Barbara Hendricks, and Leona Mitchell, to name a few—but even those without ties to the clergy found themselves ensconced in church activities during childhood. "We went to church all day Sunday—all day," remembered Betty Allen, a junior choir alumnus. "We traveled on this trolley car from Campbell, Ohio, up to Youngstown, and that was a good six or seven miles. When we got there, it was time for Sunday school, my mother went to Bible class, and then we went to church. Then we had dinner, and then there was some other club group of hers, then there was a young people's group . . . that met in the early evening, and then you went home. But you had spent all day there."

If there have been black classical singers who grew up with no church affiliation and no early experience singing in a church choir, they are the exceptions to the rule. From the church, the artist gained not only stage presence and a sense of performance style, but encouragement, financial support (once Reverend Parks passed the plate for Anderson and collected $17.02 towards a new dress for the singer), and technical benefits as well. Anderson and others attribute the breadth of their vocal ranges to having filled in needed parts in church choirs. At thirteen, she sang Rossini's "Inflammatus" with its unnerving high C, but she was also able to supply the lower line in a quartet to replace a missing tenor or baritone. Grace Bumbry's voice was stretched to its highest and lowest limits in similar situations.

Metropolitan Opera soprano Leona Mitchell, who sang in a family gospel group, claims the church "is where you can learn to get your nerves under control." Another young soprano, Wilhelminia Fernandez, whose mother was a pianist and church organist, was first presented in recital at her church in South Philadelphia. "Without the church experience, I don't know that I would have been able to sing in front of the public." The church was a place where the classical black artist could sharpen her wares in a sympathetic setting before putting them up before the critical scrutiny of the predominantly white world. But more importantly, it was, according to Bumbry, "the rock that we depended on. It was the one place that we could go to that was ours. Nobody was there to tell us what to do. It was black, it belonged to black people, it was our social element as well as our religious element. It played a great part in our lives."

Much has been written and conjectured about the so-called connecting link between blacks and religion. When Virgil Thomson cast *Four Saints in Three Acts* he declared that the use of blacks was "a purely musical desideratum, because of their rhythm, their style and especially their diction," but allowed that it was because of their "innate spirituality" that he found blacks believable as saints. James Weldon Johnson spoke freely of the "innate and deep religious emotion of the race." That this affinity for religion is rooted in the emotion-charged oppression of slavery is generally acknowledged. J. Rosamund Johnson, prefacing his first *Book of American Negro Spirituals*, asserted that black slaves embraced Christianity as "the religion which implied the hope that in the next world there would be a reversal of conditions, of rich man and poor man, of proud and meek, of master and slave." Consequently, the most tangible and lasting manifestation of this belief of future compensation is a body of music that implies devotion to the basic tenets of the Christian faith—love, patience, selflessness, tolerance, hope—in essence, the spirituals.

The spirituals of slavery, sung by uneducated, misery-inspired men and women in open fields and camp meetings, may hardly have seemed a portent of the noble music that has since become the authentic American folk song. A humbler birth of a musical art form is unimaginable. Yet the spiritual has taken its position as the cornerstone of indigenous American music and has found a place of exalted respect in the repertory of the black concert artist. Spirituals reached the concert halls in the 1920s and figured importantly in the recital programs of the aforementioned elite black quartet: Hayes, Anderson, Robeson, and

Maynor. Hayes emoted them from the core of his soul, with eyes closed and, as one writer observed, "with a tear on his cheek." Anderson's earthen delivery was enough to elicit, as Vincent Sheean wrote, "a silence instinctive, natural and intense, so that you were afraid to breathe." Paul Robeson's honey-rich, mellifluous basso, wrote a *New York Times* critic, projected an "intense earnestness" that "gripped his hearers." And Dorothy Maynor's vibrant (albeit somewhat more pristine) interpretations further propelled the spiritual to the level of distinction and acceptance it has now achieved.

When John Rosamund Johnson introduced his second *Book of American Negro Spirituals* in 1925, he wondered, "What is to be the future of this music? Will it continue only as folk song . . . or is it to be a force in the musical art of America?" Johnson might have been pleased at the current state of the music of the early American tragedians: A recital by a black artist without the inclusion of at least one spiritual, either in the body of the program or as an encore, is rare. Some artists find the omission of the spiritual unthinkable. Said Leontyne Price, "I have spent all of this time as an artist exposing my faculties towards perfecting the music of a folklore that I don't know, because I'm not born into it, and I am not going to include the folklore that I *am* born into? It doesn't make sense."

What are the spirituals, and how did they make the journey from the plantations of the American south to the concert halls of the world? These simple songs, containing the full range of emotions from immense sorrow to unbounded joy, were the spontaneous outpourings of faith and cathartic release from a people for whom freedom was an unattainable goal.

The story of the spirituals as we know them, or at least the beginning of their international popularity, began on October 6, 1871, now a landmark date at Fisk University in Nashville, Tennessee. That day a group of nine students boarded a northbound train with the lofty and, as some saw it, preposterous purpose of conducting a singing tour in order to raise funds to save their financially troubled institution. The group consisted of four men and five women; all except one of them were former slaves. Organized in 1865 by the American Missionary Association to educate freed slaves, Fisk opened its classrooms the following year, but by 1871 its nearly empty coffers had brought the school to the brink of bankruptcy. No one was more concerned than George L. White, a blacksmith's son born in Cadiz, New York, who served as the school's treasurer and director of its choir.

White had served with the Freedman's Bureau in Nashville and learned the slave songs from his Sunday school students. As director of the Fisk Singers, White centered the repertory of his group around popular ballads, temperance songs, anthems, and some classical music.

The slaves' songs were sung as diversion—in private—but even then some members of the group recoiled in embarrassment at this reminder of unhappier, strife-filled days.

White's proposal that the Fisk singers embark on a tour to raise money for the school fell on deaf ears. The school's administrators and trustees thought the idea ridiculous and offered no support, financial or moral. White was not dissuaded; redoubling his resolve, he financed the tour from his own meager resources, and the Fisk Singers' mission began. Wearing borrowed broadcloth gowns and suits, they gave their first performance in Ohio. After an opening concert at the Vine Street Congregational Church in Cincinnati, the group traveled throughout the state singing their normal repertory. At Chillicothe, their efforts brought in a collection of $50, but they donated the money to victims of the recent Chicago Fire, which had left 100,000 homeless. During concerts in Columbus, Ohio, White adopted a new name for his ensemble—the Fisk Jubilee Singers.

Times were difficult in the North for the determined group of southern black singers. The northern winter was bitterly cold, and the racial climate not much better. Lodging was hard to find; the singers were turned away from hotels and passed many nights in railroad stations. In Springfield they slept in a cramped space above a grain store. But in December their luck changed. The Jubilee Singers performed at the Council of Congregational Churches in Oberlin, Ohio, and were heard by Henry Ward Beecher, the firebrand abolitionist and minister of the Plymouth Church in Brooklyn, New York. There White unveiled the slave songs for the first time—"Steal Away" and "Swing Low, Sweet Chariot"—to the delight of the audience. Beecher was so moved by the Jubilees' performance that he emptied his own pockets into the collection plate, causing his colleagues to do likewise, and invited the ensemble to sing at his church. That evening the Jubilee Singers raised $1,300.

After the Oberlin concert, the success of the Jubilees was assured. The group continued northward, and the racial animosity they met with was assuaged by their dramatically improved financial prospects. In Newark they were turned away when an innkeeper realized they weren't the minstrel group he'd been led to believe they were. But their Connecticut concerts brought $3,900, and in Washington, although forced to leave a hotel because of complaints from white guests, they were invited to the White House and warmly received by President Arthur. Perhaps their most important performance, which brought them national acclaim, took place in Boston at the World Peace Jubilee in June 1872. There they sang their spirituals before some 40,000 people, engendering a tumult of cheers and shouts of "The Jubilees! The Jubilees forever!"

In the spring of 1873, the newly famous Jubilee Singers of Fisk University, having long since exceeded their goal of $20,000 for the school's treasury, traveled to Europe. The reaction was the same. In England they sang for the Prime Minister and Queen Victoria, who presented them with a tapestry carpet that still hangs in Fisk's Jubilee Hall. Monarchs of Europe praised their singing of the spirituals; in Germany the Kaiser squired them through the streets in imperial carriages, and the crown princess was moved to tears at the heart-rending poignancy of "Nobody Knows the Trouble I've Seen." The tour continued through Scotland, Ireland, Wales, France, the Netherlands, Switzerland, Spain, Italy, and Belgium. The success of the Jubilee Singers became legendary, and the music of the spirituals was recognized and praised globally. By 1875 the tours had raised enough money not only to save the institution from extinction, but to sponsor the building of a new dormitory—appropriately named Jubilee Hall. The contribution of the group of nine singers, three years after their initial trek north from Nashville, was estimated at $150,000. In 1878 the original singers disbanded for a few years, but today the Fisk Jubilee Singers still travel and sing, continuing the legacy of the pioneering group.

Naturally, the success of the Jubilee Singers spawned imitations, and among the most successful offspring ensembles was the Hampton Institute Jubilee Singers, who in 1873 set off on a concert tour of spiritual singing to raise $25,000. They, too, were successful. Thus the spiritual was not only responsible for the salvation of major black institutions of learning, but also, through song, introduced the experience of the black American to other parts of the world. Its powerful pathos reached remote people and forged a new understanding of an art form that is intrinsically American and characteristically black.

Scholars still argue vehemently whether the melodic and harmonic basis of the spiritual is grounded in white Western hymnody or in the primal cries, chants, and work songs of black Africa. But few argue that the heart of the spiritual—its inspired, often richly symbolic text, its rhythm, and its soul-stirring delivery—is unequivocally black. The more plaintive, melancholy songs urged forbearance until deliverance from an unhappy life or—if subscribing to the theory that some songs signaled an organized plan of escape—from slavery itself:

> Steal away, steal away,
> Steal away to Jesus.
> Steal away, steal away home.
> I ain't got long to stay here.

Other spirituals were lighter in mood, sometimes deliberately comical:

> There's no hiding place down here,
> There's no hiding place down here.
> Oh, I went to the rock, to hide my face,
> The rock cried out, "No hiding place!"
> There's no hiding place down here.

Still others were full of promise and jubilation—"In that great gettin' up morning, fare thee well, fare thee well"—where "morning" implied the long-awaited heavenly reward, while some bespoke the inconsolable loneliness of man's life on earth and his search for solace and final peace:

> I am a poor pilgrim of sorrow,
> I'm tossed in this wide world alone.
> No hope have I for tomorrow,
> I've started to make heaven my home.
>
> Sometimes I am tossed and driven, Lord.
> Sometimes I don't know where to roam.
> I've heard of a city called heaven,
> And I've started to make it my home.

It would take nearly fifty years for the spiritual to travel from college chorales to the concert stage, and historians acknowledge Roland Hayes, the Georgia-born tenor and one-time Fisk Jubilee Singer, as the first major classical artist to bring about the transition. Born in 1887, Hayes was the son of slaves—his father died when Hayes was twelve, and his mother raised her three sons alone. Hayes helped support his family by working in a machine shop when he was barely in his teens. His introduction to classical music came when he met a young black music student of Oberlin College, W. Arthur Calhoun, who sang with Hayes in a choir while on leave from school. On hearing Hayes sing, Calhoun urged him to consider music as a profession, but Hayes was wary. His mother had warned him, "Son, they tell me Negroes cannot understand good singing, and even if they can, white people don't want to hear it from them." But Calhoun was persistent, playing opera recordings for Hayes on a borrowed phonograph. Hayes was enthralled and decided to study music at Oberlin.

Hayes started for Oberlin with $50 in his pocket, but his money lasted only as far as Nashville. There he entered the preparatory department at Fisk, earning his keep by doing housework. Eventually he became a touring member of the Jubilee Singers. When the group sang in Boston, the young tenor took a liking to the city and decided to settle there. Supporting himself as a bellboy and a messenger, he studied voice, particularly the singing of Lieder, with Arthur J. Hubbard. In 1917, Hayes set out to prove himself to the musical world—he audaciously rented Boston's Symphony Hall for a recital, a gamble that paid off richly. After the success of his Boston debut, Hayes went to England, where after only two concerts he was commanded to appear before the King and Queen of England. More concerts and more successes followed Hayes throughout Europe.

It has been said that the surge in popularity of the spiritual in the twentieth century coincided with the return of Roland Hayes to the United States in 1922. Hayes' recitals, which always included several spirituals, caused some reviewers to compare them to a religious experience. While critics generally agreed that Hayes was not the most gifted of singers in terms of vocal endowment, they acknowledged that his interpretive powers, fundamental in the singing of both Lieder and spirituals, were unmatched. Like Anderson, Hayes' moving interpretation of such spirituals as "The Crucifixion" ("They crucified my Lord, and he never said a mumblin' word") was known to move audiences to tears. He was wildly popular in America after his European triumphs, and his 1926 Carnegie Hall recital was, as described by a *New York Times* writer, "sold out to the doors." Commented the *Times* reporter, "From the start of his program to the hushed finish in those 'spirituals' that he sings with profound conviction, the artist again made the audience forget the singer in the song." Of Hayes' singing of spirituals, J. Rosamund Johnson wrote: "Through the genius and supreme artistry of Roland Hayes these songs undergo, we may say, a transfiguration. He takes them high above the earth and sheds over them shimmering silver of moonlight and flashes of the sun's gold; and we are transported as he sings."

Likewise, Paul Robeson's renderings of the spirituals were enthusiastically received. Generously and variously gifted in the areas of sports, law, theater, and music, he chose singing and acting from a number of possible careers. When the young bass was starring in *The Emperor Jones* in London in 1925, he announced his future plans to the British press: "I want to sing—to show the people the beauty of Negro folk songs and work songs. I will not go into opera, of course, where I would probably become one of hundreds of mediocre singers, but I will concentrate on Negro music, which has never been properly handled." Robeson fulfilled his promise. After Carl Van Vechten introduced him to pianist Lawrence Brown, the two partnered to give programs consisting entirely of spirituals and black folk music.

Unlike Hayes', Robeson's voice was untrained, but what he lacked in training he more than made up for in mood, projection, and sheer quality of sound—his dark, weighty timbre reminded many listeners of the Russian bass Feodor Chaliapin. His first recital packed the Greenwich Village Theater in New York and inspired a *Times* critic to write: "His Negro spirituals have the ring of the revivalist, they hold in them a world of religious experience. It is this cry from the depths, this universal humanism, that touches the heart. These spirituals...were all well known, but it was Mr. Robeson's gift to make them tell in every line, and that not by any outward stress, but by an overwhelming inward conviction. Sung by one man, they voiced the sorrows and hopes of a people."

With the powerful voices of Hayes and Robeson (and later Anderson) ennobling the music of the black American, the popularity of the spirituals grew. Written arrangements began to appear. As early as 1917 H. T. Burleigh had published his versions of the folk music, and soon thereafter followed the arrangements of R. Nathaniel Dett, Hall Johnson, Margaret Bonds, and others. The spiritual became the subject of musicological discourse—examined, analyzed, and dissected ad infinitum. Carl Van Vechten, whose fascination for the spiritual bordered on obsession, wrote about them copiously. "Negro folk songs differ from the folk songs of most other races through the fact that they are sung in harmony," Van Vechten, writing for *Vanity Fair* in 1925, astutely observed.

Opinions abounded on performance style, from white observers as well as black authorities, and advice was freely offered to singers of the rediscovered art form. Samuel Chotzinoff, in a *Vanity Fair* article that appeared in 1924, described his perception of common gyrations normally accompanying the singing of the spiritual: "A lifting of shoulders, a rolling of eyes, a swaying of the head.... There is an inevitable longing to let this extraordinary rhythmic force take possession of one's body and work its will...." Van Vechten went so far as to determine who should and should not sing them. "I do not think white singers can sing spirituals," he boldly wrote, and even more audaciously added, "Women, with few exceptions, should not attempt to sing them at all."

Van Vechten's fatuous statement about women, made in 1925, obviously predated Marian Anderson's public singing of spirituals in America; in any case, she might have been one of his "exceptions." Having heard the spiritual early in its popularity, Van Vechten, more than likely, had only heard them sung to his liking by men—principally Hayes, Robeson, and male ensembles. Therefore, to him they were the expressions of a masculine muse. So it was all the more interesting that an article appeared in the *Musician* magazine a few years later written by a so-called authority on the spiritual who was not only female but white. Marion Kerby, a singer as well as a collector of black folk music, wrote "A Warning Against Over-Refinement of the Negro Spiritual" in 1928. Kerby's antiquarian fascination for the music of black slaves led her to the Mississippi delta on an expedition to receive the songs first-hand: "I went right down to the sunny South...and got the material direct from the Negroes," she effused. "It was one of the great experiences of my life."

Kerby's argument that the spiritual was advancing toward "over-refinement" is as popular today as it was in the 1920s. Kerby maintained, "It should be borne in mind that this music is primitive, no matter what the musical frame or concert presentation, and it must not be set...with the same polish and form of other musical expressions." Kerby was referring to the dialect and casual inflection of black slaves; once very pronounced, it rapidly fell into disuse as the spirituals grew in popularity and respectability. Even in 1925 Van Vechten feared too many blacks "not only avoid the natural Negro inflections, but are inclined to avoid the dialect as well." He compared the spiritual to the music of other ethnic groups: "It is to be remembered that when Caruso sang Neapolitan folk songs he sang them in dialect, as much as possible in the manner of the authentic interpretation." Sylvia Olden Lee, former Metropolitan Opera coach and now a member of the voice faculty at Philadelphia's Curtis Institute, laments the fact that spirituals often are "glossed up" and rendered totally devoid of dialect. (An example is Dorothy Maynor, whose articulate speech and Italianate rolling of the r's while singing spirituals might have been considered less than authentic.) "Some of the spirituals don't have a trace of dialect, so that you don't have to feel that you have to butcher the English," Lee allows. "But even then, they are to be sung in a leisurely, primitive speech."

Mezzo-soprano Betty Allen, on the subject, says; "First of all, spirituals are folk music, and folk music is earthy. And if you get too far out of the ground, off the earth, I find myself uncomfortable."

But Allen adds, "I have tried not to make what I call a terrible, terrible dialect. When I teach singers, I tell them, 'Don't sing "I'se gwine to ride up," just say "I'm gon' ride up," because that is what people say.' I tell them just to use sloppy English. Nobody these days [uses the hard dialect]—it's so stereotypical, it makes your flesh crawl."

Thus the concert artist is faced with balancing the spirituals' intrinsic earthiness and her own emotional freedom with sound vocal technique and modern colloquial speech. The result is a modified dialect, at no cost to the singer's classical training and sense of correctness. "I heard a young lady who was studying sing Mozart, and it sounded gorgeous, but then she sang, 'Pre-shus Lord, take mah haan'," said Martina Arroyo, imitating the singer's heavy-throated delivery. "I told her, 'If you ever do that again, I'll kill you.' Vocally, she was doing something that would go against her technique—she was singing straight from the throat. I'm not saying she shouldn't feel what she's singing. I'm saying you don't technically sing from the throat. I don't sing spirituals from here, that's all there is to it. I'm not going to ruin my technique for the sake of making an effect.... Whether it's spirituals or Stockhausen, you don't do that if you want to keep a healthy technique."

Interestingly, Van Vechten's argument that whites would sing the spirituals too antiseptically has never really been resolved. But many artists feel it is a problem that has more to do with spiritual "temperament" or "feel" than skin color. Rosamund Johnson contended that the problem came when a singer, black or white, sang the spiritual to extremes—as high "art" (with no loyalty to its primitive origins) or "exhibition" (overdoing the primitive aspect). "There are a few blacks who can't sing spirituals," said Shirley Verrett. "They don't have the innate rhythm for it—the post—that spirituals really need ... and these people, just like whites who don't have the feeling, shouldn't do them.

"I have heard a couple of white people sing spirituals and have deep feeling for them.... It's the same as saying, 'Should a black person sings Brahms' songs?' I think it's a matter of learning, if you have the ability inside of you. It's something I don't think you really can be taught—you either have a gift for it or you don't. And if you have, I think there's no reason why anyone can't sing spirituals. I know lots of blacks who say, 'Why don't whites leave our spirituals alone?' But it is the same as [a German] saying, 'Leave my Brahms alone, leave my Schubert alone.' That may have been okay in the old days, but not anymore. Music is too international."

Music is indeed more international than, say, fifty years ago—thanks to media technology—and the popularity of the spiritual is worldwide. Many singers notice a particular fascination for the spiritual among Europeans. Verrett recalled recitals in Europe in which she had omitted them from her written program and then was obliged to sing them anyway after vociferous requests for the "Spiri-chu-elles" resounded from the back of the auditorium. Sylvia Lee, during a seven-year stay in Germany, taught spirituals to German choruses (from published German versions) at the request of the German government. And there is no question that the spiritual has formed the basis for modern popular music in America—gospel and rhythm and blues.

In the late twentieth century, the future of the spiritual seems well assured. It has survived a multitude of fashionable phases in concert and popular repertory, and even in the era of the current recording industry–upsetting phenomenon, the compact disc, the spiritual is a thriving representative of the industry's standard fare. Modern recordings of spirituals vary greatly in style and mood, and in fact it is spirituals' ability to reflect the individual personality of each artist that heightens their appeal. Each artist's approach is different—varying from lavishly extravagant, heavily produced symphonic arrangements to the solo voice backed by an a capella choir—and the differences in voice and temperament allow for the interesting exploration into the singer's artistic imagination.

Of the more recent recordings of spirituals, the collections of Jessye Norman, Barbara Hendricks, and Simon Estes are exemplary of the art form's broad range of stylistic approaches. Estes' *Spirituals* (Philips LP 412631-1, CD 412631-2) is an example of the spiritual painted with a broad brush and grand, sweeping strokes. Assisted by the Howard Roberts Chorale and sometimes aided by a full symphony orchestra, Estes' baritone voice is at its best in the more plaintive Roberts arrangements, such as "City Called Heaven" and "Let Us Break Bread Together." *Barbara Hendricks Sings Spirituals* (Angel EMI DS 38024, CDC 47026) is a more intimate encounter (her only collaborator is a Russian pianist) and has the informal, infectious style of a gospel jam session. Indeed, the light lyric soprano's approach is more "gospelized" than usual, with improvisatory liberties taken in the melodic lines, and with some inspired and strongly supportive accompaniment by Dmitri Alexeev, particularly on "Roun' about de Mountain" and "Hold On." Norman's recording (*Spirituals*, Philips CD 416462-2) offers the artist with England's Ambrosian Singers and pianist Dalton Baldwin and features Norman's awesome dynamic vocabulary—from soaring fortes to reverential pianissimos in one syllable. Improvisationally more restrained than Hendricks, Norman stays close to the traditionally written musical line and shines best when her full melodic and dynamic ranges are explored, especially on "My Lord, What a Morning" and "Were You There?" The stability of the spiritual as art form is evidenced in these recordings; it is clear that the future of the spiritual lies in the willingness of black singers to continue singing and recording them. Estes, Hendricks, and Norman, all with burgeoning careers in the 1980s, show a deep affection for the music of their forebears and appear committed to its long life.

Whether the spiritual, in the hands of the great modern classical artists, has lost any of its humility, its authenticity, or its rough-hewn power over the years may not be easily determined, but it seems not to have lost any of its popular appeal. The spiritual is a tradition and, like all traditions, has evolved to suit the times in which it finds itself. Regardless, one thing is certain: The modern black classical artist reveres the spiritual as fundamental to her musical legacy. It is, as she sees it, folk music as richly tapestried and earthbound as the Hebraic melody and the German Lieder. And through its bond with the artists of the past, it illuminates the emotional and musical wealth of the people it represents.

# 11

# *Ethnicity:*
# *Vocal and Visual*

*R*AISE the question of vocal ethnicity—of the supposed individual-
ity of the black singer's voice, of casting situations where race is
an issue, and of racism in opera in general—and a multitude of
responses springs forth. Among black singers, reactions to the subject
of the relationship of their art to their blackness range from boredom
to annoyance to hypersensitivity to fascination. Some artists are open
on the subject; others feel that belaboring the differences between black
and white singers, vocally or visually, only serves to delay the assimila-
tion process. Many cringe, and justifiably, at the thought of being
regarded merely as a "black singer"; they feel being singled out for
special attention, however noble or innocent the motive, is a means of
separation. And to be separate, as the 1954 Supreme Court decision in
*Brown* vs. *Topeka Board of Education* stated, is not to be equal.

   Still, one cannot help but look at the strong presence of blacks in
recent years in the rarefied world of opera and marvel at the quality and
quantity. In 1985 Samuel Niefeld, then vice-president of Columbia
Artists Management (which has represented a number of black artists)

estimated that blacks comprised about 25 percent of the Metropolitan Opera roster—a considerable jump from the two percent participation of the 1970-1971 season. True enough, the company had recently mounted a production of *Porgy and Bess*, requiring a sizeable number of blacks for cast and chorus. But once on the roster, many were retained, and even in 1989, during a season without *Porgy* the figure dropped only to fourteen percent.

The numbers are even more astounding when one looks outside of opera at other classical music arenas. In the enlightened 1980s, opera was the only area of classical performance where black employment even slightly resembles a foothold. In professional symphony orchestras, of which there are hundreds in the United States, one or two black members on a roster of 85 to 105 is normal, but many orchestras employ no black players. Hence, black professional orchestra players comprise about one percent of the population. On the recital stage, the figures are worse. Of the internationally known performing instrumental artists, only two blacks, pianists Andre Watts and Natalie Hinderas, have managed major careers of long standing.

Why the difference? It may come down to a matter of socio-economics, and other more natural factors. Instrumentalists require years of training, at no small expense, from an early age; it is an expense many blacks cannot afford. A talented soprano, on the other hand, may receive her first intensive training as late as her teenage years (when scholarships often are made available from reputable schools) and still launch a major career. In the early stages of the career, age also works to the singer's advantage. At twenty-five years old, when the bulk of the instrumentalist's training is under his belt and he is ready for a symphonic position, the singer's developing instrument is still only nearing vocal maturity. Thus the singer has the luxury of time to nurture her resources before she is expected to fulfill her early promise.

While blacks are showing up in impressive numbers on the opera stage, to say that the battle for an equal position has been won would be naive. As many blacks see it, things are clearly better, but an operatic Utopia has not yet arrived, nor is it in sight. While the older New York companies, the Met and City Opera, have bolstered their rosters with talented blacks, some smaller companies throughout the United States have been less than thrilled at the prospect. Incidents of typecasting (the maid/slave-girl/gypsy syndrome) or outright discrimination, while not as prevalent as a few decades ago, still occur. And as long as some opera managers continue to make a distinction between the black singer and her white counterpart, there will be some discussion about whatever differences exist between them.

In the case of the so-called "black" sound, that distinction is almost unanimously complimentary. Black singers (but not all of them) have been said to possess inordinate ranges and an indescribably warm, dark sound. Here, though, is a sensitive area. For many black singers feel a discussion of the voice's peculiarities is akin to an analysis of the jumping ability of black basketball players or the "natural rhythm" of black dancers—it is blind categorization at its best. Sylvia Olden Lee, who served as the Met's first black staff interpretative coach in the 1950s, warns against making too much of the "black sound" and argues that too much attention to it only dredges up old stereotypes and narrow thinking, particularly if vocal differences are said to be rooted in racial anatomy. "They said we couldn't do ballet, because of the shape of our feet, or that we couldn't learn certain languages," Lee says. "Well, they can't say that anymore."

When Sissieretta Jones appeared before the public in the 1890s, everything about her was peculiarly alluring to her white observers— her hair, the tint of her skin, the shape of her head. Her physical attributes were described in almost embarrassing detail. To whites, she was a fascinating, attractive anomaly. It is not surprising that her voice fell prey to the same magnifying scrunity. A *Chicago Tribune* reporter described her voice as possessing a "peculiar, plaintive quality" that "no amount of training could eradicate. Not that anyone would want to have it eradicated. It is the heritage the singer has received from her race, and it alone tells not only of the sorrows of a single life, but the cruelly sad story of a whole people."

Interestingly, Jones did not sing spirituals (though she surely must have heard them sung by the Jubilee Singers of Fisk University). But even in such standards as "Comin' Through The Rye" and "The Cows in the Clover" Jones projected a mystifying pathos that enthralled, inspired, disarmed. One hundred years later, that quality of sound in black voices still sends critics groping about in a fog of abstract adjectives—"smoky," "dusky," or "husky" are the most recurring ones— and struggling to divine the origin and mechanics of its production. While whites and blacks generally agree on the existence of a black sound, they also agree it is a quality not easily described.

"The words that come to mind are 'rich,' 'velvety'—some people describe it as a 'deep-throated' sound," said Cynthia Clarey. "It is something that you really can hear, and there are people who say that it is not right for classical music. I'm of the opinion that anything is right—it's between you and the audience. If the audience believes you, then it's right." But in his provocative article for Britain's *Opera* magazine titled "Yes, But Are We Really Colour Deaf?" (July 1985), Martin Bernheimer cites a curious statement from Dr. Geerd Heinsen, editor of the German magazine *Orpheus*. Reviewing Clarey's performance as Nicklausse in *The Tales of Hoffman* with the Deutsche Oper in Berlin, Heinsen (the sole dissenting voice amid overwhelming praise) dismissed Clarey's tone as "too Negroid for the French vocal line." Too Negroid a voice? It would be interesting to know whether Heinsen has heard voices too Oriental, too Slavic, or too Jewish for the French vocal line. These days, such thinking is outdated, and has been, for the most part, since the voice of Anderson plunged critics into a semantic quandary. For Clarey's part, she brushes off opinions that the black sound is too unusual or, as one worn-out sentiment goes, that it contains too much of the gospel intonation of black church music. Says the mezzo-soprano, "I think classical music could use a little bit of that."

Joan Sutherland describes the black voice as a "beautifully rich, mellifluous and warm sound" with a "great sympathy, a loving sound." Richard Bonynge, Sutherland's husband and conductor, says in black singers "the middle voice seems covered, smoky, emotional-sounding." Bonynge also suggests that the dark quality may be an extension of the speaking voice, which, he observes, "sits" low among black singers. "Some have managed to become high sopranos, but that seems to be the exception," Bonynge said. "It seems as if the high voice is constructed more from intelligence than from a natural inclination." But, Bonynge hastens to qualify, the black sound is not to be found in all black singers.

Certainly there are many black high sopranos, and very successful ones. But some observers feel that even in the high voices (with the exceptions of the lighter lyric or coloratura) the lower end of the black voice is deeper, richer, more voluptuously shaped than that of many white singers. In fact, many highly successful sopranos, among them Leontyne Price, Dorothy Maynor, Shirley Verrett, and Grace Bumbry, began singing early as mezzos. Barbara Moore, chairman of the voice department at Dallas' Southern Methodist University and herself a black soprano, says this phenomenon is partly a matter of cultural taste. Many of her black students grew up hearing and emulating the decidedly low-voiced inflection of gospel singing and rhythm and blues. And the pitch of the speaking voice, she maintains, is a factor. "Speech patterns are learned," she says. "If your mother and father and others in your family speak low, you also tend to speak low. I've had students come to me singing lower than they should. They had been told they were altos, mezzos, or basses just because the quality of their voice is deeper and richer than other voices."

Moore says it is typical of her black students to experiment with the low end of the voice, while her white students are more fascinated with the prospect of extending the top. "Black singers come to me with no idea of their top voices. It doesn't mean they have had any damage, it just means that they haven't experimented with the top tones, and did not find it attractive to do so."

Moore is not alone in her belief that criteria for vocal attractiveness vary from culture to culture. Reri Grist, who teaches blacks as well as white Europeans in Berlin, agrees that vocal beauty is as relative as physical beauty. "A lot of singers try to produce the sound they think is attractive, the most beautiful sound—or what they grew up thinking is beautiful," said Grist. "I have a case here in Germany where very many of the singers, particularly the sopranos, try to create what I call a 'hole' in the voice, a h-o-o-o sound, because that is their concept of what is beautiful. And you will find young basses trying to emulate the dark, so-called black bass of Boris Christoff, to get that dark guttural sound which is identified as black—not black in our terms, but in their terms."

So blackness as a description of the voice is not necessarily racial, as many artists point out. It is a quality of vocal darkness, found in as many Russian basses as black basses. Sylvia Lee points to the dark sound of the Russian Feodor Chaliapin and the Italian Ezio Pinza. But a case is made for the particularly identifiable sound of certain geographic regions; the Australian-born Sutherland maintains that the local speech habits of a country affect the timbre of the voice and describes her own Australian sound as having "a nasal, lazy quality that gives it a kind of sweep." Likewise the Italianate, the Welsh, and the Slavic sounds all are determined by what the individual culture, through language and ethnic tradition, determines is beautiful.

But is the sound of certain blacks so specific as to be recognizable at a casual hearing? Many artists have been fooled. "When I first heard Marilyn Horne sing," said Shirley Verrett, "she was auditioning for a conductor at the Hollywood Bowl the same time that I was there. I didn't know her, and I thought it was a black singer singing. When I found out it was a white person I said, 'Hmmm, there goes that.' But that doesn't happen very often, I do admit. It's very rare when I would mistake a white singer for a black singer, but I have mistaken black singers for white singers many times, especially the lighter voices. When you get down to the mezzo voices, the dramatic soprano voices, somehow the weight of the voice gives it away."

If Horne's sound is indeed a "black" one (and perhaps that is why she was chosen as the voice of Dorothy Dandridge in the film version of *Carmen Jones*), then the theory that blacks sound as they do because of certain anatomical differences is discredited, if not disclaimed. While science has proved that there are no such things as distinctively black vocal cords (it would be as ridiculous to suggest black tonsils), claims have been made that African bone structure may affect sound. Even some black singers allow for the possibility, given variations in the size and breadth of nostrils, cheekbones, etc., among blacks. "There are theories on bone structure," said Metropolitan Opera mezzo-soprano Florence Quivar, who believes in the existence of an innate black voice.

"High cheekbones make for a very resonant sound." But can bone structure color a sound black? In a 1953 book titled *Manual of Bel Canto*, Ida Franca claims that the chest and head of black women singers are larger than those of whites, and further states: "the range of the Negro tenor can be developed to outdo any white singer's range." Even in 1953 such bold, general assertions seem a little strange, especially as there is no sophisticated scientific data to back up the theory.

Says Reri Grist, "I think there are certain sounds, certain colors in voices, that are specifically associated with language and how one speaks—certainly, with parts of one's culture. But there is nothing—medical, organical, or biological—which says that one can identify a voice as being a black voice, a nonblack voice, etc." But Grist adds, "I can, however, turn on the radio and hear someone sing 'Embraceable You,' and I can very often tell whether a black person is singing. How do I tell that? By the inflection of vowels, the placement of consonants."

Grist and Clarey agree that there may exist an inexplicable vocal similarity between blacks and Koreans. "When I was at school in Juilliard, we had a lot of Korean singers, and they had a sound that was very similar," Clarey said. "So I thought, because of the broad flat face, maybe it does have something to do with structure." Grist taught a Korean student in Europe whose sound resembled an American black. "I gave her spirituals to sing," Grist said. "I hadn't talked about them, I'd only assigned them and worked on them technically. You would have thought this girl was someone from Tallahassee! She hadn't listened to records, because she didn't have them. How do you explain that? It baffled me, because I thought I would get a very clean polished Mozart-like spiritual, but no I didn't. I sat there and I was dumbfounded."

It seems to be a question that will always defy satisfactory explanation. George Shirley, a Metropolitan Opera tenor during the sixties, says there is more to a black sound than American acculturation or bone structure. "It has to do somehow with our history," he says. "True, we've been out of Africa some four hundred to five hundred years, but there are Africanisms that remain very strong within us that don't seem ever to be eradicated." However elusive or inexplicable this quality of vocal blackness, most listeners, black and white, find it moving, appealing, attractive. "It is something I am very proud of," says Clarey. "I like it when people tell me I have that quality in my voice."

While the appreciation of a black sound among black singers is largely a positive one, the visual appreciation is often not so favorable. In opera, a world of fantasy, illusion, and unbounded imagination, artists are hired, supposedly, for their abilities as singers and their appropriateness for a particular role. But that is where the problem arises. Appropriateness is left to the subjective discretion (and sometimes capricious whims) of opera management. And while more blacks are being hired in opera than ever before, for some managers the possibility of a black Manon or Don Giovanni causes them to lose their sense of illusion and imagination. Under the cloak of attempted "realism" and "authenticity," they feel a black singer in a particular role would at the least distract, and possibly offend, some viewers' sensibilities. One black singer tells of being turned down for the role of Desdemona in *Otello* because she was black. For a Glyndebourne Festival production of *Don Giovanni*, director Sir Peter Hall ignored suggestions to hire Leona Mitchell for the role of the Spanish aristocrat Donna Anna; her presence, he said, would "ruin the realism and social structure which were to form the very heart of the production." Mitchell responded in an *Opera News* article: "You'd think people wouldn't even consider all that any more. They just shouldn't be saying that somebody doesn't look the part when certain singers are 350 pounds fat. Now are they gonna play a nice young Donna Anna?" Clarey was turned down for a role when a director claimed he wanted to do an "authentic" production of a particular opera. "If the director feels that way, fine," said Clarey. "I don't like it—it's a job that I could have had. But if he really feels that way, I think I'd be a lot happier not doing it." And subtler forms of discrimination are even more difficult to pinpoint. "Opera is such a subjective art," said Mitchell. "They can always hide behind words like 'She's just not my type.'"

Realism. It is a word that, in opera, is conveniently invoked. The reality, of course, is that opera is an art form that is, by definition, unrealistic. (Is it realistic for people to go about singing their thoughts and conversations, rather than speaking them?) But as the popularity of video and televised productions makes opera more vision-oriented, producers and directors continue to search for the visual ideal. Nothing is more desirable in opera than a singer who not only sings well but also looks the part. Some black artists and directors have managed to solve the problem of visual authenticity, if indeed there is one, through makeup.

In his article for *Opera News* titled "The Black Performer" (January 1971), George Shirley discusses his views on the subject. "In my opinion," he writes, "theatrical tradition should be respected within reason; that is, a singer should resemble a character as closely as possible. This means makeup to a point, but not to the point of appearing ridiculous. Just as a white Otello should look bronze but not like a blackface minstrel, a black Iago shouldn't look as though he had been dumped into a flour barrel." Grace Bumbry, who has played both Amneris and Aida many times, advocates the use of a lightening makeup, especially when a contrast in skin color is crucial to the fabric of the opera. As Amneris, the Egyptian, she uses a light compound; as Aida, the Ethiopian, she wears none at all. "You have to show the difference between the two races," says Bumbry. "I think it's very important that the audience see the Egyptians and Ethiopians on either side, and with my dark skin they would be thinking that I'm one of the Ethiopians. That's why I really so much enjoy singing Aida, because I don't have to worry about that stuff. As Amneris, I'm the first person in the theater, and the last one leaving at night."

Both Shirley and Bumbry take a dim view of those black artists who, for whatever reason, refuse to lighten their coloring for roles. "I hold to the view that ethnic self-consciousness should stop at the footlights and the singer should do his best to portray the character naturally," said Shirley. Adds Bumbry, "Not only is it a mistake [not to use makeup], but I think it is unprofessional. I went to the opera to see Tosca, and there was a black fellow singing the role of Angelotti—not a significant role, I grant you. But it bothered me to see this person with a black face, without the wig, without the makeup. Actually, I thought it was like a high school performance."

The consensus seems to be that while opera may never truly achieve realism, directors and singers ought at least try to construct a plausible picture. However, it is a two-way contract—the audience must be willing to suspend disbelief in order to accept certain visual incongruities, for the sake of good music. But makeup and imagination do not completely solve the problem, especially as it applies to the hiring of black men. While the number of black women with major careers has increased dramatically in recent years, black males have been noticeably less successful.

"They have not been guided in," said Mitchell, who feels the path to professional opera has been made smoother for black women. Reasons range from the smaller number of available male roles to allegations that some opera boards look with fearful disdain on a black man playing a romantic lead opposite a white woman. The black woman, supposedly, is seen as less threatening. But the reasons may be even more complex. Samuel Niefeld, who once represented the bass Simon Estes, says the medium itself is partly to blame, having always catered to the dazzle and fashion-conscious glamor of its female stars. "Opera has always been essentially a diva's medium, so that men have trouble getting noticed," said Niefeld. "Opera is so costume-oriented, men can't compete with what a good designer can do for a woman."

But even Niefeld admits there is more to the problem. "There are many young black male singers on the scene, but they are making so-so careers, they are not making the big careers," Niefeld said. "They are singing in France, in Italy, even in Germany, but they are not getting the big new productions, that sort of thing. Simon Estes, in that respect, is somewhat unique. He is a commanding presence on stage, and he sings a repertory which very few people, black or white, sing."

Estes' repertory may have helped him in recent years, but the dramatic baritone (who essays the roles of Wagner and Verdi) spent the early years of his career struggling to reach the position he now holds as the most successful black male ever to sing opera. Despite early triumphs in Europe, he did not make his debut at the Metropolitan until he was past forty, and then it was in the less than spectacular role of the Landgrave in *Tannhäuser*. Until then, his American career left much to be desired. Today, however, he shares the position of black male opera superstar with no other singer.

Estes is outspoken on the issue of race and opera, and particularly on the situation with black men. "There seems to be some fear of romantic involvement between the black man and the white woman," he candidly told *Opera News* in a 1983 interview. And he becomes specific when the question of racism arises. When he was turned down for a role in a 1983 *Ring* at Bayreuth, discrimination, Estes says, was the reason (though both the director, Sir Peter Hall, and conductor, Sir Georg Solti, claim his audition was not impressive). The frustration for both black men and women lies in the nature of the hiring process; selection of an opera cast will be a subjective undertaking, and there-fore discrimination always will be difficult, if not impossible, to prove.

For black tenors, who generally play romantic leads, the problem of discrimination is even more critical. Vinson Cole, a tenor who has performed at most of the major opera houses in America and Europe, says the fear of a black male/white female romantic angle exists mostly in the minds of management and board members. "In this day and age a person cannot come out and say, 'I'm not going to hire you because you are black,'" Cole says. "But I'm sure that there are instances where I'm not engaged basically because people have the belief that if they hire a black lyric tenor...the board would not accept such a thing. I don't think it really matters to an audience, but they seem to have the feeling that it would matter."

Though Estes stands out in the lineup of contemporary black male singers, there are a number of talented young artists deserving of prominent places in the opera and concert worlds—Bruce Hubbard, Michael Austin, Curtis Rayam, Steven Cole, Gregg Baker, Philip Creech, and Willard White, to list a few—and the number is ever increasing. But competition is fierce, and most black artists feel they must be extraordinarily prepared. "It has never been that a black male can just be good," Vinson Cole says. "He has to be excellent. You can't be anything less than that. If you are, it just won't work."

Presumably, as more and more blacks enter opera, whatever visual and vocal differences exist between black and white singers will be relegated to a position of less significance. Or better still, those differences will be respected as unique cultural distinctions, adding a measure of variety and texture to the colorful fabric of the vocal music scene. The black-sounding voice can only enhance the musical color spectrum; it would be a dull world that allowed or appreciated only a single sound. And visually, the appearance of blacks on the opera stage can only serve as a testament to musical democracy. In opera, as in society, ethnic differences should not divide and disturb; rather they should enrich and enlighten. Where opera as a theatrical and musical medium is headed remains to be seen. But if the present is any indication of future direction, the coming years will yield a presence of black opera artists, both men and women, heretofore unequalled and unimagined.

# 12

# Voices of
# a New Generation

$B$Y the 1970s, American activists who had predicted the birth of a black revolution in the 1960s were mourning its stillborn state. Civil rights had underscored the era, but barely had the theme taken hold when the light of the movement dimmed. Giant strides had been made since the 1950s in every area of achievement—sports, education, government, the arts—but two decades later blacks pondered the degree of gain. Had the years of struggle been effective, or had the movement died prematurely? Clearly, the push for social change had lost its surge. Momentum slacked, charismatic leaders vanished, conservatism displaced radicalism, and the torch of idealism that had blazed at the beginning of the era flickered at the end.

But a movement cannot prescribe its own distance. Though the feverish days of the civil rights struggle had passed, calmer times revealed significant progress. Nowhere could change be seen more vividly than in the vocal arts. Without the drama of grand demonstrations, marches, or sit-ins in American concert halls, progress in the arts still paralleled that of the greater movement. Activism had been, of course, alien to Marian Anderson's style, but she so strongly engraved her image on the face of American music that even in the 1970s it still bore her powerful imprint. She did not require the tools of outrage and anger; instead she tore at the heart of the American conscience like a silent, beleaguered saint. Leontyne Price commanded equally powerfully, but differently, defying injustice and abuse through talent and sheer attitude.

In opposing ways, both women helped produce in the 1970s and 1980s an era unlike any other. The younger prima donnas no longer combatted racial discrimination as policy. The battles had been waged and won, the trenches cleared, and even though residual racism marred the picture here and there, the prospect of major careers for black women in opera was no longer in serious doubt. When race problems did occur, they took on subtler shadings, usually obscured by subjective prerogative and almost always unprovable. Generally, though, the black diva not only flourished in the major opera houses of the world, but sometimes even benefited from discrimination. Black women often were preferred over their white counterparts as old trends from the Harlem Renaissance were renewed: the all-black production, black opera companies, and operas written by black composers for black casts.

Virgil Thomson's *Four Saints in Three Acts* played in 1973 at New York's Mitzi Newhouse Theater, still honoring the composer's casting wishes. This time Betty Allen, Benjamin Matthews, Clamma Dale, Hilda Harris, Arthur Thompson, Barbara Hendricks, and Henry Price played the Spanish saints. In 1975 ragtime fever climaxed when Scott Joplin's barroom-bred tunes, enjoying a trendy resurgence sixty years after the composer's death, made a leap from cathouse to opera house; his forgotten jewel *Treemonisha* was staged at New York's Uris Theater after a run in Texas with the Houston Grand Opera. And *Porgy and Bess* was performed in unexpurgated form with the Houston Grand Opera in 1976, and in 1985 at the Met.

But by the time of *Porgy*'s Met debut, what was once seen as innocent casting now raised a few bemused eyebrows. When the Met signed with the Gershwin estate to hire only black singers, critic Donal Henahan voiced his disapproval in the *New York Times*. Admitting his preference for an all-black cast over one that might feature whites masquerading as blacks under layers of skin darkener, he argued, "but a legal agreement at the Metropolitan... involving race? That is hard to countenance."

Nevertheless, the Met complied with the long-standing Gershwin stricture. The composer's heirs carried out his obsession with preserving *Porgy*'s natural state, but Gershwin had chiefly wanted to prevent an eventual white occupation of Catfish Row. Henahan argued that

Gershwin's reasoning made better sense in the 1930s, before legal civil rights. In the 1980s, Henahan maintained, favoring blacks by discriminating against whites was equally egregious, and a dangerous precedent. After all, a contract demanding an all-white cast for, say, *The Marriage of Figaro* surely would incite an uproar. So the questions rear up with reversed implications: Should a singer belong to a particular race to play a member of that race on an opera stage? Is such a compensatory move, an operatic "affirmative action," constitutional? Could a white singer barred from a *Porgy* production effectively invoke the Civil Rights Act of 1964 in a court case? The plaintiff would, after all, be suffering employment discrimination based on color.

But Gershwin's logic prevailed theatrically and socially. He sought the patois and style peculiar to black culture and could hardly fathom the cork-blackened visage of an Al Jolson as Porgy. Moreover, he knew blacks were the ones who needed protection from racism, not whites. Therefore, with his curious stipulation, Gershwin determined to supply the repertory with at least one opera from which blacks could never be barred. Fighting discrimination with discrimination, he knew total fairness to both sides would have been achievable only in a perfect world.

With the 1985 *Porgy*, the cause of blacks in opera triumphed. Never before had so many black artists populated the stage, and new stars shone brilliantly. It was perfect irony; suddenly by written agreement, there were more than a hundred black singers, dancers, and choristers in a company that, only thirty years before, shunned black voices. Some who made their debut were new to opera itself—baritone Gregg Baker, straight from Broadway, so impressed the part of Crown with his personal stamp that he practically redefined the role. Other young singers made their mark: Bruce Hubbard and David Arnold were equally effective alternating the role of Jake, as were the three singers portraying Clara: Marvis Martin, Myra Merritt, and Gwendolyn Bradley. Florence Quivar's torchy "My Man's Gone Now" brought the house down, while Isola Jones, according to one reviewer, "covered herself with glory" in the small but musically sublime role of the Strawberry Woman. And despite protestations that this *Porgy* was too "high-falutin," younger members of the cast promised much for the future of blacks in opera.

The black voice continued to reverberate as New York City Opera reaffirmed its faith in black themes with a new production in 1986. When black composer Anthony Davis penned *X, the Life and Times of Malcolm X*, City Opera's general manager, Beverly Sills, selected it for production, hailing it "a very good work on a relevant topic...a necessary work for the company to do." City Opera's posthumous connection with the dark prince of the Civil Rights era—an establishment endorsement of an anti-establishment hero—reflected a respectful look at the life of the notorious Muslim leader. In this opera could be found the antithesis of Porgy. Where Gershwin's hero had been submissive, servile and crippled by nature and white society, Davis' was erect, strong, defiant, and in his early days militantly anti-white. Set to music derived from a blend of black music styles—including American jazz and African motifs, the opera captured the frenzy and unrest that characterized the sixties.

And if that era yielded anything, it created an awareness among blacks of the need for economic independence. Blacks realized opera was no different from any other enterprise; to ensure work, one had to create it. Black opera companies resurfaced, reviving the pre-Anderson days, but this time with an expanded purpose: to offer a testing ground for young black singers, dancers, technicians, directors, and composers and to prepare them for competition in the larger market. One such company, Opera Ebony of New York (which also hires white artists), was founded in the early 1970s by baritone Benjamin Matthews, Wayne Sanders, Margaret Harris, and Sister Mary Elise of the Sisters of the Blessed Sacrament. The company set new standards for black opera organizationally and musically. Its small-budgeted but well-executed productions drew praise from the press and a strong following. While offering work for black artists, the company also provided a repertorial home for little-known operas; works such as Leo Edward's *Harriet Tubman* and Dorothy Rudd-Moore's *Frederick Douglass* were staged by the ensemble. Through the years the company's circle of performers included Hilda Harris, Alpha Floyd, Joyce Mathis, Gurcell Henry, Ruby Hinds, Esther Hinds, Cynthia Clarey, Gwendolyn Bradley, and Jennifer Jones.

As the number of black women artists has increased, so in recent years has the need for their services, and the greatest talents among them are rarely unemployed. The vast number of European opera houses (Germany alone has more than seventy) and the sprouting of regional operas in America account for the success of many singers, and supply and demand has become a factor. Singers of a particular *Fach*—the spinto, the coloratura, or leggiero soprano—are in perpetual short supply; for these rare types, the stock value is high, and opera companies vie for contract commitments years in advance. So despite occasional racial typing and outright discrimination, some artists are unaffected and freely admit that problems of race have never been a major issue.

One such artist is Kathleen Battle, one of the brightest stars of the 1980s. A lyric coloratura with a voice of burnished silver, Battle has transcended the usual limitations of her vocal type. Not since Roberta Peters' career in the 1950s and 1960s has such an artist, who does not take on the heroines of Verdi and Puccini, achieved such household name popularity. Instead, her domain is the repertory of the lighter voice, chiefly the soubrette roles of Mozart—Despina, Susanna, Zerlina, and Blondchen—Rossini's Rosina, and Strauss's Zerbinetta and Sophie. With a voice that lacks the power to command by sheer volume, Battle derives amplitude from trueness of pitch and focus, and critics praise her enunciation and ability to communicate mood and meaning. Like the voices of Marilyn Horne and Leontyne Price in terms of their ability to impress and linger in the mind, Battle's voice, once heard, is instantly recognizable.

Battle's career began in the industrial town of Portsmouth, Ohio, where she grew up the youngest of seven children. Hers was a musical family—her father, a steelworker, was a tenor in a gospel quartet, and her mother once displayed the source of her daughter's industriousness by rebuilding the family piano. Grounded in the gospel music of the African Methodist Episcopal Church, Battle began piano lessons at thirteen and played and sang regularly at church functions.

Even within her own family of singers Battle's voice was not the one most likely to captivate opera house audiences. As a youngster she was overshadowed by her older sister Carol, who owned what Battle called "a major voice." Kathleen's "small but pretty" instrument was usually sheltered beneath a mass of sound in the school chorus, while Carol reaped attention for her larger, more substantial voice. However, Carol opted out of music early. Kathleen, though she showed a penchant for math and science, entered the University of Cincinnati College Conservatory and majored in music education. Led by a strong practical nature, Battle looked warily on singing as a career. At college she tested the waters cautiously, studying with Franklin Bens and, rarely, auditioning for student productions. Soprano Eleanor Steber coached her in a master class and encouraged her with generous praise, and bass Italo Tajo, the school's opera director, provided constant confidence-bolstering and inspiration.

But Battle still wasn't convinced. She was keenly aware of the possibility and consequences of failure, of having nothing to "fall back on." After college she plunged into a teaching career. Working with black children had been a dream, and in Cincinnati's mostly black inner-city schools Battle dispensed rudimentary basics to classrooms full of ten-, eleven-, and twelve-year-old music students. Performance, though, was not sidelined entirely, and occasional auditions yielded promising results. In 1972 Thomas Schippers, then conductor of the Cincinnati Symphony, adjudicated Battle's bid for a part in the upcoming Spoleto Festival of Two Worlds, and delegated her to sing the soprano solo in Brahms' *A German Requiem* in Spoleto, Italy. Later, she met James Levine, then a bright, young conductor with a burgeoning

Kathleen Battle in *Giulio Cesare*
*Photo by Winnie Klotz, Metropolitan Opera Association, Inc.*

reputation. He chose her to sing the Mater Gloriosa in Mahler's Eighth Symphony at the Cincinnati Symphony's May Festival in 1974.

The careers of Battle and Levine progressed almost in tandem. When Battle moved to New York to understudy Carmen Balthrop in the title role of Treemonisha, Levine was there conducting at the Metropolitan. Levine adored Battle's voice, and whenever he had an opportunity to hire her, he did. Battle bowed at the Met as the Shepherd in a 1977 *Tannhäuser*—a small role but one that brought deserved attention—and subsequent performances of Sophie in *Werther and Susanna* at City Opera followed.

As Battle's name became familiar, other offers came—some suitable, some outrageously inappropriate for her voice. But with counsel from advisers such as Tajo and Levine, Battle resisted the allure of the more glamorous roles that would have led not only to unfair comparisons but eventual vocal damage. By declining the star vehicles, Battle became known as a stubbornly sensible artist, and one of the foremost exponents of the light lyric repertory.

Within a few years, Battle became one of the most ardently pursued artists of her generation, inspiring routine praise at nearly every major opera house in the world. Her fans pointed to her Mozart interpretations as definitive; at Salzburg she made a huge success of her performance as Despina in *Così Fan Tutte*, and the same result ensued at the Met with her portrayal of Susanna. After her Covent Garden debut as Zerbinetta in Strauss's *Ariadne*, the British gave her the Laurence Olivier Award, their top theatrical prize. She sang at the Vatican for Pope John Paul II with the Vienna Philharmonic under Herbert von Karajan. As a recitalist and singer of Lieder and spirituals, Battle was equally popular; her New York recitals were touted as major events and sold out within days of their announcement.

Battle's effect as an artist stems largely from her ability to invest her art with a soul-felt spirituality, admittedly a residue of her early ties to gospel and black American popular music. In a 1987 televised interview Battle said: "The culture I come from is just as rich as any Western European culture, therefore I believe what I'm bringing to it only enriches opera. Many times I am asked, 'How can you be from a small town in the Midwest and sing Mozart?' Mozart was a human being with emotions and a sense of humor…we all share these qualities as human beings. As a black performer in opera…I grew up on the music of the sixties, the Motown sound, and I was touched and moved and formed in some way by that."

At the midpoint of her career, Battle's discography already rivaled the output of the most popular Motown artists. A favorite of the world's most revered conductors, she has been among the busiest recording artists of the decade, with laudable performances of *Così Fan*

*Tutte*, under Riccardo Muti; *Ariadne*, with James Levine; *Don Giovanni*, under Herbert von Karajan; and *Un Ballo in Maschera*, conducted by Sir Georg Solti. Her recordings consistently reach the top of the charts, and among her major offerings are the *Salzburg Recital* album with partner James Levine and a voice-guitar duo album with guitarist Christopher Parkening.

At the other end of the vocal spectrum is Jessye Norman, a dramatic soprano of stentorian power who rocketed to fame and, like Battle, accrued an enormous international following. Norman's big voice does not conquer simply by virtue of its opulence; rather it does so with its voluptuous shape, timbre, vast melodic and dynamic range. It is a voice of contradictions, combining liquid warmth and molten steel with the agility to soar from reverential mezzo-voces to fiery, passionate fortes and back. Throughout her early career Norman clearly preferred recital work, focusing on the chanson, Lieder, and contemporary compositions, but in the early 1980s she began to relent in the direction of opera. And on the opera stage, Norman's Olympian stature supports the bigger-than-life theme that pervades her selective opera repertory: the mythological heroines Dido, Cassandra, Helen of Troy, and Ariadne. She has planned her career instinctively, refusing to be seduced by a repertory for which she feels she is not suited. To those who would have made Norman into a singer of the Leontyne Price brand, Norman has demurred with, "My voice is different."

"I'm not interested in so-called mainstream repertory," Norman told John Gruen in a *New York Times* interview in 1984. "I have not become a Verdi heroine soprano, and, of course, that's what's needed in opera houses. But roles such as Lady Macbeth, Eboli, Leonora, or Amelia are not part of my temperament. To sing roles with which I have no empathy would be wrong. I sing Aida because it's right for me. I sing Mozart, Wagner, and Richard Strauss, because I love them. But what really interests me is the music of Monteverdi, Rameau, Purcell, Berlioz, Stravinsky. It's music I can relate to, and it's music of immense beauty."

A native of Augusta, Georgia, Norman is one of five children born to Silas and Janie Norman. Her early singing experiences took place in Augusta's Mount Calvary Baptist Church, where her father, who managed an insurance company, also sang. Her mother played piano, and each of the five children studied the instrument. At age seven, Norman entered a singing contest sponsored by the church and won third prize—a memory slip in "God Will Take Care of You" precluded greater success. Though she was musically gifted, Norman's parents thoughtfully withheld voice lessons, a move Norman now counts as a wise one, until she entered college. "The very best thing that could

**Jessye Norman**
*Photo by Winnie Klotz, Metropolitan Opera Association, Inc.*

happen to a voice, if it shows any promise at all," Norman told Matthew Gurewitsch of *Connoisseur* magazine, "is when it is very young to leave it alone, and to let it develop quite naturally, and to let the person go on as long as possible with the sheer joy of singing—rather than being concerned with what comes later; the necessary concern for vocal technique."

At sixteen, Norman entered her first important vocal competition, the Marian Anderson Award contest held in Philadelphia. The teenager sang two arias, "Mon coeur s'ouvre à ta voix" from *Samson and Delilah* and an aria from *Il Trovatore*. But her youth and lack of training brought her only sincere words of encouragement from contest judges. The trip, however, did prove propitious. On the way back from Philadelphia, Norman stopped off in Washington, D.C., to visit relatives, and sang for Carolyn Grant at Howard University. The Howard voice teacher was so impressed she recommended Norman for a full tuition scholarship to the school.

Norman began voice training at Howard under Grant's supervision in 1963. After graduating cum laude she went to Baltimore to study with Alice Duschak, then on to the University of Michigan to work with the French baritone Pierre Bernac. Norman endured the stipulations of her fellowship—she had to teach voice to fellow students, string players who only studied singing to fulfill curriculum requirements. But her own hard work and patience paid off quickly; after a year of study at Michigan she won her first major award, the vocal category of the International Music Competition given by the German Broadcasting Corporation in Munich. In 1969 Norman settled into the lifestyle of a young diva in Europe; she signed a three-year contract with the Deutsche Oper in Berlin, having debuted as Elisabeth in Wagner's *Tannhäuser*. But as a member of a European opera company, Norman soon realized she was hired to fill in needed parts, with little regard for her brand of talent, level of experience, and temperament. Out of a "need for survival," she resigned.

Years passed, and Norman abandoned opera temporarily, filling her calendar with recital dates and recording sessions in Europe. After a brief period in Paris, she settled in London, where she established a permanent base. Meanwhile, she carved herself a niche in the international music community and accomplished an unusual feat: She built a career of mammoth proportion as a recitalist in a world that panders to the opera diva. In Europe her fans were legion, drawn to her like metal filings to a magnet. Her every stage appearance was received with a shower of accolades—at the Salzburg Festival she was once called back for six encores—and it is little wonder she is said to have inspired the premise and title character of Jean-Jacques Beineix's film *Diva*.

Norman returned to opera, and by the time she made her Metropolitan debut—as Cassandra in *Les Troyens* in 1983—she was already a figure of legendary stature. It was a major debut worthy of its advance publicity. The *New York Times* called Norman "a soprano of magnificent presence who commanded the stage at every moment." Norman's queenly countenance served her equally effectively in other Met productions, particularly in telecasts as Madame Lidoine in *Dialogues of the Carmelites* and as Ariadne in Strauss' *Ariadne auf Naxos* (which also got a tumultuous reception at Covent Garden). In 1989, she made Metropolitan Opera history, performing as the Woman in Schoenberg's *Erwartung*, the company's first one-character production. She preceded the performance by singing Judith in Bartók's *Bluebeard's Castle*, opposite bass Samuel Ramey.

But it is chiefly as a recitalist exploring the music of Poulenc, Satie, Brahms, Schubert, and Strauss that Norman continues to garner the bulk of her worldwide acclaim. She remains one of the few artists whose recorded repertory covers an unusually expansive range, from the Countess in *The Marriage of Figaro* with Sir Colin Davis, to Strauss' *Four Last Songs*, to a moving performance of Dido in Purcell's *Dido and Aeneas*. Norman has even followed the trend of many modern artists in delving into popular or "crossover" repertory with a recording titled *With a Song in My Heart*, featuring guitarist John Williams and the Boston Pops Orchestra. In 1987 she gave a concert in New York to benefit the Duke Ellington Memorial Fund, singing songs by Ellington and Cole Porter. Said Norman of her newfound eclecticism (in a *New York Times* interview before the event): "If you send up a weather vane or put your thumb up in the air every time you want to do something different, to find out what people are going to think about it, you're going to limit yourself. That's a very strange way to live."

Another soprano ranking among the busiest in the world is Leona Mitchell, who belongs to perhaps the rarest breed of female artists, at least in recent years—the spinto soprano. Like Leontyne Price, Mitchell essays the heroines of Verdi, Puccini, and Mozart. She represents the new group of young American singers whose principal training took place in the United States. Mitchell bypassed the usual rite of passage— the obligatory tour of duty in Europe's smaller houses. There was an engagement in Barcelona, Spain, and a few regional opera dates early in her twenties, but otherwise she went directly from San Francisco Opera's acclaimed Merola Program to the Metropolitan, where she sang, at age twenty-five, opposite Placido Domingo. As Micaela in *Carmen*, Mitchell displayed a voice that effortlessly combined dramatic power with lyric sweetness, and became the heir apparent to Price's repertory and status among black sopranos.

Born in Enid, Oklahoma, the daughter of a Pentecostal minister, she was the tenth child of fifteen in a musical and deeply religious family. Gospel music figured heavily in the family's recreational time, and Mitchell recalled singing in front of a church congregation from the age of eight. In Enid, a small town sixty-five miles from Oklahoma City, opera was practically nonexistent; the fine arts were overshadowed by oil and agricultural interests. In fact, Mitchell was never exposed to opera until college. As with Battle, Mitchell's position as a younger child did not allow her an early spotlight. Instead, the Musical Mitchells, a gospel group composed of the five oldest children, traveled through-out Oklahoma, Texas, and Kansas, singing occasionally on radio and television. Mitchell took chorus class at school and played piano ("by ear") and violin at home. Eventually she became a church choir director, inspired by the gospel singers of the sixties, notably James Cleveland and Mahalia Jackson. Before the church congregation, Mitchell acquired professional poise, confidence, and stage presence, even though the raspy wailings of gospel weren't exactly beneficial to her classical studies. "I would sing gospel music and get hoarse on the weekends," Mitchell recalled, "and then go back and sing 'Moon River' and try to find my voice."

In high school, when Mitchell's music teacher Maureen Priebe heard the young girl's voice soaring above the others in chorus class, she pulled her out for special attention. With Priebe's encouragement and coaxing, Mitchell's interest narrowed to opera. Recordings of Price and Callas mesmerized her, and an *Aida* aria, learned phonetically, got her into the vocal department at Oklahoma City University. Mitchell indulged her mentor's interest in her potential, but the shy youngster was skeptical about a career in music. In college Mitchell studied with Inez Silberg, who groomed her for professional music and turned her into a champion contest competitor; under Silberg's guidance Mitchell won more than thirty competitions in college. She warmed to the idea of a music career with each encouraging result. Her success led not only to San Francisco's Merola Program, but also to a $10,000 Opera America Grant allowing her to study with Ernest St. John Metz in California.

But the most fortuitous contact was with Kurt Herbert Adler in San Francisco. The San Francisco Opera conductor took Mitchell under his wing and paved the way for her Met audition with a word to a former colleague in Met casting. Mitchell had only sung Micaela in English, and her only performance in the role had taken place in San Francisco. Yet she managed to dazzle critics with her warm full-bodied tone, and praise was unanimous. In a few years she became one of the most reliable exponents of Puccini and Verdi heroines: Mimi, Butterfly, Manon Lescaut, Leonora, and Aida.

With a repertory that so resembled Price's at a time when the older

Leona Mitchell in *Aida*
*Photo by Kranichphoto*

soprano was tapering off her itinerary and planning retirement, the press labeled Mitchell "best of the black opera singers" in the early 1980s—an awkwardly racial compliment. Expectations loomed and brought stress and unexpected pressure. Burdened with the sobriquet "Price's protégée," Mitchell was suddenly nagged with self-doubt at the busiest time in her career. "I went through a bad case of nerves," Mitchell recalled, "the kind of nerves where I could have quit singing. I was going up the ladder and I wasn't ready." Some critics were unsympathetic, and Mitchell raised the question of unfair treatment of black artists in a *Life* magazine article: "In Europe they say my language is wonderful. In the States they say I'm dropping phrases. Are they judging me differently because I'm black?"

But after soul-searching, reassessment, and hearing Laurence Olivier on a TV talk show confess to a mid-career crisis ("He went through the same thing—he couldn't remember his lines and yet he was well established"), Mitchell regained her confidence. She became one of the Met's most often employed artists, drawing warm receptions for her performances of Liù in *Turandot* and Micaela on "Live from the Met" as well as in her standard repertory: Butterfly, Aida, Mimi, and the Leonoras. She performed regularly with the Rome Opera, the Sydney Opera in Australia, and Covent Garden, and her 1975 recording of *Porgy and Bess* with Lorin Maazel and the Cleveland Orchestra still stands as one of the most definitive.

Keen intellect and philosophical instinct mark the life and career of soprano Barbara Hendricks. And though she places life decisions ahead of career moves, Hendricks nevertheless has emerged as one of the most important concert artists of her generation (her recital commitments number as many as forty-five a year), with an ever increasing repertory of opera roles. With a lyric voice of silvery purity, Hendricks has placed her stamp on such operatic characters as Sophie in *Der Rosenkavalier* (the vehicle for her Met debut in 1987), Susanna in *The Marriage of Figaro*, and Massenet's Manon.

Hendricks was born in Arkansas and raised in Arkansas and Tennessee, the daughter of a Christian Methodist Episcopal minister and an elementary school teacher. A church pulpit was her first singing platform. Her first contact with classical music came in the school chorus, where she sang Bach cantatas and Handel's *Messiah*. Attending college at the University of Nebraska, she studied science and earned a degree in chemistry, while meeting expenses by singing with a jazz band.

A college summer spent at the Aspen Music Festival in Colorado proved pivotal. It was there that Hendricks met the great French-Canadian mezzo Jennie Tourel, who became teacher, adviser, and

Barbara Hendricks in *Der Rosenkavalier*
*Photo by Winnie Klotz, Metropolitan Opera Association, Inc.*

guiding force in her career, actually convincing her to consider a career in music. "It was never really a decision that had to be made," Hendricks recalled. "At the end of those nine weeks it was obvious to me this is what I should be doing." Hendricks returned to finish her last year in college and applied immediately to Juilliard to continue working with Tourel.

In Tourel Hendricks found artistic wisdom and purpose. "My whole week revolved around my lesson," she said, "the energy it gave me, the inspiration—I always came from my lessons wanting to go back to the practice room to study harder and dig deeper. We didn't spend the whole hour working on scales and placing the voice. We were both interested in working on the music—getting to the music."

When Tourel died of cancer in 1973, Hendricks struggled to find new direction and motivation, but fortunately Tourel's wisdom and guidance left a residual confidence in her young student. "When she died I spent a lot of time seeking for someone to replace her, until I realized I would have to become my own light to myself. That was a very strong and important time—those five years we spent together. I realized what was important, and that what I was searching for was not outside myself, but inside of me. I had to get to know myself better and delve deeper inside myself to find out what the truth for me would be."

Part of that truth was the knowledge that her personal life would take priority over her professional goals, that fulfillment as a person eclipsed achievement as a singer. She met Martin Engström, an aspiring artists' manager, married him in the mid-seventies, and moved to Paris, against the advice of friends who feared the move might stunt her career. Instead, it had a positive effect. In the next few years Hendricks became a recognized star in Europe, and in America she was engaged by the Chicago Symphony and the opera companies of San Francisco, Boston, and Santa Fe. Her New York recitals drew crowds and her recordings mounted; in addition to her spirituals album, there were recordings of Mozart concert arias, David del Tredici's *Final Alice* (which she created), *The Marriage of Figaro*, and a collection of Gershwin songs.

Hendricks credits Tourel's guidance with much of her success and gets inspiration from a quote of Chaliapin given to her by her teacher: "My life has a leitmotif, a struggle against the sham glitter that eclipses inner life, the complexities that kill simplicity, and the vulgar externals that diminish grandeur."

"It means that what I am concerned with in my life and work is what is essential—nothing artificial," Hendricks explained. "Simplicity—no glitter. Only that which has to do with the essence of what I'm about or the essence of what music is about. It's not the easy way, but then I have never been one to look for the easy way. And I don't pat myself on the back and say, 'I'm full of virtue'—I only live the way I can. I have only myself to answer to; the choices I make are because that's how I can live with myself."

Mezzo-soprano Florence Quivar established herself in the 1970s and 1980s as a major artist specializing in recitals and orchestra appearances, but her opera performances have also brought her substantial recognition. Her dark, velvet-textured timbre has made her a favorite among conductors, among them Riccardo Muti, Lorin Maazel (with whom she recorded the role of Serena in *Porgy and Bess*), and James Levine.

Born in Philadelphia, Quivar became interested in music with exposure to her mother's private piano teaching. Her interest peaked when she heard the Met perform in Philadelphia during its spring tour. "I heard the company do *Butterfly* and I was hooked," she said. Meanwhile, music pervaded her household. Quivar's mother, a pianist and organist, taught eighty voice and piano students at home. Quivar herself made her singing debut at age six in church.

When Quivar's mother formed the Harmonic Choraliers, a group of gospel singers from local church choirs, her daughter sat transfixed during rehearsals. "They would give concerts, and I'd be on the first row," Quivar recalled. "I knew all the words. I grew up hearing that kind of music all my life—I think you bring those elements [of gospel] to classical music." Quivar showed talent as a singer early but, for practical reasons, entered a teaching college with elementary education in mind. She lasted one day in the program—realizing music would have but minor emphasis, she quit. She transferred to the Philadelphia Musical Academy and after graduation attended the Juilliard School.

Her first time in New York, Quivar lasted only a year in the city. ("It wasn't the right time—I wasn't experienced enough.") She returned to Philadelphia, where she taught privately, and signed with the Franklin Concert Series, a young artists program. Master classes with contralto Maureen Forrester sparked an interest in Lieder. While time spent in a Boris Goldovsky workshop exposed her to opera, she chose to concentrate on concerts and oratorio.

Later Quivar decided to try New York again, and this time made it her permanent home. After winning the Marian Anderson Award, her confidence swelled. Her first job paid about $150 a week, performing "for young kids in the public school system." Other modest engagements followed. As a concert artist, Quivar found the struggle difficult but workable. She was signed by Harold Shaw's management, and later by Columbia Artists, and was soon in demand as a recitalist and oratorio singer internationally. She began to appear with the country's top orchestras: the New York Philharmonic, the Philadelphia

Florence Quivar in *Prophete*
*Photo by Winnie Klotz, Metropolitan Opera Association, Inc.*

Orchestra, and the Boston Symphony. She sang in opera but kept her roles to a minimum. Following her Met debut in 1977 as Marina in *Boris Godunov,* she was Mother Marie in *Dialogues of the Carmelites,* Jocasta in *Oedipus Rex,* and Isabella in *The Italian Woman in Algiers.*

Quivar's success as an artist living in New York may have allayed some of her early fears about the life of an artist in the city, but when asked about the best path for young artists, she advises caution. "I go to schools and students want to know, 'What do you advise?' For sure, I tell them *not* to come to New York. It's very, very hard. I tell them to look for the colleges—find someone who is out there performing and get to that school. Indeed, you need talent, but you also need some connection to pull you through, something that will set you apart from the others. And it is still very difficult—it never becomes easy. As they say, you are as good as last night's performance. Every time you walk out there you are still proving."

Among the group of young artists now proving themselves is mezzo-soprano Cynthia Clarey. Raised in Rocky Mount, North Carolina, and born in Smithfield, Virginia, Clarey first sang as a child in the Hill Street Baptist Church in Smithfield. She studied voice at Howard University and later at the Juilliard School. Based in New York State, Clarey affiliated with the Tri-Cities Opera Company of Binghamton, which allowed her a forum for experimentation with new vehicles. Like Verrett and Bumbry, Clarey also changed registers in midcareer. However, Clarey made the transition in reverse, switching from a soprano with a top D to a mezzo. She tested the waters in a Tri-Cities production of *Carmen,* and the result encouraged her. While she missed the soprano heroines, particularly Butterfly, Clarey is not bound to labels when it comes to choosing roles. "I still get offered soprano roles," she said. "I just have to look at them and say yes, I can or no, I can't. Unfortunately, singers are pigeonholed and people get very nervous when they can't figure out what you are. Sometimes they would rather not deal with you than have to figure it out."

But the change proved a wise one. When Clarey stepped in to replace an indisposed Frederica von Stade for a production of *L'Incoronazione di Poppea* at Glyndebourne in 1984, critics raved, praising her voice as well as her feel for gesture and movement onstage. Since then, variety and innovation have characterized her choices. When theater director Peter Brook searched for a theatrically and vocally convincing Carmen for his controversial treatment of the Bizet classic titled *La Tragédie de Carmen,* Clarey was one of the several choices to alternate the role. She toured with the critically lauded production throughout Europe and so impressed Brook that he offered her a straight acting role in his next production, which she turned down.

Cynthia Clarey in *La Forza del Destino*

Clarey preferred to remain a singing actress. She debuted with the New York City Opera in the world premiere of Thea Musgrave's *The Voice of Ariadne* and took part in the American premiere of Michael Tippett's *The Ice Break*. Since standing in for Von Stade at Glyndebourne, Clarey became a house favorite there and returned for a number of productions, including the popular Trevor Nunn production of *Porgy and Bess*, in which she played Serena.

Soprano Wilheminia Fernandez was on her way to establishing a career in opera and recital when she was offered the role of the eccentric singer Cynthia Hawkins in *Diva*. The worldwide popularity of the film propelled Fernandez to screen stardom and gave her visibility outside of classical music. Since then she not only has become strongly linked with the film, now an art house favorite, but takes some credit for making popular Catalani's aria from *La Wally*, which recurs through-out the movie like a romantic theme.

Born in Philadelphia, Fernandez grew up hearing the music of her mother, a church pianist and organist, and began singing in church when she was seven. A high school teacher encouraged her to plan a singing career, and she studied voice at Philadelphia's Academy of Vocal Arts. She began her career in the chorus of the Houston Grand Opera's production of *Porgy and Bess*. Later she auditioned for the lead role and alternated as Bess with Clamma Dale in New York.

The *Diva* offer came while Fernandez was in Europe in the middle of a Paris Opéra stint, playing Musetta in *La Bohème*. "On reading the script, my first opinion was to say no," said Fernandez. "I didn't want to be associated with a film then because it wasn't my true art. Later I was convinced to do it because I felt it was going to be something positive. It was a way of introducing opera to people who don't necessarily know what opera is about. I find a lot in my performances that there is a new wave of young people coming through. Their first reaction when they come back to meet me, is that they are there because they saw the film. They got interested in opera and they want to know more about it. And if they are interested, that's great. That's all I wanted to happen."

Soprano Gwendolyn Bradley grew up in the pre-integration days of South Carolina's predominantly black Lee County, in the small town of Bishopville. The daughter of two school teachers, Bradley attended Athens College in Athens, Alabama, the North Carolina School of the Arts, and the Curtis Institute in Philadelphia. Equipped with flexibility and an unusual range—from a low C to a G above high C—Bradley has sung at the Metropolitan Opera since the 1980–81 season in roles such as Olympia in *The Tales of Hoffmann*, Zerbinetta in *Ariadne auf*

Gwendolyn Bradley as Olympia in *The Tales of Hoffmann*
*Photo by Winnie Klotz, Metropolitan Opera Association, Inc.*

*Naxos*, Blondchen in *The Abduction from the Seraglio*, and the Forest Bird in *Siegfried*.

Bradley began singing at age seven with the encouragement of an elementary school teacher, and played piano for her church choir and Sunday School. Educational facilities were limited in Bishopville, a town seated in one of South Carolina's poorer counties, so Bradley traveled daily to school in Hartsville, seventeen miles away. In high school she sang a solo at a music festival and won a scholarship to Athens College. Though she planned a career as a pediatrician and had no exposure to opera, she entered the college and studied music. "Athens had about twelve hundred students, with about twelve blacks," said Bradley. "That was somewhat of an adjustment, coming from a segregated high school."

When Bradley explored her musical potential and leaned toward a career in music, her theory teacher recommended finding a music school to continue her studies. He persuaded her to enter the Miss Alabama pageant, which offered as one of its prizes a four-year scholarship to the Manhattan School of Music in New York. "It was a joke to me, and I didn't take it seriously," Bradley said, but she won the talent competition and the scholarship. When Bradley arrived at the school, however, there were no records of her application or scholarship. "A lady who did some research found out that no one had won that scholarship in ten years," Bradley said. "It was only a screening process to get singers up from the South to the North." Instead, Bradley attended the North Carolina School of the Arts, where she studied with the noted American tenor Seth McCoy.

"That was where I really learned about opera," Bradley said. "Before that the closest thing to opera I had experienced was Leontyne Price singing 'We Shall Overcome' on a record." After completing studies at North Carolina, Bradley entered Curtis and studied with Margaret Harshaw. She extended her studies another year at Philadelphia's Academy of Vocal Arts "because I needed more time to really prepare myself for the New York scene." To help support herself she entered and won twenty-six vocal competitions between 1976 and 1978. After moving to New York, she was presented in recital by the Concert Artists Guild at Carnegie Recital Hall. Reviews were good and word spread; soon afterwards she was invited to audition for the Met and debuted in Ravel's *L'enfant et les Sortilèges* during the 1981 season. In the following years Bradley became a Metropolitan favorite, taking on high lyric and leggiera roles. In Europe she made the rounds of the major houses, singing at the Paris Opéra, the Hamburg Staatsoper, Deutche Oper Berlin, Nice Opera, and Glyndebourne.

Mezzo-soprano Hilda Harris, a native of Warrenton, North Carolina, made the unusual transition from New York recording studio backup singer and Broadway musical chorister to performing with opera companies and symphony orchestras in America and Europe. Her youthful appearance and petite size made her a favorite mezzo for "trouser" roles, such as Cherubino in *The Marriage of Figaro* and the child in *L'enfant et les Sortilèges*. As Carmen, though, she was popular throughout Europe where she drew packed houses for twenty-eight consecutive performances in Switzerland and Brussels.

Harris had no designs on a music career until she was already a student at North Carolina State University, and didn't begin working seriously until her senior year. On the recommendation of her teacher, she traveled to New York to study with Lola Hayes, who dispelled her notion that she was a coloratura soprano. "I had that kind of flexibility, but it wasn't my true voice," Harris said. While developing her technique and learning the mezzo repertory, she supported herself in a number of jobs, first working in a photographic studio ("I would close the door, practice the songs I was working on and vocalize") and later singing "doo-wahs" in recording sessions behind Dionne Warwick, Aretha Franklin, and Roberta Flack. "It was very interesting because of the technique that one had to use in doing that kind of music—a much straighter tone, with less vibrato. I would sometimes leave a voice lesson and go straight to a recording studio. I'd turn one voice off and the other voice on."

In the next few years Harris juggled voice lessons with work on Broadway, where she appeared in *110 in the Shade*, *Golden Boy* with Sammy Davis, Jr., and *Mame* with Angela Lansbury. On a night off from *Mame*, after a week of eight shows, she gave her recital debut at Carnegie Recital Hall. "Sunday night I did the recital and Monday I was back in the show," Harris remembered. "It was rough, but it was what I wanted to do. With the Broadway shows my days were free, so it allowed me time to study, go to coaching, and take other languages."

Harris took a leave from Broadway to make her opera debut with a Martha Baird Rockefeller Foundation production of *The Marriage of Figaro* at Brevard, North Carolina, and New York's Chautauqua Festival. It was a successful effort (encouraging enough to allow her to retire from the Broadway stage) and led to her four-month run of Carmen in Europe. Harris' vocal abilities and stage presence made her a mezzo in high demand; she debuted with New York City Opera in 1972 and with the Metropolitan in 1977 in a production of Alban Berg's *Lulu*. Other roles include Stephano in *Romeo and Juliet*, Smeton in *Anna Bolena*, Nicklausse in *The Tales of Hoffmann*, and the child in *L'enfant et les Sortilèges*. As a symphony guest she appeared with the Chicago Symphony, the New York Philharmonic, the Dallas Symphony, and the Concertgebouw Orchestra of Amsterdam.

Hilda Harris in *The Martydom of St. Magnus*
Photo by Peter Maxwell Davies

Roberta Alexander in *The Marriage of Figaro*
*Photo by Winnie Klotz, Metropolitan Opera Association, Inc.*

Another major artist of the last decade is Roberta Alexander, described by *Opera News* as possessing a voice of "rich low notes and crystalline, brilliant top notes, excellent diction, and clear execution." Alexander became known as an exponent of lyric roles such as Mimì and Pamina, but her technique, which the *Berliner Zeitung* once called "as close to the ideal *bel canto* as it is possible to come," allowed her to vary her repertory with roles like Violetta, Zerlina, and the title role in Janáček's *Jenufa* at the Met.

Born in Lynchburg, Virginia, and raised in Yellow Springs, Ohio, Alexander attended Central State University in Ohio and the University of Michigan at Ann Arbor. She debuted at the Met in 1983 in *Don Giovanni*, and alternated Bess with Grace Bumbry at the Met in 1985. Alexander took up residence in Amsterdam and performed with the major Dutch orchestras, including the Concertgebouw and the Rotterdam Philharmonic. Highlights of her career include an eleven-city tour of the Soviet Union and an American joint recital with Simon Estes, with whom she recorded excerpts from *Porgy and Bess*.

In the mid-1980s soprano Marvis Martin more strongly evoked the musical image of the young Leontyne Price in tonal quality, phrasing, and sweep of sound than any sprano of her generation. Even early in her career she was generally embraced by the press for her warmth of style, richness of timbre, and effortless technique. After a recital in Dallas in 1986, critic John Ardoin called her "the most communicative and musical young singer before the public" and called her singing of Charpentier's "Depuis le jour" "as rapt and unfettered a performance as I have heard since Dorothy Maynor's twenty-fifth anniversary concert at Town Hall."

Martin was born in Tallahassee, Florida, graduated from the University of Miami, and studied also at the Manhattan School of Music. In 1980 she won three prizes in the Concours International de Chant in Paris and first prize in the 1980 WGN-Illinois Opera Guild "Auditions of the Air." The following year she won the Kathleen Ferrier Prize from the Young Artist's International Competition, and as a result gave her New York recital debut at the 92nd Street Y. She joined the Metropolitan Opera's Young Artists' Development Program in 1981 and gave her first performance with the company on tour in 1982 as Pamina. She made her European opera debut at Aix-en-Provence in *Mitridate*, a rarely performed early Mozart opera. Her solo recital at Aix was broadcast throughout France. Her voice and presence made her popular with both American and European conductors; she performed with Sir Georg Solti and the Chicago Symphony, Zubin Mehta and the New York Philharmonic, and with James Levine and the Chicago Symphony at the Ravinia Festival. In addition to Pamina and Clara in *Porgy*, other opera roles include Ilia in *Idomeneo*, Liù in

Marvis Martin in *Idomeneo*
*Photo by Winnie Klotz, Metropolitan Opera Association, Inc.*

*Turandot*, Echo in *Ariadne auf Naxos*, and the Princess in *L'Enfant et les Sortilèges*.

The list of notable black artists goes on to include, among others, contralto Marietta Simpson, mezzo-sopranos Barbara Conrad, Isola Jones, Jennifer Jones, and Gwendolyn Killebrew, and sopranos Faye Robinson, Harolyn Blackwell, Carmen Balthrop, Cynthia Haymon, and Clamma Dale. In his engaging book *The Singing Voice*, Robert Rushmore wrote, "Now that blacks have broken the barriers that used to keep them out of the opera house, they are making an almost disproportionate contribution to the art of great singing." That may be true, but unfortunately the number of blacks on stage is not matched proportionately in audiences. Even in cities such as New York, Philadelphia, and Washington, D.C., which claim a progressive arts community as well as a sizeable black population, blacks comprise a negligible fraction of the audience at operas and classical concerts. Yet we recall that in the 1800s, when Col. James Henry Mapleson attended a concert to hear Marie Selika, he was the only white among 2,000 blacks. The difference in support in one hundred years may be due to a division in cultural interest; since the beginning of jazz and rock music, black classical artists have had strong competition for audience support. But some artists are optimistic about the future of black support of the classical arts. "I think we still have a ways to go as far as the audience is concerned, because our black audiences still consider it 'their' music and not 'our' music," said Gwendolyn Bradley. "But the awareness that it is not a so-called 'white' art now—that it is okay to be a part of the opera—is such that we have more people who want to be involved in it."

Despite lagging black audience support, the numbers of black artists heading opera company rosters bears proof of Rushmore's statement; black participation at the top of the profession has exceeded most expectations. But perhaps those expectations were too low. Excellent singing has never been alien to the black culture, as pure vocal talent has never been a respecter of ethnic origin. In the 1890s, an era less self-conscious about racial generalizations, a *Chicago Tribune* reporter wrote, "The richness of the Negro's singing voice has long been recognized, and the belief has been expressed that were such a voice cultivated and trained, an artist of exceptional warmth would be the result." Fortunately, the milieu that made training for Elizabeth Taylor-Greenfield impossible has passed in America. But even among the untrained, the black woman's contribution to song is enviable. The great black divas of jazz and blues, Billie Holiday, Ella Fitzgerald, Sarah Vaughan, and, more recently, rhythm and blues/pop singers Aretha Franklin, Patti LaBelle, and Whitney Houston have drawn from the same repositories as their classical counterparts—the spiritual ethos of the black church and the emotion-filled pathos of common life experiences. Neither group of artists has escaped the plaintive strains of gospel or the raucous rhythms of urban streets. Likewise, neither has gone unimpressed by the message of Martin Luther King, Jr., the image of Marian Anderson, and the memory of Mahalia Jackson. Indeed, there is probably no social group in the world where more common ground is shared between the practitioners of the popular art and the classical.

As the black diva becomes assimilated in a profession so dominated by European culture, one wonders if the umbilical ties to black culture—the affinity for the spiritual, the imprint of gospel, the elusive, indefinable black voice—will become strengthened or frayed. If a black sound indeed exists, will its attractiveness and appeal affect the modern style of singing and find its way into contemporary fashion, or will the character of that sound become diffused in the vastness of the classical singing arena? In short, will the black artist more strongly affect or become affected by the culture surrounding her? One thing is certain. The transformation of the black artist in the past century is staggering. The persistent voices of the pioneers—the voices of Greenfield, Jones, and Anderson—unquestionably opened the door for the modern black diva. And the indomitable spirit of her forerunners has created a population of black women whose love for that legacy shines in their unyielding desire to create beautiful music.

# Selected
# Bibliography

## Books

Abdul, Raoul. *Blacks in Classical Music*. New York: Dodd, Mead & Co., 1977.
Anderson, Marian. *My Lord, What a Morning*. New York: Viking Press, 1943.
Bing, Sir Rudolf. *5000 Nights at the Opera*. New York: Doubleday & Co., 1972.
Bontemps, Arna. *Chariot in the Sky*. New York: Holt, Reinhart and Winston, 1971.
Christiansen, Rupert. *Prima Donna*. New York: Viking Press, 1985.
Cottrol, Robert. *The Afro-Yankees*. Westport, Conn.: Greenwood Press, 1982.
Cuney-Hare, Maud. *Negro Musicians and Their Music*. New York: Associated Publishing Co., 1970, 1986.
Daughtry, Willia. *Sissieretta Jones, A Study of the Negro's Contribution to Nineteenth Century American Theatrical and Concert Life*. Dissertation, 1967.
Durante, Jimmy and Kofold, Jack. *Night Clubs*. New York: Alfred A. Knopf, 1931.
Ewen, David. *George Gershwin, His Journey to Greatness*. New York: Ungar Publishing Co., 1970.
Franca, Ida. *Manual of Bel Canto*. New York: Coward, McCann, 1953.
Franklin, John Hope. *From Slavery to Freedom*. New York: Random House, 1969.
Gilliam, Dorothy. *Paul Robeson: All American*. Washington, D.C.: New Republic Books, 1980.
Hurok, Sol. *Impresario*. New York: Random House, 1946.

Jacobson, Robert. *Reverberations—Interviews with the World's Leading Musicians.* New York: William Morrow, 1974.

Johnson, J. Rosamund. *The Book of American Negro Spirituals* and *The Second Book of American Negro Spirituals.* New York: Viking Press, 1925, 1926.

Kirk, Elise. *Music at the White House.* Urbana and Chicago: University of Illinois Press, 1986.

LaBrew, Arthur. *Elizabeth Taylor Greenfield: The Black Swan.* Detroit: Authur LaBrew, 1969.

Litwack, Leon. *Been in the Storm So Long.* New York: Random House, 1980.

Litwack, Leon. *North of Slavery.* Chicago: University of Chicago Press, 1961.

Lash, Joseph P. *Eleanor and Franklin.* New York: W. W. Norton & Co., 1971.

McLoughlin, William. *Rhode Island: A Bicentennial History.* New York: W. W. Norton & Co., 1978.

Mordden, Ethan. *Demented: The World of the Opera Diva.* New York: Franklin Watts, 1984.

Murrow, Edward. *The Lady from Philadelphia.*

Nathan, Hans. *Dan Emmett and the Rise of American Negro Minstrelsy.* Norman, Okla.: University of Oklahoma Press, 1962.

Pleasants, Henry. *The Great Singers,* 2nd ed. New York: Simon and Schuster, 1986.

Rushmore, Robert. *The Singing Voice.* New York: Dembner Books, 1984.

Schonberg, Harold C. *The Glorious Ones.* New York: New York Times Publishing Co., 1986.

Shaw, Arnold. *Black Popular Music in America.* New York: Schirmer Books, 1986.

Sheean, Vincent. *Between the Thunder and the Sun.* New York: Random House, 1943.

Sheean, Vincent. *First and Last Love.* New York: Random House, 1956.

Sims-Wood, Janet. *Marian Anderson, An Annotated Bibliography.* Westport, Conn.: Greenwood Press, 1981.

Southern, Eileen. *Biographical Dictionary of Afro-American and African Musicians.* Westport, Conn.: Greenwood Press, 1982.

Southern, Eileen. *The Music of Black Americans.* New York: W. W. Norton & Co., 1983.

Thomson, Virgil. *Virgil Thomson.* New York: Afred A. Knopf, 1966.

Toll, Robert. *Blacking Up.* New York: Oxford University Press, 1984.

Trotter, James. *Music and Some Highly Musical People.* Chicago: Afro-Am Press, 1969.

Vehanen, Kosti. *Marian Anderson.* New York: McGraw-Hill, 1941.

## Periodicals

*Sissieretta Jones*

More than 200 news clippings of concert reviews (mostly undated) are found in the singer's personal scrapbook, now the property of the Howard University Moorland-Spingarn Collection in Washington, D.C.

"At the Theaters." *Fort Worth Star-Telegram,* October 12, 1912.

"Black Patti at the California." *The Bulletin,* December 30, 1901.

"Dvořák Leads for the Fund." *New York Herald,* January 24, 1894.

"Her Favorite Is L'Africaine," unsigned. *Detroit Tribune,* February 12, 1893.

"In Summer's Whirl." *Daily Saratogian,* August 16, 1892.

Letters to the Editor. *The Conservator,* September 9, 1893.

"Patti's Dusky Rival." *Morning Advertiser,* April 27, 1892.

*Marian Anderson*

"Anderson Ban Protested." *New York Times*, February 23, 1939.
"A Door Opens," Olin Downes. *New York Times*, October 17, 1954.
"Good-Will Triumph Scored on Asian Tour by Marian Anderson," Harry Harris. *Philadelphia Inquirer*, December 31, 1957.
"Marian Anderson Ban Arouses Wide Protest." *The Crisis*, March, 1939.
"Marian Anderson in Concert Here." *New York Times*, December 31, 1935.
"Marian Anderson's Svengali Is Hypnotized by Her Voice!" *Philadelphia Record*, December 25, 1938.
"Marian Anderson Thrills Salzburg," Herbert Peyser. *New York Times*, August 29, 1935.
"Marian Anderson Wins Ovation in First Opera Role at the Met." *New York Times*, January 8, 1955.
"Miss Anderson 'Stops Music' in Tremendous Met Debut." *New York Times*, January 8, 1955.
"Music Will Out," Marcia Davenport. *Collier's*, December 3, 1938.
"Noted Singer Barred from Exclusive Club." *The Chicago Defender*, May 2, 1944.
"Opera: 'Masked Ball' Given at Met," Olin Downes. *New York Times*, January 9, 1955.
"The Other Voice of Marian Anderson," Harold Schonberg. *New York Times*, August 10, 1958.
"Over Jordan," Ruth Woodbury Sedgwick. *The Reader's Digest*, March, 1940.
"Roulades and Cadenzas," Carleton Smith. *Esquire*, July 1939, p. 79.
"Singer and Citizen." *Newsweek*, April 25, 1949, pp. 84–86.
"Singer Marian Anderson Says She'll Work for Understanding in Role of UN Delegate," Bernard Cavzer. *Philadelphia Evening Bulletin*, September 9, 1958.
"Throng Honors Marian Anderson in Concert at Lincoln Memorial." *New York Times*, April 10, 1939.
"250 White Persons in Florida Get Refunds at Marian Anderson Recital in Armory." *New York Times*, January 24, 1952.


*Dorothy Maynor*

"Classical Arts Come to Harlem," Doris Black. *Sepia Magazine*, October, 1971.
"Dorothy Maynor Berkshire Soloist," Noel Straus. *New York Times*, August 10, 1939.
"Dorothy Maynor in Debut Recital." *New York Times*, November 20, 1939.
"Dorothy Maynor Extolled by Rubinstein at Gala for School of the Arts." *New York Times*, March 18, 1976.
"Dorothy Maynor: The Musical Wiz of Harlem," Maurice Peterson. *Essence Magazine*, December, 1977.
"Dry Springs," Nancy L. Ross. *Washington Post*, February 4, 1969.
"Million-Dollar Voice," Howard Taubman. *Collier's*, March 2, 1940.
"Music: Dorothy Maynor," Ross Parmenter. *New York Times*, November 21, 1959.
"An Oasis Grows in Harlem," John Herbert. *The Village Voice*, February 21, 1977.


*Lillian Evanti*

"Mme. Evanti Wins Acclaim of Capital." *Washington Post*, March 21, 1932.
"National Negro Opera Co. Acclaimed at WaterGate," Alice Eversman. *Washington Star*, August 29, 1943.

## Carol Brice

"Carol Brice Sings Unusual Program," Noel Straus. *New York Times*, March 31, 1952.
"Mahler in Brief." *Saturday Review of Literature*, August 31, 1946.
"Music by Virgil Thomson." *New York Herald Tribune*, December 11, 1946.
"Voice Like a Cello." *Time*, March 11, 1946.

## Anne Brown

"Good Enough to Launch a Ship, But Not to Sing in 'White' Theater," Sally Winograd. *PM Magazine*, December 14, 1943.
"I Gave Up My Country for Love," Anne Brown. *Ebony Magazine*, November, 1953.

## Martina Arroyo

"Madame Butterball," Alan Levy. *New York Times Magazine*, May 14, 1972.
"Martina Arroyo Is Back After a Five-Year Absence," John Gruen. *New York Times*, April 17, 1983.
"No Nerves." *The New Yorker*, April 8, 1967.

## Leontyne Price

"Collard Greens and Caviar," Robert Jacobson. *Opera News*, July, 1985.
"Conversation with Leontyne Price," Samuel Chotzinoff. *Holiday Magazine*, March, 1964.
"Leontyne Price: 'I'm Not Scared Anymore,'" Stephen E. Rubin. *New York Times*, September, 1973.
"Leontyne Price—Still the Diva," Susan Heller Anderson. *New York Times*, February 7, 1982.
"Mistress of Stage and Score." *Time*, May 30, 1960.
"A Voice Like a Banner Flying." *Time*, March 10, 1961.

## Grace Bumbry

"Amazing Grace," Stephen Rubin. *Opera News*, October, 1981.
"Carnegie Recital by Grace Bumbry," Raymond Ericson. *New York Times*, January 7, 1964.
"Hurok's Venus at $250,000," John Rosenfield. *Dallas Morning News*, August 21, 1961.
"Tannhäuser at Bayreuth," Ronald Eyer. *New York Herald Tribune*, July 25, 1961.
"Yankee Parsifal." *Time*, August 4, 1961.

## Shirley Verrett

"Shirley Verrett Sings Met Debut," Allen Hughes. *New York Times*, September 23, 1968.
"Shirley Verrett Takes Up the Challenge," Marcia Chambers. *New York Times*, October 22, 1973.
"Why They all Want to Sing 'Norma,'" John Ardoin. *New York Times*, March 11, 1979.

*Other Writings*

"The Black Performer," George Shirley. *Opera News*, January 30, 1971.
"A Bravo for Opera's Black Voices," Harold C. Schonberg. *New York Times Magazine*, January 17, 1982.
"The Folksongs of the American Negro," Carl Van Vechten. *Vanity Fair*, July, 1925.
"Living with Gershwin," Ned Rorem. *Opera News*, March 16, 1985.
"A Long Pull," Ethan C. Mordden. *Opera News*, March 16, 1985.
"The Negro Spiritual." *Etude Magazine*, October, 1924.
"Rediscovering the Spiritual," Abbe Niles. *The Nation*, December 1, 1926.
"A Warning Against Over-Refinement of the Negro Spiritual," Marion Kerby. *The Musician*, July, 1928.
"Yes, But Are We Really Colour Deaf?" Martin Bernheimer. *Opera*, July, 1985.

# Index